THAILAND

WESTVIEW PROFILES
NATIONS OF CONTEMPORARY ASIA
Mervyn Adams Seldon, Series Editor

† Available in hardcover and paperback.

ABOUT THE BOOK AND AUTHOR

Thailand is exceptional among modern states in Asia in that it has built and retained a national culture around a traditional monarchical institution. Moreover, this culture has also been based on a dominant religious tradition, that of Theravada Buddhism. The process of creating the modern nation-state of Thailand out of the traditional Buddhist kingdom of Siam began in the nineteenth century when the rulers of Siam, confronted with increasing pressure from the colonial powers of Britain and France, were able to preserve their country's independence by instituting revolutionary changes that established the authority of a centralized bureaucracy throughout the country. The new state asserted its authority not only over Siamese who lived in the core area of the old kingdom but also over large numbers of Lao, Yuan or Northern Thai, Khmer, Malays, tribal peoples, and other groups, all of which had previously enjoyed relative autonomy, and over the sizable immigrant Chinese population, which was assuming an increasingly significant role in the economy. Because the rulers of the Siamese state strove to incorporate these diverse peoples into a Thai national community, how this community should be defined and what type of state structure should be linked with it have been dominant questions in modern Thai history. Significant tensions have arisen from the efforts by members of the Thai elite to make the monarchical traditions of the Bangkok dynasty, Buddhism, and the central Thai language basic to Thai national culture. Other tensions have arisen as monarchy, military, bureaucracy, the Buddhist sangha, business interests, and elected political representatives assert or maintain an authoritative position in the state structure. This book examines these tensions with reference to the major changes that have taken place in Thai society, economy, polity, and culture in the twentieth century, especially since World War II.

Charles F. Keyes, professor and chairman of the Department of Anthropology at the University of Washington, Seattle, has conducted research in Thailand over the past twenty years. He is the author or editor of numerous publications, including *The Golden Peninsula: Culture and Adaptation in Mainland Southeast Asia.*

THAILAND

Buddhist Kingdom as Modern Nation-State

Charles F. Keyes

Westview Press / Boulder and London

Westview Profiles/Nations of Contemporary Asia

Published in 1987 in the United States of America by Westview Press, Inc.; Frederick A. Praeger, Publisher; 5500 Central Avenue, Boulder, Colorado 80301

Library of Congress Cataloging-in-Publication Data
Keyes, Charles F.
 Thailand, Buddhist kingdom as modern nation-state.
 (Westview profiles. Nations of contemporary Asia)
 Bibliography: p.
 Includes index.
 1. Thailand. I. Title. II. Series.
DS563.5.K49 1986   959.3   86-15764
ISBN 0-86531-138-2 (alk. paper)

Printed and bound in the United States of America

The paper used in this publication meets the requirements of the American National Standard for Permanence of Paper for Printed Library Materials Z39.48-1984.

10   9   8   7   6   5   4   3   2   1

for Jane,
who has shared my quest to understand Thailand

Contents

)

Tables and Illustrations

Acknowledgments

Several years ago, Westview Press approached me about writing a book on Thailand for their Nations of Contemporary Asia series. Although I began work on the book shortly thereafter, it was not until I took a sabbatical leave in 1984-1985 that I was able to finish writing the book. I am grateful both to the University of Washington and to the John Simon Guggenheim Memorial Foundation for support that enabled me to take this leave. I have benefited from comments on the book in manuscript form by John Girling, Chai-anan Samudavanija, and Ruth McVey and especially from the comments by Jane Keyes, Benedict R. O'G. Anderson, and Mervyn Seldon. I also want to thank Nancy Donnelly for her help in preparing the index. I am grateful to Dr. Amara Pongsapich for helping me obtain some statistical information used in the book. I owe a deeper debt to the many people in Thailand who have made me aware of aspects of their society and culture.

Charles F. Keyes

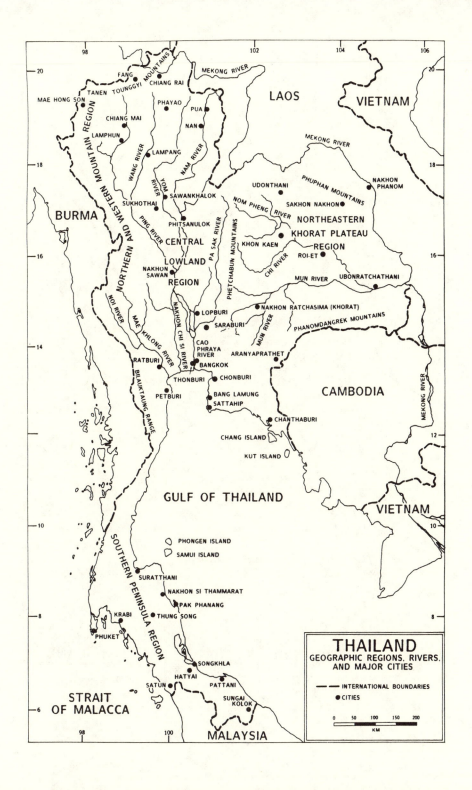

THAILAND
GEOGRAPHIC REGIONS, RIVERS, AND MAJOR CITIES

— INTERNATIONAL BOUNDARIES
● CITIES

0   50   100   150   200
KM

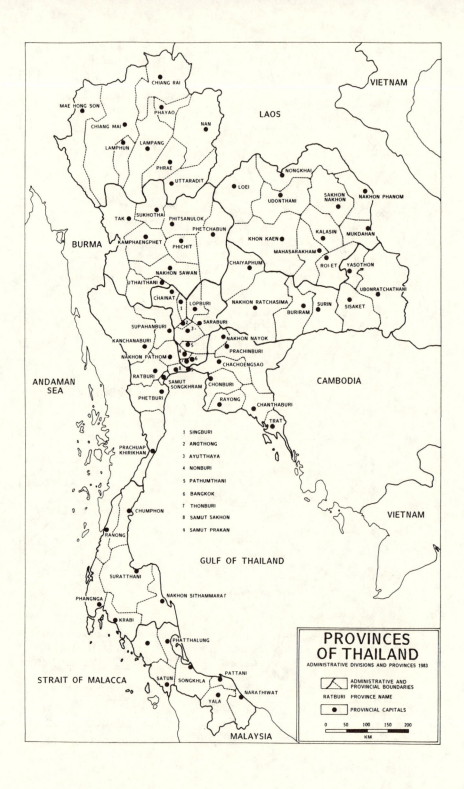

PROVINCES
OF THAILAND

ADMINISTRATIVE DIVISIONS AND PROVINCES 1983

Prologue

In mid-1968, King Bhumibol Adulyadej, the ninth monarch of the present Chakri dynasty of Thailand, flew to the remote northwestern Thai town of Mae Hong Son. Here he was to present to representatives of this province, as he was doing in every province in the kingdom, an image of the Buddha he had had cast. To Thai government officials posted to the province, Mae Hong Son had long been regarded as the "Siberia" of Thailand, for even into the 1970s it was largely cut off from the rest of the country. This separation was not only geographical but also cultural, for almost the only Siamese or Central Thai people living in the province were the officials themselves. The local population was mainly divided between Shans, Tai-speaking peoples[1] who are found mainly in the Shan State of Burma, and a number of different hill tribal peoples. The king's visit to Mae Hong Son in 1968, the first visit to the province by any Thai monarch, thus entailed the ceremonial display of the essential elements of Thai national culture for people whose connection to the Thai state was tenuous owing to their residence in a remote border area and their ethnic distinctiveness.

I was fortunate enough to be able to observe the ceremonies attending the visit of the king; his wife, Queen Sirikit; and an entourage of palace and government officials to Mae Hong Son.[2] The event conjured up images of the durbars held in India in the last century at which representatives of the diverse peoples of a particular district were brought together to demonstrate their fealty to the British raj. The town of Mae Hong Son at the time was strikingly different from any other provincial capital in Thailand. Most of the buildings in the town were wooden—mainly teak—structures, built in the Burmese Shan style. The temple-monasteries (called *wat* in Thai) with their distinctive reliquary shrines or stupas (*cedi* in Thai) and associated buildings with their tiered roofs and towers and carved wooden decorations were typical of Burma rather than Thailand. The peoples who came together for the visit of the royal

1

couple were dressed in distinctive ethnic clothing. There were Shan girls wearing Burmese-style blouses and silk skirts; Akha tribal peoples in their distinctive turbans; and Hmong (Meo, Miao), Lahu, Lisu, Kayah (Red Karen), Sgaw Karen, and Lua (Lawa), each dressed in their own costumes.

Although the overall setting was quite alien to the world of Bangkok, the ceremonies took place within a context that was quintessentially Thai—the grounds of the provincial government office (sala klang). The office building itself was in a style that would be immediately recognizable no matter what province one happened to find oneself in. The Thai flag and the national colors (red, white, and blue) flew from the building and from poles along the edge of the grounds. Near the office building a temporary pavilion had been erected, and there were two elaborate chairs on a raised platform at one end for the king and queen, ordinary chairs on a lower platform for the ranking members of the Buddhist clergy (the sangha), and still more chairs on the floor of the pavilion for the dignitaries from the province and members of the entourage of the royal couple. Below the pavilion seating was provided for lesser officials, and around the edges of the grounds covered booths without chairs had been set up for representatives of each of the ethnic groups in the province. The arrangement of the grounds for the ceremony thus made evident the constituent elements of the Thai state: the monarch (phra maha kasat), the Buddhist sangha (phra song), the officials (kha-ratchakan, literally, "servants of the crown"), and the populace (ratsadon).

The participants in the ceremony arrived in reverse order of importance: the representatives from the general populace took their places in ethnically distinct groupings; then came the lesser officials followed by the higher officials and those accompanying the royal couple; next the members of the sangha were shown to their seats. Last, after considerable anticipation among the others present, the king and queen arrived in a motorcade that had brought them from the airport. After they took their places, the ceremonies began. First, the king presented the provincial governor and the provincial head of the sangha with the statue of the Buddha that thenceforth would be primarily used in ritual events involving officials. Next came presentations by the people, consisting of dances and cultural entertainments by members of the local ethnic groups. The king and queen then toured the grounds, stopping to talk with representatives of each ethnic group and to receive gifts offered them on behalf of a group. Within a few hours the ceremony was over, and the king and queen departed for their northern palace in Chiang Mai.

Although the events described took place in a remote corner of Thailand, they serve to define the essence of the national culture of

King Bhumibol and Queen Sirikit at ceremony in Mae Hong Son, northern Thailand, 1968. (Photo by author)

modern Thailand. Since the reign of King Chulalongkorn, who ruled from 1868 to 1910, there has been a conscious effort on the part of the central government in Bangkok to bring all the diverse peoples living within the political boundaries of Thailand under its authority. The assertion of this authority has been exercised not primarily through the use of force, although from time to time force has been directed against groups that have resisted central government control. Rather, it has been asserted by emphasizing a set of national symbols that hold a strong appeal for the vast majority of the populace. At the center of this set lies the monarch (*phra maha kasat*), upon whom the legitimate power of the state is based. Today the king is a constitutional monarch, and most actual power is wielded by a prime minister and Council of Ministers or cabinet, but the latter's authority still has to be sanctioned by the king. Moreover, the administration of the state is carried out by members of the civilian and military bureaucracies, collectively known as "servants of the crown" (*kharatchakan*). The legitimacy of the monarch, in turn, is predicated upon his association with the Buddhist religion (*satsana*, from Pali, *sasana*). The king demonstrates this relationship through his acts of public piety and especially by his patronage of the sangha, or clergy. As in the ceremony at Mae Hong Son, the king is also often linked symbolically with an image of the Buddha. The loyal subjects of the monarch—no matter, as the ceremony at Mae Hong Son demonstrates, what their ethnic background might be—constitute the Thai nation (*chat Thai*).

In Thailand today, national cultural themes are so pervasive that most people accept them without question; they are, nonetheless, much more problematic than would first appear. Although the Thai national culture has its roots in premodern Siam, its present form was formulated only in the latter part of the nineteenth century in the wake of efforts to create a modern nation-state. Because of the relative newness of the present form of the national culture, it has not been equally well established even to this day among all segments of the populace. Indeed, the assembly at Mae Hong Son probably provided some of the tribal peoples who attended it with their first demonstration that they were considered citizens of a Thai nation-state.

The central elements of the national culture have been reformulated by successive Thai governments. This fact is particularly evident in the case of the monarchy, which has been presented quite differently during the reigns of the absolute monarchs who ruled Thailand before 1932, under the somewhat antiroyalist constitutional governments that guided national affairs from 1932 to 1957, and by the proroyalist military and civilian governments that have been in power since 1957. Since the 1970s there has also been a growing debate, at least in urban circles, about the future of the monarchy.

The Buddhist religion, too, has been cast in different lights by different governments and competing political elites. In the early stages of national integration, the government promoted Thai Buddhism over Buddhist traditions associated with other ethnic groups. Although Thai Buddhism has become the national religion, there still remain serious differences as to what roles members of the sangha can play in national life. Moreover, since Buddhism is the national religion, people who follow non-Buddhist faiths have been relegated to somewhat ambiguous positions within the national order. Finally, the notion of "Thai" as a national identity has been the subject of considerable debate, and the promotion of different constructions of what it means to be Thai has bred a series of conflicts.

The evolution of a Thai national culture and the salience of that culture for life in contemporary Thai society can be explored only by considering, on the one hand, the degree to which Thai society has been transformed by political and economic forces that have impinged upon Thailand from the outside and, on the other, the degree to which Thai society perpetuates premodern social forms. Since the middle of the nineteenth century, the Thai economy has been increasingly tied to the world economic system, and integration into the global economy has steadily transformed life in even the most remote villages in the society. Since the early 1960s, the Thai "open" economy has grown at a rate faster than that of most Third World economies. Associated with the recent economic growth has been a marked expansion of a middle class and, concomitantly, a marked expansion of an urban underclass and a growing gap between urban rich and rural poor. During the same period that Thailand has been brought increasingly into the world economic system, the Thai state has also been reshaped as a bureaucratic polity, thereby permitting it to function in ways comparable to other states. The bureaucratic polity, like the market, has intruded to a marked degree into the lives of the people in Thailand. Although today's Thai society shares many of the same characteristics of other Third World societies, which have also been transformed by the preeminently modern forces emanating from international capitalism and the incorporation of peoples into nation-states, social life in Thailand still retains distinctive features that can only be understood with reference to the character of premodern Siam.

NOTES

1. On the usage of the term "Tai" as distinct from "Thai," see Appendix A.

2. At the time, I was carrying out research on the relationship between tribal peoples and the Thai in Mae Sariang district, located in Mae Hong Son Province.

1

The Land and the People

Thailand is located in the tropical region of Asia, and despite the recent introduction of air-conditioning and other means of climate control, the tropical environment continues to constrain and shape life in the country. Although there are microenvironmental differences, the climate throughout most of monsoonal Asia is characterized by alternating rainy and dry seasons. The rains are generated by monsoonal storms originating, in the case of Thailand and other parts of mainland Southeast Asia, primarily over the South China Sea, and the dryness comes from other monsoonal winds originating over the Asian landmass. In most of Thailand, the southern isthmus being an exception, the southwest monsoon begins to bring rains in May or June or sometimes as late as July; for the next three months, the rains grow in intensity, then taper off, and finally stop in about October. The winds then shift, and the northeastern monsoon ushers in a period of dryness that becomes most pronounced in December, January, and February.

Because the storms are not predictable, the rains do not always come at the same time, nor are they always of the same intensity, and these marked fluctuations in rainfall patterns create considerable anxiety among local farmers. The rains may arrive late, thereby creating problems with planting; they may stop in the middle of the growing season, thereby killing the plants; they may be too heavy in one period, thus causing devastating flooding. Efforts to control the effects of the unpredictability of the rains have been made since ancient times. Even today villagers often perform rites designed to placate or counter the supernatural forces that are believed to control the rains. In modern times, governments have built irrigation systems to control flooding and provide drought and flood relief. All such efforts notwithstanding, each rainy season brings renewed anxieties as to whether the rains will come at the right time and in the right amounts or not. Even in contemporary

Bangkok there is no escaping the annual flooding that comes with the rainy season. Indeed, the sinking of Bangkok, caused by the heavy population concentration in the area, has made floods even more of a problem there than in many other parts of the country.

Throughout monsoonal Asia the average temperatures are significantly higher than in temperate zones. Microenvironmental differences—especially ones connected with altitude and with proximity to the sea—are associated with different temperature ranges. The cooler temperatures of the "hill stations" of Simla in India, Taunggyi in Burma, or Dalat in Vietnam made these places very appealing to colonial officials and others seeking to escape from the heat of the plains. In Thailand, except for the king's summer palace, no such hill station was ever built, and most of the populace lives in areas where the temperature ranges are much the same. Although temperatures over 100° F (38° C) and as low as 45° F (7° C) have been recorded, the typical range is between about 65° F (18° C) and 96° F (35° C). Even in the hill areas of the country temperatures rarely drop to freezing. The high temperatures have permitted the peoples of Thailand to erect buildings that do not require the insulation needed in more temperate climates. Only since World War II has the preference for the more regulated interior temperatures permitted by air-conditioning required the construction of more substantial, and expensive, houses and other buildings. Nor has it been necessary for people in Thailand to invest in heavy, expensive clothing because the high temperatures permit people to wear light clothing throughout the year.

SETTLEMENTS OF RICE-PRODUCING PEOPLES[1]

The peoples of Thailand have adapted themselves to a tropical climate and have distributed themselves throughout the country with reference primarily to mountains and rivers. Mountains (hills by comparison with the Himalayas, Alps, or Rockies) have retarded movement from east to west while the rivers have facilitated movement north and south.

Northern Thailand is characterized by the ridge-and-furrow type of geography found throughout most of northern mainland Southeast Asia and southern China. That is, hill ranges are separated by rather narrow valleys. The main valleys of northern Thailand are drained by the Nan, Yom, Wang, and Ping rivers with only the valley of the latter—the Chiang Mai valley—constituting a relatively wide lowland. These four rivers come together in the north central part of the country to form the Cao Phraya River, the river that dominates the wide central plain. A long cordillera, the Tennasserim range, runs from the northern part of the country down the western border of central Thailand, connecting with the peninsular ranges that continue down the center of the Thai isthmus into Malaya. In the west central part of the country there is a small valley centered on the Mae Khlong River and its main tributaries, the Khwae Yai (better known as the River Kwai) and the Khwae Nọi.

The Phetchabun range, which in its lower reaches turns to the east and becomes the Sankampheng range, divides central Thailand from the Khorat Plateau. This plateau is drained by the Mun and Chi rivers, which run across it, and by the Mekong into which these rivers ultimately flow. The Mekong today forms the border between northeastern Thailand and central and southern Laos. The Khorat Plateau is separated from Cambodia by an escarpment known as the Phanom Dongrak range. In peninsular Thailand, the sea is a more important orienting feature than the rivers, and, in this regard, the peninsula is similar to Malaya and the coastal areas of Indonesia.

Even into the twentieth century, much of Thailand was covered by tropical forests. These forests supported a significant variety of animals and plants, which humans made use of for food and housing materials. Since World War II there has been rapid deforestation and a concomitant decline of natural resources found in the forests.

The earliest humans to live in what is today Thailand supported themselves entirely through hunting and gathering in the forests, fishing in the streams and rivers, and collecting shellfish from both freshwater and sea sources. Somewhere around 10,000 years ago, some peoples, living in the northern part of the country, began to make the wild rice they collected an important element of their diet.[2] Over the next several thousand years, it was discovered that rice could be cultivated through preparation of fields, planting of selected seeds, tending of plants, and harvesting the mature plants. Around 5,000 years ago, domesticated rice had become the dominant source of food for the growing population inhabiting what is Thailand today.

The first permanent agricultural settlements in Thailand were on the flanks of hills. There, villagers laid out fields on relatively level ground close to forested areas and streams flowing from the hills. By 3,000 B.C., some villagers, as is evident from the rich archaeological finds at Ban Chiang and Non Nok Tha in northeastern Thailand, began to develop quite sophisticated cultures. Not only have distinctive and elaborate ceramic artifacts (Ban Chiang pottery, for example) been found at these sites, but both bronze and iron tools have also been discovered. Although questions remain about whether prehistoric bronze metallurgy in northeastern Thailand was independent of external influences, there

Terraced rice fields in northern Thailand. (Photo by author)

is no doubt that the foundations of later civilizations in Thailand were laid by the peoples living in these prehistoric rice-producing communities.

Rice was to become the staple crop of all agriculturalists in the country from prehistoric times on. Rice is not, however, cultivated by everyone in the same way. Different types of cultivation have been and continue to be associated with different types of settlement patterns. The dominant form of cultivation, today as well as in the past, is one in which agriculturalists cultivate the same fields year after year. As continuous cultivation leaches nutrients from the soil, this mode requires that the cultivators employ some method to renew the fertility of their land. Until quite recently, most agriculturalists depended on the annual floods of streams and rivers that follow the end of the rainy season to bring new nutrients. To take advantage of these floods, farmers reshaped the topography of their fields so as to guide water into them and retain it there for the proper amount of time. An area planted to rice on a flood-plain is immediately evident from the dikes used to control the flow of water through the area, and more elaborate forms of irrigation, which make possible the use of the regular flow of water through streams and rivers, were created by peoples living near hills in north central and northern Thailand. These forms of irrigation were constructed and maintained primarily by villagers themselves with little involvement on the part of higher-level authorities, such as had been the case, for example, in the Tonkin Delta of northern Vietnam. Not until the twentieth century, and then mainly since World War II, has there been any significant state involvement in irrigation in Thailand.

Since prehistoric times, the people who have cultivated permanent rice fields have used animal power to plow and harvest those fields and to transport rice and other products from fields to storage areas. By far the most important source of animal power has been provided by water buffalo, although oxen have also been used in some areas. Today, both water buffalo and oxen are rapidly being replaced by machines for transporting goods, but animals remain dominant for agricultural purposes. Houses in rural Thailand have long been built on stilts (or piles) so that buffalo, cattle, and other animals can be kept underneath them at night.

Settlements by villagers cultivating rice on permanent fields have constituted and continue to constitute the basic elements of Thai society. On the margins of these settlements, in upland areas, live other peoples who have followed different modes of production and whose relationships with lowland polities have been tenuous. Upland-dwelling peoples, who are found mainly in northern and western Thailand, also cultivate rice as their main crop, but most uplanders grow rice by what is known as the "swidden" or "slash-and-burn" method. Fields are prepared by burning off the vegetation on a hillside, the residues from the burning providing much of the required nutrients. The fields are watered entirely through available rainfall rather than through any system of controlling floodwaters or through irrigation. Because the upland method leads to a rapid leaching of nutrients from the soil, swidden fields can be planted for only one or two years before they are allowed to return to fallow for a period that, ideally, should be about twelve to fourteen years long. To produce sufficient rice year after year, even small communities of swidden cultivators must therefore have access to very large amounts of land. To remain within walking distance of their fields, swidden farmers move their settlements relatively often, so their settlements are less permanent than those of lowland rice cultivators. The remoteness of most settlements of swidden cultivators from centers of state power has contributed to the maintenance of cultural distinctiveness among uplanders in relation to the dominant lowland peoples. Today, most uplanders belong to one or another tribal group.

RICE IN THE FIELDS AND FISH IN THE WATER: THE FOOD OF THE PEOPLES OF THAILAND

Whether an upland swidden cultivator, a lowland permanent-field farmer, or even a nonfarming town dweller, rice is basic to life for all who live in Thailand. Rice (*khao*) is equated with food in a basic sense, all other foods being considered as "that which is eaten with rice" (*kap khao*). From rice one acquires not only nutrition but something that is also spiritual in essence. All the peoples of Thailand, like their neighbors elsewhere in Southeast Asia, conceive of rice as having a "vital essence" (*khwan*) that is the same as that possessed by human beings.

Rice not only unites peoples in Thailand, it also serves to distinguish them. Hill rice (*khao doi*), that is, the rice raised in swidden fields, is considered by valley peoples to be coarse, but uplanders consider it far more flavorful than the rice raised in lowland fields. Glutinous rice (*khao niao*), which has to be prepared by soaking it for several hours before steaming and which has a distinctly "sticky" quality, is the staple for most of the lowland peoples of northern and northeastern Thailand as well as Laos. This rice is considered by the lowland peoples of central Thailand to be appropriate only in desserts. For them, like most of the other lowland dwelling peoples of Southeast Asia, the staple rice is a nonglutinous type the Thai call "lordly rice" (*khao cao*) or "beautiful rice" (*khao suai*).

For most of the people of Thailand, the main food "to be eaten with rice" is fish (*pla*) in some form. Many communities along the coast of the Gulf of Thailand specialize in fishing. Although some of the catch is eaten fresh—more today than in the past because of improved means of transportation and refrigeration—much of it is dried or salted. Preserved fish from the coastal communities is traded far into the interior; today there is scarcely a marketplace up-country that does not have for sale salted *plathu*, a type of mackerel that is extremely popular. In the interior, freshwater fish from rivers, streams, lakes, ponds, and mudflats provides the main supplement to rice. Fish sauce (*nam pla*), made from salted fish; fermented shrimp, made into a paste called *kapi*; or fermented fish, made into a sauce called *plara*, are ubiquitous constituents of the diet, used either as the base for hot sauces or as seasoning. Fish sauce in particular is to Thai food what soy sauce is to Chinese or Japanese food.

Meat is consumed far less than fish except among the affluent middle and upper classes. Nonetheless, on festive occasions, villagers feel that it is essential to have chicken, beef, or, more rarely, pork. It might seem surprising to some that in a Buddhist country like Thailand there is no prohibition against eating meat. In point of fact, people throughout South and Southeast Asia who adhere to the tradition of Buddhism known as Theravada, "the way of the elders," are not vegetarians. They can, and often do, point to scriptures that attest to the fact that the Buddha himself ate meat offered to him. It is thought, nonetheless, that the people who deprive animals of their lives—fish are considered to be an exception since they are not killed but simply allowed to die after being removed from the water—commit a sin in the Buddhist sense. Thus it is rare to find Buddhist Thai working as butchers; more commonly the butchers are either Chinese or Muslim, although in rural communities where there are no Muslims or Chinese slaughtering is performed by local village men. Few Thai men have qualms about killing chickens, and there are usually one or two men in any village willing to chance their fate by slaughtering larger animals on those occasions when meat is in demand.

A distinctive feature of Thai food, whether eaten in the villages or in the most expensive restaurants in Bangkok, is its spicy hotness, a characteristic produced by the use of very hot chili peppers. Almost all rural families own small garden plots where they raise chilies and a variety of vegetables, of which a type of cabbage and vegetable marrow are perhaps the most common.

People in Thailand also eat a variety of tropical fruits—bananas, papayas, mangoes, coconuts, custard apples, jackfruit, and in some areas, longans, litchis, mangosteens, rambutans, and the smelly but highly prized durians. The "milk" made from squeezing the meat of the coconut is used to make curries (*kaeng*), which although similar in some respects to those of India, Malaya, and Indonesia have their own distinctive Thai character—a result of the particular spices used.

Until quite recently, few Thai suffered from malnourishment. The relatively low population density of Thailand as compared with, say, Bengal, the Red River Delta in northern Vietnam, Java, or southeastern China made it possible for most Thai to find, as King Ramkhamhaeng said in his famous inscription of 1292 A.D., that "there is fish in the water and rice in the fields." Only with the rapid population growth of Thailand in the twentieth century, and especially since World War II, have provisioning problems, previously unknown to the country, begun to emerge.

THE POPULATION OF THAILAND

Rough estimates suggest that the population of what is today Thailand grew from around 4 million people in 1800 to perhaps 7 million in 1900.[3] Since the beginning of the twentieth century, the population has grown at a much faster rate, expanding from 8.3 million in 1911, the year of the first modern census, to 44.8 million in 1980. The highest rate of population growth has occurred since World War II, especially between about 1950 and 1970. During most of this two-decade period, the rate of growth was over 3 percent per year. This high rate of growth was strongly supported by the governments in power between 1947 and 1973, which viewed the expansion of a Thai population as essential to fend off a perceived threat from the Chinese living both in China and, as immigrants and descendants of immigrants, in Thailand.

Beginning in the 1970s, even before the government abandoned a pronatal policy, women in many parts of the country began to adopt birth control methods.[4] Initially, these were made available through private organizations, and even today, the work of the Planned Parenthood Association and the Population and Community Development Association led by Meechai Veeravaidya has played a major role in persuading people to adopt birth control measures. Meechai's image, as one who passes out calling cards with condoms attached and who gains the attention of children by having them blow up condoms as balloons, is well known not only in Thailand but throughout the world. By the mid-1970s, the government had also undertaken a major birth control program. The response to these private and public efforts has been extremely positive in both urban and rural areas, making Thailand one of the major success stories among Third World countries in cutting the rate of population growth. By the late 1970s, the rate had dropped from over 3 percent in the 1950s and 1960s to 2 percent per year, and it has been lower since 1980.[5]

Like many other Third World countries, Thailand has also recently experienced a dramatic growth in its urban population. In 1947, only 5 percent of the people were living in places having populations of 20,000 or more, and only 10 percent were living in centers designated as "urban places" in the Thai census. By 1967, the number of people living in centers with 20,000 or more inhabitants had reached to 12 percent of the total population, and the percentage of people living in census-designated "urban places" had jumped to 14 percent.[6] According to data in the 1980 census, the percentage living in urban places by that date had increased to 23.6 percent.[7] Urban growth has been particularly marked in the greater Bangkok metropolitan area. Indeed, in few other countries of the world is the disparity between the principal city and secondary cities as great as it is in Thailand. In 1970, the greater Bangkok metropolitan area was more than thirty times larger than Chiang Mai, the next major city in size, and three times larger than the combined populations of the nineteen next-sizable cities in the country.[8] The disproportionate growth of Bangkok has exacerbated long-standing differences between the rural and urban populations of Thailand as well as creating many problems for those who dwell in Bangkok.[9]

TABLE 1.1
Citizenship, Language, and Religion of Population of Thailand According to
Censuses of 1960, 1970, 1980

Characteristic	1960 Census %	1970 Census %	1980 Census %
Citizenship, Country of[a]			
Thailand	98.2	98.7	----
China	1.6	1.1	----
Other	0.2	0.2	----
Language, Ability of Population 5 years of Age and Older to Speak Thai[b]	97.0	----	----
Religion			
Buddhism	93.6	95.2	95.0
Confucianism[c]	1.7	----	----
Islam	3.9	3.9	3.8
Christianity	0.6	0.6	0.5
Hinduism[d]	<0.1	----	<0.1
Other and none	0.2	0.2	0.1
Unknown	<0.1	0.1	0.5

Sources:
  Thailand. Central Statistical Office, National Economic Development
  Board, Thailand Population Census 1960: Whole Kingdom (Bangkok, 1962);
  Thailand. National Statistical Office, Office of the Prime Minister,
  1970 Population and Housing Census: Whole Kingdom (Bangkok, 1973);
  Thailand. National Statistical Office, Office of the Prime Minister,
  1980 Population and Housing Census: Whole Kingdom (Bangkok, 1983).

Notes:
  a. Category not included in 1980 census.
  b. Category not included in 1970 and 1980 censuses.
  c. "Confucianism" combined with "Buddhism" in 1970 and 1980 censuses.
  d. "Hinduism" combined with "other" in 1970 census.

THE PEOPLES OF THAILAND[10]

From Thai censuses, one gains the impression that the population
of Thailand is largely culturally homogeneous. Recent census figures
(see Table 1.1) show that nearly 99 percent of the populace are citizens
of Thailand, 97 percent of them speak Thai, and 94–95 percent of them
adhere to Buddhism. This appearance of cultural homogeneity is, however,
deceptive. The people who have constructed Thai censuses have been
led by political guidelines to avoid asking the kinds of ethnic self-
identification questions raised in censuses in other countries, such as
the United States. Moreover, categories such as "ability to speak Thai"

and "Buddhism" have been defined so as to subsume considerable cultural variability.

If a survey were made in which ethnic self-identification were taken into account, the population of Thailand would appear to be much more ethnically diverse. Such a survey would take into account the fact that many people assume that certain cultural attributes which they share with others are indicative of a common ethnic identity. Language acquired from parents and spoken at home, the religious tradition inherited from one's parents, memory of descent from immigrants to Thailand, and stories of past political independence from or discrimination by the government in Bangkok are the most salient attributes for those who claim distinctive ethnic identities in Thailand. In Table 1.2 I have estimated what percentages of the population of Thailand would belong to different ethnic groupings if such a survey were to be conducted.

The Thai Peoples

The vast majority of the peoples of Thailand—over 80 percent— speak related languages belonging to the Tai or Daic language family.[11] Tai languages are spoken not only by peoples in Thailand but also by several tens of millions more living in Laos, the Shan State of Burma, northern Vietnam, and southern China. In Thailand, it became government policy early in the twentieth century to consider all who spoke Tai languages as being speakers of Thai, the national language. Such a determination has obscured the fact that many people continue to consider their own language to be quite different from Thai. "Standard Thai"—that is, the national language taught in the schools, used on all official occasions, and employed, in written form, in almost all printed materials—is based on only one of the Tai languages spoken in the country, namely that of the Siamese or Central Thai. People who speak Siamese as their domestic language, that is, the language of the home, constitute only about a quarter of the total population or 30 percent of all Tai speakers in Thailand.

The large majority of those who speak Tai languages consider their domestic language to be other than Thai. Most people living in northeastern Thailand speak related dialects that, although somewhat different from one another, are all referred to as Lao or Isan (literally, northeastern) by those who speak them. Most of the people of the northern provinces call their local language Kham Mɨang (literally, "language of the principalities"), although in its written form it is called Yuan. Lao and Kham Mɨang are as different from Siamese as, say, Portuguese is from Spanish, but since peoples in northeastern and northern Thailand have been educated in government schools they are quite able to communicate in standard Thai. The Tai dialects of southern Thailand, although more

TABLE 1.2
Estimates of Ethnic Composition of Thai Population
(Not Including Refugees)

Ethnic Group	Location	Percentage of Total Pop.
Tai-Speaking Groups		(83.0)
Siamese (Central Thai)	Central Thailand	25.0
Northeastern Thai (Isan, Thai-Lao)	Northeastern Thailand	31.0
Northern Thai (Khon Myang, Yuan)	Northern Thailand	20.0
Southern Thai	Southern Thailand	4.0
Thai Muslims	Central & Southern Thailand	1.0
Other (Phu Thai, Yǫ, Lue, Shan, Lao Song, Lao Phuan)	Northeastern, Northern & Central Thailand	2.0
Austroasiatic-Speaking Groups		(2.3)
Mon	Central Thailand	0.2
Khmer	Borderlands with Cambodia	1.5
Kui (Suai)	Northeastern Thailand	0.5
Tribal (Lawa, Thin, Khamu)	Northern Thailand	0.1
Malay	Southernmost provinces	3.0
Immigrant Groups		(10.8)
Chinese (Including Sino-Thai)	Urban areas	10.5
Vietnamese	Northeastern Thailand & Urban areas	0.2
Indians and Other (Burmese, Europeans, Japanese, etc.)	Urban areas	0.1
Tribal (Other than Austroasiatic)		(0.9)
Karen	Northern Thailand	0.5
Hmong (Miao, Meo) & Mien (Yao)	Northern Thailand	0.2
Other (Akha, Lahu, Lisu)	Northern Thailand	0.2
Total		100.0

Sources:

Estimates are based on census data and on the following sources: Peter Kunstadter, ed., Southeast Asian Tribes, Minorities, and Nations (Princeton: Princeton University Press, 1967), 1:397-400; United States Department of the Army, Ethnographic Study Series: Minority Groups in Thailand (Washington, D.C.: U.S. Govt. Printing Office, 1970); Paitoon Mikusol, "Social and Cultural History of Northeastern Thailand from 1868-1910: Case Study of the Huamuang Khamen Padong (Surin, Sangkha and Khukhan)," Ph.D. Dissertation, University of Washington (1984) (for Khmer and Kui); Peter A. Poole, The Vietnamese in Thailand (Ithaca, N.Y.: Cornell University Press, 1970) (for Vietnamese); John McKinnon and Wanat Bhruksasri, eds., Highlanders of Thailand (Kuala Lumpur: Oxford University Press, 1983); Paul and Elaine Lewis, Peoples of the Golden Triangle (London: Thames and Hudson, 1984) (for tribal peoples).

closely related to Siamese, are still considered by those who speak them as belonging to a distinctive language. This language is usually referred to as Pak Tai, which literally means "southern tongue." In northeastern and central Thailand there are small pockets of people, descendants of immigrants or resettled prisoners of war who came from Laos in the nineteenth century, who speak at home such distinctive Tai languages as Phu Thai, Yǫ, Lao Song, and Lao Phuan. In northern Thailand there are also other pockets of people whose ancestors came from northern Burma, northern Laos, or southern China, and they speak still two more distinctive Tai languages, Shan and Lue.

The ethnic distinctiveness of many of the Tai-speaking peoples of Thailand is not based on linguistic differences alone. Those who call themselves "Thai" without any qualification are speakers of Siamese or Central Thai who trace their descent to forebears who were subjects of the several premodern kingdoms known as Siam, i.e., Ayutthaya (1350–1767), Thonburi (1767–1782), and Bangkok from its founding in 1782 until the end of the nineteenth century when the Siamese state was radically transformed. Historically, the Siamese followed a Buddhist tradition that was different in significant ways from the traditions of the Tai-speaking peoples in northern and northeastern Thailand. The Siamese tradition was closely linked to the tradition of the Khmer of Cambodia while the traditions in the north and northeast had greater affinities to those in Burma. Although all Buddhist traditions in modern Thailand have been reshaped by the same religious reforms, which began in the mid-nineteenth century, customary practices persist and distinguish the Siamese from other Tai-speaking peoples.

In northern Thailand, a number of monks and lay persons have actively maintained the distinctive Yuan religious tradition. This tradition is linked with language differences; the orthography used for writing Northern Thai traditionally was quite different from that used for writing Siamese. Northern Thai speakers share with Northeastern Thai and the Lao of Laos a preference for glutinous rice as their staple food, and the customs associated with this food further distinguish them from the Siamese. Northern Thai or Khon Mɥang identity is further rooted in the separate history of the region, a history of a group of principalities known collectively as Lanna Thai. These principalities, of which Chiang Mai was preeminent, enjoyed either independence or autonomy from the Siamese courts until the end of the nineteenth century.

Although Northeastern Thai speakers, also known as Khon Isan (literally, "people of the northeast") or Thai-Lao (namely, the Lao who live in Thailand), were under Siamese control for much longer than were the Northern Thai, they also have a history of relative autonomy. From the latter part of the eighteenth century, when the area was brought under Siamese control, to the end of the nineteenth century, the region was divided into dozens of small feudalities, each under a hereditary "lord" who paid obeisance to the Siamese king. Since the elimination of this system of indirect rule at the end of the nineteenth century, there have been numerous incidents of suppression of political dissent in the region by the Thai government. Memories of these incidents and of the period of semiautonomy in the premodern period have helped to shape Northeastern Thai identity. In addition, Northeastern Thai follow a distinctive Buddhist tradition, one closely related to both the Northern Thai and the Lao, and follow other distinctive customs such as those associated with the cultivation and eating of glutinous rice.

Southern Thai identity is rooted primarily in the political-religious history of the region, especially the history of the towns of Nakhon Si Thammarat (historically known as Ligor) and Chaiya. Because this history is closely linked in a positive way with the Siamese kingdoms, and because Southern Thai language and customs are not so clearly distinguishable from those of the Siamese as those of the Northern and Northeastern Thai are, Southern Thai identity has tended to be rather muted, although in recent years Southern Thai regionalism has become more evident.

Most of the peoples speaking one of the lesser Tai languages maintain their identities only within local contexts and with reference to the Siamese tend to associate themselves with some other identity. Thus, Phu Thai and Yǫ speakers see themselves as Northeastern Thai and Lue and Shan speakers consider themselves Northern Thai vis-à-vis the Siamese. Even the Lao Song and Lao Phuan speakers who live in central Thailand tend to identify themselves as Northeastern Thai because of the connection between their languages and customs and those of the Northeastern Thai.

Non-Tai Minorities

Tai-speaking peoples are not the original inhabitants of what is now Thailand. Prior to the eleventh century, when Tai first became historically significant, peoples speaking languages belonging to the Austroasiatic or Mon-Khmer language family were dominant in the area. This family includes not only the major languages of Mon and Khmer but also dozens of smaller languages spoken by peoples from Assam in India to the highlands of southern Vietnam. In Thailand, there are groups of Mon and Khmer as well as smaller groups of such Austroasiatic-speaking tribal peoples as the Lawa, Thin, and Khamu.

The Mon, who in the period from around the third century A.D. to the thirteenth century had kingdoms in central and northern Thailand as well as in lower Burma, have the longest tradition of being Buddhist of any other people in mainland Southeast Asia. When Tai-speaking peoples settled in Mon areas, they adopted the Buddhism of the Mon. In turn, many descendants of the Mon became speakers of Tai languages. Such mutual assimilation between Mon and Tai in Thailand, comparable to a similar mutual assimilation between Mons and Burmans in Burma, has resulted in the almost total eclipse of Mon as a distinctive identity. Western Thailand and the area around Bangkok retain, however, small Mon populations, consisting mainly of descendants of refugees from Burma in the late eighteenth and early nineteenth centuries. These Mon continue to speak their own language, although they are almost universally bilingual in Thai, and continue to observe some distinctive customs that are mainly associated with their own Buddhist temple-monasteries.

Contacts between Tai and Khmer were less peaceful than those between Tai and Mon. When the first Tai states emerged in the thirteenth and fourteenth centuries, they challenged the dominance of the Khmer empire of Angkor over much of central mainland Southeast Asia. Not only were Khmer governors of provinces in what is today central Thailand ousted, but the Siamese state of Ayutthaya attacked and conquered the capital of Angkor itself. By the middle of the fifteenth century, Ayutthaya had replaced Angkor as the dominant power in the area. Subsequently, the kings of Ayutthaya borrowed many of the court traditions of Angkor and emulated Angkor by extending their power throughout the central part of mainland Southeast Asia. This expansion of the Siamese state brought under Siamese control areas in which much of the populace spoke Khmer or such Khmer-related languages as Kui (called Suai by the Siamese). Even after being forced by the French in the late nineteenth century to renounce sovereignty over what is today northwestern Cambodia, the Siamese court continued to rule over areas of eastern and northeastern Thailand that contained significant numbers of Khmer speakers or speakers of Khmer-related languages. Today, there are close to a million people living on Thailand's border with Cambodia who continue to speak Khmer or Khmer-related languages at home and who follow distinctive traditions.

Almost all Tai-speaking peoples and Austroasiatic-speaking peoples in Thailand, except for a small number of tribal peoples, find a shared identity in religion, for although they follow variant traditions of Theravada Buddhism they adhere to the same basic doctrines and accord respect to all members of the Buddhist clergy, the sangha, no matter what ethnic background a member of the sangha may come from. Even most of the small population of Austroasiatic-speaking tribal peoples consider themselves to be Buddhist. Those Tai-speaking peoples (mainly speakers of Southern Thai or of Siamese) who follow Islam clearly stand apart from the Buddhists who speak the same languages; the former believe that they constitute a separate group, the (Thai) Muslims.

Adherence to Islam is also a primary component of the distinctive identity of the Malays who live in the southernmost provinces of Thailand. For them, Malay language and pre-Islamic customary practices are also significant markers of their identity. In addition, many of the Malays living in the province of Pattani accentuate their separate identity by referring to the history of the formerly semiautonomous sultanate of Pattani.

Malays, like Tai-speaking and Austroasiatic-speaking peoples in Thailand, can claim to be a "people of the place," that is, to be a people whose ancestors settled in what is now Thailand in the distant past. Such "peoples of the place" distinguish themselves from people who are immigrants or descendants of immigrants. The Chinese constitute by far the largest immigrant population in Thailand. Although a few Chinese came to the country before the middle of the nineteenth century, most came during the period from about 1860 to 1940. Mass immigration of Chinese was effectively brought to an end when World War II began. The Chinese who settled in Thailand (a significant percentage of migrants returned to China) assimilated to Thai society to a greater extent than did Chinese migrants to almost any other society in Southeast Asia. There still remains, however, a significant population, located primarily in Bangkok, which continues to identify itself as Chinese (*khon cin*). A far larger number of people recognize their Chinese ancestry (*luk cin*, literally, "children of Chinese") but also identify as Thai; those belonging to this group are usually termed "Sino-Thai." Most Sino-Thai do not speak any Chinese language or retain Chinese names, and most consider themselves to be Theravada Buddhists rather than followers of Mahayana Buddhism, Confucianism, or Taoism. Many Sino-Thai, like the people who identify as Chinese, do, however, continue to practice some form of ancestor worship.

A small number of the Vietnamese living in Thailand today trace their descent to Catholic refugees who fled Vietnam in the middle of the nineteenth century. Most Vietnamese immigrants came, however, following the end of the French-Indochina War in 1954. To this day, few of this latter migrant group or their descendants have been permitted to become Thai citizens. Some were repatriated to Vietnam in the 1960s, but most remain in settlements in northeastern Thailand. More recent refugees from Vietnam, as well as the much larger number of refugees from Laos and Cambodia, have also been prevented from taking up permanent residence in Thailand. The presence of these refugees has, nonetheless, influenced the attitude of the government toward related peoples living permanently in the country.

A very small population of Indians who are also immigrants or descendants of immigrants also exists in Thailand. Indians, who are internally divided into Hindus, Sikhs, and Muslims, are found mainly in Bangkok and other urban centers. Most are connected with trade, especially the textile trade. In addition to Indians, Vietnamese, and Chinese, there are also other small immigrant communities in Thailand, with the Burmese forming perhaps the largest of these. In Bangkok there are conspicuous Western and Japanese communities, but very few members of these communities become citizens of Thailand or remain in the country longer than a few years.

Owing to the wide publicity given to the opium trade as well as to the promotion of tourism, tribal peoples are perhaps the best-known distinctive ethnic groups in Thailand. In fact, tribal peoples—whom the Thai refer to as "highlanders" (*chao khao*)—constitute only about 1 percent of the total population of the country, a smaller percentage than that of any other country of mainland Southeast Asia except Cambodia. Speakers of Karen languages, who live in the hill areas of northern and western Thailand, account for over half of the tribal population. Many Karen people, like the Austroasiatic-speaking Lawa, Thin, and Khamu, see themselves not only as tribal but also as "people of the place" with close relations to the local Tai-speaking populace. By way of contrast, most other tribal people are relatively recent immigrants to Thailand and maintain a much greater sense of distinctiveness. The second largest tribal group, and perhaps the best known because of its association with opium production and involvement in the tourist trade, are the Hmong (called Meo by the Thai and also known as Miao). Closely related to the Hmong are the Mien or Yao. While the Hmong and Mien migrated into northern Thailand from southern China by way of Laos, the Akha, Lahu, and Lisu migrated to northern Thailand from Burma.

In recent years, the Thai government has moved to stop the immigration of tribal peoples into northern Thailand. This effort has been most conspicuous with regard to those tribal peoples—mainly Hmong—who have fled from Laos since 1975. These peoples have been confined to refugee camps, and many have been resettled outside of Thailand, mainly in the United States. There remains, however, a sizable tribal population living in refugee camps, many of whom have some contact with members of the same groups (mainly Hmong and Mien) who are permanently settled in Thailand.

Some tribal people have been converted to Christianity, but such conversion does not necessarily entail any change of ethnic identity. In contrast with both Buddhism and Islam, Christianity is not linked with any particular ethnic identity. The very small Christian population in Thailand—numbering about 240,000 in the 1980 census—includes Tai-speaking peoples (mostly Northern Thai), Chinese and Sino-Thai, and Vietnamese as well as tribal peoples. Although local Christian congregations sometimes assume the ethnic character of the people who belong to them, the statewide Catholic church and the Church of Christ in Thailand (the main Protestant church) have promoted national rather than ethnic identities.

The stance taken by the Christian churches reflects an effort on their part to take advantage of state policy to encourage identification of the populace with the Thai nation instead of local ethnic identities. The idea of a national community is quite recent in Thai history, dating only to the end of the nineteenth century when reforms were instituted that began the transformation of the traditional Siamese state into the modern nation-state of Thailand. The idea has been formulated, however, with reference to the premodern past, and the different interpretations of that past advanced by different governments and national leaders have determined the salience of particular ethnic identities.

NOTES

1. On the relationship between rice agriculture and settlement patterns in Thailand, see Lucien M. Hanks, *Rice and Man: Agricultural Ecology in Southeast Asia* (Chicago: Aldine-Atherton, 1972).

2. For a good review of Thai prehistory, discussed with reference to the prehistory of mainland Southeast Asia, see Donn Bayard, "The Roots of Indochinese Civilization: Recent Developments in the Prehistory of Southeast Asia," *Pacific Affairs* 53:1 (1980), pp. 89–114. A guide to an exhibition of materials from Ban Chiang also provides a good discussion of Thai prehistory (see *Discovery of a Lost Bronze Age: Ban Chiang*, by Joyce C. White [Philadelphia: University Museum, University of Pennsylvania, and the Smithsonian Institution, 1982]).

3. For discussion of these estimates, see Larry Sternstein, "A critique of Thai Population Data," *Pacific Viewpoint* 6:1 (1965), pp. 15–38, and Ralph Thomlinson, *Thailand's Population: Facts, Trends, Problems, and Policies* (Bangkok: Thai Watana Panich, 1971). Population estimates prior to 1900 are very unreliable both because no adequate census data exist and because the boundaries of the country were not the same as present-day boundaries.

4. On the politics of family planning programs in Thailand, see Ronald L. Krannich and Caryl R. Krannich, *The Politics of Family Planning Policy: Thailand—A Case of Successful Implementation* (Lanham, Md: University Press of America, 1983).

5. According to official figures, the population growth rates for the period between 1971 and 1981 have been as follows: 1971, 3.0; 1974-1975, 2.8; 1975, 2.5; 1976, 1.9; 1977, 2.4; 1978, 2.1; 1979, 2.0; 1980, 1.8; and 1981, 1.9—see Thailand, National Economic and Social Development Board, *Khryangchi phawa sangkhom khong prathet Thai, Ph.S. 2520* [Thailand, Social indicators, 1977]

(Bangkok, 1979); *Khryangchi phawa sangkhom, 2524* [Social indicators, 1979] (Bangkok, 1981); and *Khryangchi phawa sangkhom, 2524* [Social indicators, 1981] (Bangkok, 1983).

6. Percentages from Thomlinson, *Thailand's Population,* p. 56.

7. Thailand, National Statistical Office, Office of the Prime Minister, *1980 Population and Housing Census* (Bangkok, 1983).

8. Statistics calculated from data given in Wolf Donner's *The Five Faces of Thailand: An Economic Geography* (London: C. Hurst and Company, 1978), p. 59.

9. See, in this regard, Bruce London, *Metropolis and Nation in Thailand: The Political Economy of Uneven Development* (Boulder, Colo.: Westview Press, 1980).

10. For a discussion of the ethnic composition of the population of Thailand, see Peter Kunstadter, "Thailand: Introduction," in *Southeast Asian Tribes, Minorities, and Nations,* ed. Peter Kunstadter (Princeton: Princeton University Press, 1967), 2:369–400. Also see U.S. Department of the Army, *Ethnographic Study Series: Minority Groups in Thailand* (Washington, D.C.: U.S. Government Printing Office, 1970). The best discussion of linguistic diversity in Thailand is James A. Matisoff's "Linguistic Diversity and Language Contact," in *Highlanders of Thailand,* ed. John McKinnon and Wanat Bhruksasri (Kuala Lumpur: Oxford University Press, 1983), pp. 56–86.

11. On Tai dialects and languages spoken in Thailand, see Marvin Brown, *From Ancient Thai to Modern Dialects* (Bangkok: Social Science Association of Thailand Press, 1965).

2

The Legacy of Tradition

The first states in what is today Thailand appear to have emerged in the early part of the Christian era. What may be considered tribal chiefdoms, based on sedentary rice agriculture, metallurgy, and limited trade, were established sometime around the beginning of the Christian era on the Khorat Plateau (northeastern Thailand) and in the lower Cao Phraya River basin (central Thailand). Several of these chiefdoms were transformed into small kingdoms when new ideas of power based on the Hindu-Buddhist religion and expressed in an Indian-derived literary culture were introduced into the area. These Indian influences were brought to Southeast Asia, not by military conquerors, but by merchants and by monks and priests who traveled on commercial vessels. From about the tenth century A.D. on, the petty states on the Khorat Plateau were brought under the control of the Khmer empire with its capital at Angkor near the Great Lake (Tonlé Sap) in northwestern Cambodia. In the Cao Phraya basin, a distinctive Mon-Buddhist civilization known as Dvaravati emerged and became associated with a number of petty kingdoms. Sometime before the eleventh century A.D., one of the most important of the Dvaravati kingdoms, Lavo (modern Lopburi), helped establish the small state of Haripuñjaya with its capital at modern-day Lamphun in northern Thailand. Lavo itself, with surrounding territories in the Cao Phraya basin was brought under Angkorean control in the twelfth century. Angkor also extended its power over areas in the lower Ping and Yom river valleys, but it did not succeed in bringing Haripuñjaya into its domain.

THE TAI AND THE ORIGINS OF SIAM

Just when Tai-speaking peoples began to move from their original homeland in southern China and to settle in what is present-day Thailand has not been clearly established by historical evidence. The earliest mention of Tai is in an inscription of the eleventh century A.D., but it

24

is almost certain that Tai had been moving into the area of central mainland Southeast Asia well before that time, perhaps since the seventh century A.D. By the eleventh century, there was most probably a substantial Tai-speaking population living in the domains of the Mon-Buddhist kingdoms of Dvaravati in the lower Cao Phraya basin and Haripuñjaya in the north as well as in the western territories of the Angkorean empire. The immigrant Tai may well have been organized as tribal peoples under petty chiefs, as such organization has been reported much later for non-Buddhist Tai such as the Black Tai, White Tai, Jui or Chung-Chia, Nung, and Tho living along the borders of southeastern China, northern Vietnam, and northeastern Laos. The Tai who migrated to central mainland Southeast Asia, however, came under the influence of the Buddhist Mon and the Hindu-Buddhist Khmer and subsequently adapted their traditions to Indian-derived culture.

Relations between the Tai and the Mon and Khmer who ruled the area appear to have been amicable, and there was probably intermarriage between families of Tai chiefs and the Mon ruling families of the petty states in the lower Cao Phraya basin. It seems likely that by the twelfth century A.D., Tai outnumbered Mon and Khmer not only in the sparsely populated hilly regions of the far north but also in the valleys of the lower Ping and Yom rivers (north central Thailand) and even in the Cao Phraya basin. By the thirteenth century, Tai lords had founded or assumed control of a number of petty states, the most important being Sukhothai in the Yom River valley, Chiang Mai in the north, and probably Nakhon Si Thammarat on the peninsula.

The kingdom of Sukhothai, founded in the middle of the thirteenth century, has a special place in Thai history primarily because Ramkhamhaeng (ruled 1279?–1299?), who according to official genealogies was Sukhothai's third king, claimed to have devised (in 1283) the first writing system for a Tai language. His famous inscription of 1292 is also taken today to be the first work of Thai literature. The orthographic system ascribed to Ramkhamhaeng, one that influenced both modern Siamese and modern Lao scripts, was not the only system of writing devised for Tai languages. In northern Thailand, Mon models were used for a script for writing the Yuan language, and this orthography was employed until quite recently in northern Thailand, in Kengtung in the Shan State of Burma, and for religious texts among the Lao of Laos and northeastern Thailand. Its use has all but disappeared, however, as a modernized version of Sukhodayan orthography has been adopted as the official script for today's standard Thai. Sukhothai also figures prominently in modern Thai history as having been an important center for Buddhist culture and art in the thirteenth and fourteenth centuries.

Standing image of the Buddha at the medieval capital of Sukhothai. (Photo by author)

Although Ramkhamhaeng was a warrior king who brought a large area of what is today central and southern Thailand under the control of Sukhothai, this kingdom was not long preeminent among the new Tai states. In the middle of the fourteenth century, a man first known as Uthong and later, after becoming king, as Ramathibodi (ruled 1350–1369), and who may well have been Chinese or of Chinese descent and who was married to a (Mon?) princess of Suphanburi, founded a new kingdom known as Ayutthaya (Ayudhya). Although the ethnic background of Uthong was probably not Tai, Ayutthaya was, nevertheless, to become a Tai kingdom, one that would subsequently be known as Siam. Within a very short time after its founding, Ayutthaya became the dominant power in the area. Ayutthayan history begins with the uniting of the domains of the formerly independent principalities of Suphanburi and Lavo (Lopburi), and the kingdom then extended its control further southward down the peninsula to include Nakhon Si Thammarat. In the late fourteenth century, Ayutthayan forces attacked and conquered Angkor, the capital of the Khmer empire. Faced with these attacks as well as suffering internal weaknesses, the Khmer kings abandoned Angkor in the 1440s and moved their capital to Phnom Penh. At the same time, Ayutthaya had been seeking to extend its authority over Sukhothai. In 1438, the Sukhothai dynasty came to an end, and Sukhothai became an integral part of the Ayutthayan kingdom.

While Ayutthaya was consolidating its power in the lower Ping and Yom river valleys, in the Cao Phraya basin, and on the peninsula, another Tai state, Chiang Mai, was establishing its dominance in the northern valleys of the Ping, Wang, Yom, and Nan valleys. Yet another Tai state, also founded in the middle of the fourteenth century, became established in the middle Mekong valley in what is today central Laos. Although in the fifteenth century Lan Chang (as the Lao state was known) and Lanna Thai (with its capital at Chiang Mai) were roughly equivalent in power to Ayutthaya, and although Chiang Mai was a greater center of Buddhist literary culture than Ayutthaya, neither Lan Chang nor Lanna Thai were to be antecedents of the modern Thai state. It was from Ayutthaya and its successor kingdoms of Thonburi and Bangkok, all based in the lower Cao Phraya basin, that the traditional order of Siam was to develop.

TRADITIONAL ORDER IN SIAM

The boundaries of Thailand today are the product of the colonial period even though Thailand was never itself a colonial dependency. Prior to the end of the nineteenth century, the incorporation of peoples into a state system was predicated not on a notion of geographical boundaries delimiting the territories of the state but on a relationship between ruler and subject communities. The traditional state of premodern Siam had its roots both in organizational patterns that the Tai brought with them and in Indianized models that the Tai borrowed from the Mon and Khmer.

Village, Mµang, and Bureaucracy

In the Tai system, the basic unit of political life was the village (*ban*),[1] and villages were grouped together in larger political entities known as *mµang*. As David Wyatt, in his history of Thailand, has observed, *mµang* "is a term that defies translation, for it denotes as much personal as spatial relationships. When it is used in ancient chronicles to refer to a principality, it can mean both the town located at the hub of a network of interrelated villages and also the totality of town and villages which was ruled by a single *chao* [*cao*], 'lord.'"[2] The geographical boundaries of a *mµang* were always rather vague because in traditional thought, the head of a *mµang*—a man who might be a lord (*cao*) in his own right or an appointed representative of a higher lord—exercised authority not over territory but over the people who lived in the villages in the jurisdiction of his *mµang*.

The *mµang* was a relatively small entity until the Tai came under the influence of the Indianized Mon and Khmer. The Tai rulers who formed the kingdoms of Sukhothai, Ayutthaya, Lanna Thai, and Lan Chang sought to make their *mµang* into what in Thai is termed a *ratcha-anacak*, a kingdom. This term, which is derived from Sanskrit, refers to a type of polity whose model is based on Hindu-Buddhist theories of statecraft. This model was widely employed throughout Southeast Asia, and states that seem to have been based on the model have been termed "Indianized states."[3] The ruler of a *ratcha-anacak* is more than simply the lord of a *mµang*; he is a *raja* (the term from which the Thai *ratcha* is derived). Such a *raja* exercises authority (*ana*) based on his personal identification with sacred power, an identification that is manifest in the public rites the king performs. The *raja* occupies a throne at the center of a circle (*cak*, from Skt. *cakra*), also known in Indian manuals of government as a *mandala*, which is a "this-worldly" reflection of the sacred cosmos. Within this circle are lesser polities whose lords recognize the overlordship of the king so long as he is able, through ritual performance or successful warfare, to demonstrate that he possesses divine authority.

At its inception Ayutthaya, like its Mon predecessors and like Sukhothai, was a relatively unstable kingdom, dependent on the personal qualities of its king. It, too, might have been eclipsed by some other kingdom whose ruler had emerged from what had previously been a subordinate *myang* within the Ayutthayan circle to challenge successfully the Ayutthayan king's claim to be at the center of a divinely constituted world. However, King Trailok, who reigned from 1448 to 1488, instituted a new version of the old model, one that was to make the structure of his kingdom much less dependent on the actual personal qualities of the man who sat on the throne. Trailok created a state comprising what might be termed concentric circles, each focused on the capital. Although the domains in the outer circles retained considerable autonomy, being either vassal kingdoms (*prathetsarat,* from Skt. *pradesa raja*) with their own hereditary kings (*raja*) or "outer *myang*" with hereditary lords (*cao*), those in the inmost circle, the "inner *myang*," were placed under governors who became part of a state bureaucracy.

The type of bureaucratic system instituted by Trailok had as its basic unit not a *myang* but a *krom,* usually translated as a "department." The traditional *krom,* in contrast with the *krom* as it came to be construed after the reforms of King Chulalongkorn at the end of the nineteenth century, was defined with reference to both function (e.g., military and treasury) and administrative control over a segment of the populace; in this latter characteristic, the *krom* was more similar to the traditional *myang* than to the modern unit of administrative bureaucracy. People appointed to positions within the *krom* differed in a fundamental respect from those who exercised authority over the traditional Tai *myang.* The latter were linked by descent to previous *myang* lords and had extended kin ties to many who lived within the same *myang.* The *nai,* or nobility, who were appointed to *krom* positions might well be related to other *nai,* but they had no hereditary rights within a particular *krom.* Rather, they held their positions only by royal appointment and could be removed from office at any time by royal command. The nobles who were appointed to *krom* positions thus became "servants of the king" rather than "lords of *myang.*"

The Sakdi na *System*

Under King Trailok, a common standard was developed for ranking all people within the kingdom by whether they lived in outer or inner *myang* and whether they were commoners or of the nobility, hereditary *myang*-based aristocracy, or royalty. This system of ranking, called the *sakdi na* system, has been the subject of considerable controversy among the scholars who have attempted to understand the social system of premodern Siam and to trace the persisting influence of this system on modern Thai society. *Sakdi na* combines an indigenous Tai term, *na* meaning "rice field," with a Sanskrit-derived term, *sakdi* (from *śakti*), that in India carries the primary meaning of "energy" or "active power" of deity, especially a female deity. The Siamese phrase, *sakdi na,* has typically been translated as "degrees of dignity or rank . . . giving the right to rule over certain grants of land."[4]

The notion of "power over land" has been taken as indicating that the traditional sociopolitical system that existed in Siam from the fifteenth to the mid-nineteenth century was a "feudal" system. The people who argue for the salience of the feudal model have focused attention on the usage of *na*, rice field, in the legal treatises that detail the ranking of people within the *sakdi na* system. Quaritch Wales, in his pioneering study of the Ayutthayan system, gives a succinct interpretation of why he thinks this usage implies a feudal system:

> The time is now ripe for us to explain the origin of the *śakti nā*, which literally means "power" (*śakti*) of "fields" (*nā*); and the survival of the use of which in these laws is one of the strongest pieces of evidence for the basis of the Siamese feudal system having originally been territorial. Under this type of feudalism the *śakti nā* evidently expressed the area of land in *rái* which a vassal held from his lord, and this in the case of an ordinary freeman was not more than 25 *rái*; while a lord with a *śakti nā* of 5,000 *rái* had that area of land with its conjoined serfs under his control.[5]

Wales recognizes that those who held high *sakdi na* ranks in Ayutthayan times rarely controlled anywhere near the amount of land, and associated "serfs," that their rank indicated. He suggests that the *sakdi na* system was "retained" and used "to tell the number of clients attached to a patron. . . . Thus, supposing each of his clients owned 25 *rái* a patron of *śakti nā* grade 400 controlled 16 men; while a minister of 10,000 *śakti nā* grade controlled 400 clients."[6]

Wales's interpretation of the *sakdi na* system as "feudal" is based on a rather conjectural reading of Siamese history and appears to have been suggested by a rather diffuse notion of feudalism drawn from Western historiography. A more rigorous attempt to construe the *sakdi na* system as a type of feudalism has been made by scholars drawing on Marxist theory. Jit Poumisak, the brilliant radical writer of the 1950s and early 1960s, initiated this line of interpretation in his *Chomna sakdi na nai pacuban*, a work whose title is usually translated as *The Face of Thai Feudalism Today*. In the 1970s, Jit's work stimulated a prolonged debate involving radical scholars, some theoreticians in the Communist party of Thailand, and other scholars about the character of Siam's "precapitalist social formation."[7] This debate has led most scholars to reject the equation of the *sakdi na* system with feudalism, but the concept of *sakdi na* has been retained as a powerful trope for talking about a "backward agrarian order," "authoritarian rule," and "exploitative relations of production."[8] It also has salience for characterizing the ideological system that was the basis for the type of Indianized state that Siam evolved following the reforms of King Trailok in the fifteenth century.

The *sakdi na* system was associated not with a fragmentation of power—as feudalism would imply—but, ideologically, with the concentration of power in the hands of the monarchy. It is important in this connection to consider not only the concept of *na* but also that of *sakdi*. In the usage that emerged during the reign of King Trailok, the latter concept came to mean, not the concrete power or energy of a deity, but an abstract sacral power that attaches to the monarchy as an institution. *Sakdi* can be parceled out to others, but only by an act of a king. Similarly, *na* should be seen, not as fief whose product has been granted to a particular lord and his descendants in perpetuity, but as a portion of the total land (*phaendin*) of a kingdom whose ultimate owner (*cao*) is the king alone. Kings held that only they were entitled to the surplus product of the labor of the subjects (*phrai*) of the kingdom and reserved for themselves the absolute right to levy demands for taxes and for corvée labor. That certain peoples—either because they were bondsmen of particular lords or temples or because they were members of the sangha—were excluded from such demands did not undermine the basic principle of the ultimate "ownership" of the land by the king. The *na* that the king invested temporarily in one of his subjects stood for a portion of the total revenue that the king received from the total product of the land, which he owned. In short, those who received *sakdi na* status held it at the will of the king.

The sacredness of the monarchy in traditional Siam was manifested in the rituals the king performed. From the fifteenth century on, each king of Siam participated in an elaborate and a conspicuously Brahmanistic set of rituals, which appeared to assert that the king of Siam, like the kings of Angkor whose model was being followed, was an incarnation or avatar of a Hindu god. These Brahmanical rituals continued to be followed even into the modern period, with King Chulalongkorn resurrecting a number that had previously all but disappeared.[9] Even the present king, Bhumibol Adulyadej, has perpetuated some of these rituals. In traditional times, the significance of the Hindu character of these rituals was most meaningful to the kings and the people closely associated with their courts. Yet, the legitimacy of traditional Siamese monarchs among their subjects generally rested less on their being viewed as Hindu gods than on Theravada Buddhist conceptions of kingship. The Siamese people derived their basic understanding of the world in which they lived, a world in which the monarch had a central place, from the Theravada Buddhist religion to which they adhered.

A BUDDHIST SOCIETY

Tai Adoption of Theravada Buddhism

The Tai peoples who first settled in what is now Thailand can be compared to the barbarians living on the edges of the Roman empire. Although the Tai lived in proximity to the Hindu-Buddhist civilizations of the Mon, the Khmer, and the Burmese, they themselves followed traditions that did not make use of written texts or require the services of priests or monks who devoted their lives to religious vocations. For these Tai, the uncertainties and inequities of life were understood primarily with reference to the presumed actions of spirits (*phi*) of various types and with reference to the status of a vital essence or soul (*khwan*), which was possessed not only by humans but also by rice, elephants, and some other forms of life.

Through contact with the Mon and Khmer, the Tai came to know of other religious ideas. In the period from about the eleventh to the fourteenth century, the prevailing religions, although labeled Buddhism in the case of the Mon and Hinduism in the case of the Khmer, were not the same as the Buddhism and Hinduism that we know today. The Mon and Khmer of this period, like the Burmese, who in the eleventh to the fourteenth centuries had developed the civilization of Pagan in upper Burma, had taken from Indian sources the theory that the world as it is experienced is but a part of a much larger cosmic order in space and time. In order for the world of experience to be satisfactory for the people who live in it, it needs, according to the theory, to be attuned to and harmonized with the cosmic order. In the medieval civilizations of Southeast Asia—in Java as well as on the mainland—monumental edifices representing the cosmos were erected by "god-kings" in order to bring their realms into harmony with the cosmic order. Although at Angkor such edifices were typically dedicated to Hindu deities and at Pagan they were dedicated to the Buddha, the underlying idea was the same.[10]

The cosmological religion of the medieval kingdoms in Southeast Asia was dependent upon a monarch who could mobilize large numbers of people to labor in constructing temples or stupas. The monuments of Angkor and Pagan, in particular, reflect a degree of political control and religious faith comparable to that required for the construction of the pyramids in Egypt. The building of large Hindu-Buddhist monuments in Southeast Asia also required the expertise of priests or monks who were well versed in the texts depicting the cosmology and in the rituals that must be performed in dedicating and maintaining the cults associated with the monuments.

When the Tai began to develop independent polities of their own, they adopted the ideas of Hindu-Buddhist cosmology from their neighbors, and the many Buddhist and some Hindu monuments found at Sukhothai re-created such a cosmology in stone. The Tai rulers at Sukhothai also assumed patronage of the sangha, or Buddhist clergy, and the Brahmins who were required for the associated cults.

At the time that the Tai were founding their first kingdoms, a religious revolution had begun that would soon result in a fundamental change in the religious traditions of mainland Southeast Asia. Among the Mon of what is today lower Thailand and lower Burma, there had been for many centuries chapters of monks who adhered to the Buddhism of the "elders" (Pali and Thai, *thera*). The Buddhism known as Theravada, or "the way of the elders," contrasts with Mahayana ("the great vehicle") Buddhism in several respects. In Theravada Buddhism, great efforts have been made to reproduce the teachings that embody the way of salvation (Pali, *dhamma*; Thai, *tham*) taught by the Buddha in precisely the same form from generation to generation ever since the original elders recited them. The sacred language of Theravada Buddhism is Pali rather than the Sanskrit that is employed in Mahayana Buddhism. Theravada Buddhism also gives little attention to distinct bodhisattvas, "Buddhas-to-be," while Mahayana Buddhism recognizes a pantheon of such bodhisattvas.[11]

The early Theravadin monks of Southeast Asia were few, mainly limited to the kingdoms of the Mons and Burmese, and they apparently lacked much influence prior to the thirteenth century. In the thirteenth to the fifteenth centuries, however, a Theravadin order of monks emerged as the dominant sangha throughout the lands of the Mons, the Burmese, the Tai, and the Khmer in mainland Southeast Asia. This major change began with a few monks from Southeast Asia who went to Theravada Buddhist centers in Sri Lanka (Ceylon). On their return, these Theravadin monks began to proselytize actively in Southeast Asia. Not only did they convert kings and their courtiers, but by the fifteenth century they had also succeeded in establishing chapters of the order, the Buddhist sangha, in villages throughout the area as well.

Tai Buddhist Worldview

Although the Tai, like their neighbors the Burmese, the Mon, and the Khmer, continued to draw upon Hindu-Buddhist cosmological notions for their religious worldviews, they also came to accept the orthodox Theravadin idea that the cosmos, like the world of experience, is impermanent and subject to change. Under the guidance of the teachings professed by monks in sermons drawn from texts written in the vernacular instead of the sacred, Pali, language, the Tai came to make the human

Shrine believed to hold relic of the Buddha on Doi Suthep, near Chiang Mai, northern Thailand. (Photo by author)

actor rather than a cosmic order the central focus of religious thought. The actions of an individual, if they contravene the moral premises recognized by the Buddha, will produce "demerit" (Thai, *bap;* from Pali, *papa*) that will manifest itself at some future time as some type of suffering. On the other hand, actions that are morally positive will produce "merit" (Thai, *bun;* from Pali, *puñña*) that in the future conduces to the experience of some valued state of being. This theory of action is embodied in Buddhist thought in the "law of *kamma*" (*karma* in Sanskrit; *kam* in Thai), the root meaning of *kamma* being action. In practice, adherents of Theravada Buddhism, including many if not most contemporary Thai, see themselves as experiencing some present combination of suffering and enjoyment as a consequence of *kamma* from a previous life and as having a responsibility to attend to the moral character of present acts in order to reap the best consequences of *kamma* in the future, either in this life or in the next one. Belief in *kamma*, thus, is associated with a belief in rebirth.

Although popular Buddhism as practiced by most Buddhists in Southeast Asia accords centrality to religious acts that produce merit, the teaching of the Buddha that ultimate religious salvation—*nibbana* (Sanskrit, *nirvana;* Thai, *niphan*) is to be achieved by transcending *kamma* altogether is not forgotten. The path to *nibbana* entails more than moral action (*sila*); it also requires concentration (*samadhi*) and wisdom (*pañña*). To tread the higher reaches of the path, it has long been held necessary to become a member of the sangha, thereby subjecting oneself to the discipline that enables one to cultivate detachment from worldly desires. Because sangha members follow the discipline devised by the Buddha, they are accorded the highest respect of anyone within a Buddhist society.

When the Tai became adherents of Theravada Buddhism, they did not abandon their previous beliefs in spirits (*phi*) and vital essence (*khwan*), nor did they reject the idea of a cosmic order. Rather, these beliefs were all subordinated to the orthodox Theravadin doctrine of *kamma* and the Theravadin message of salvation.

The Tai who came to accept the Buddhist-dominated worldview— and by the fifteenth century most Tai-speaking peoples throughout mainland Southeast Asia and southern China had done so—made the sangha the central religious institution of their societies. Those who became members of the sangha committed themselves to the study and use of the texts that contained the Buddhist *dhamma*. Thus, the sangha became essential to the perpetuation of the Buddhist religion. They also subjected themselves to the discipline (Pali, *vinaya*) that advanced them along the path to salvation. Finally, and perhaps most important, the sangha became a "field of merit" for the laity. The most positive moral act a layperson could perform was to provide support in the form of food, clothing, shelter, and medicines to the sangha. Through such acts, the laity "made merit" (*tham bun* in Thai), which would be experienced as a positive reward in the future, either in this life or in a subsequent lifetime.

The Sangha and Tai Society

In the several Tai societies, as in Burmese, Mon, and Khmer societies, the sangha never became an elite institution with members drawn only from the nobility. On the contrary, the overwhelming majority of Buddhist monks in these societies, as in contemporary Thailand, came from rural villages. The Tai, like other Theravada Buddhist peoples in Southeast Asia, adopted the ideal that every male should spend a period of time as a member of the Buddhist order. This ideal could be realized by a boy becoming a novice (Pali, *samanera*; Thai, *nen*) for a period of time. As a novice, he learned how to read Buddhist texts and to write, primarily in order to copy such texts. Novices also memorized the chants used in rituals. Because most boys in premodern Siam as well as in other Tai societies spent from a few months to several years as novices, a high degree of literacy obtained among males in these societies. Indeed, seventeenth-century visitors from France to Ayutthaya were impressed by the greater degree of literacy in Siam than in France of that time.

Among some Tai, notably the Siamese and the Lao, it was the ideal not only that a boy should become a novice but also that every man should become a monk (Pali, *bhikkhu*; Thai, *phra* or *phikkhu*). When a man took the vows of monkhood in Theravada Buddhism, he did not, as in Catholicism, necessarily commit himself to remain in the religious order for life. Rather, even a temporary period within the monkhood was viewed as instilling in a man a moral sense that would remain with him even after he returned to lay life. Such moral tempering was highly valued; among the Siamese, a man who had not yet been ordained as a monk was said to be "raw" (*dip*), while one who had spent time in the monkhood was "ripe" (*suk*). Women preferred "ripe" to "raw" men as husbands.

No adequate statistics are available on how many men in premodern Siam realized the traditional ideals of serving as novices and monks for a temporary period of time. The percentage was probably very high as there are still many villages today in which two-thirds of men follow the ideal.[12] The ideal of becoming a novice or monk for a period of time persists, and in recognition of the value placed upon this experience, the Thai government today permits male government civil servants to take leave for a lenten period of three months with full pay if they are ordained and spend the time in the monkhood.

Some men who entered the monkhood did not return to lay life but remained permanently in the Buddhist sangha, in theory at least, in order to become more knowledgeable about the Buddhist *dhamma* or to devote themselves to those practices conducing to salvation. The truly adept meditation monk has always been rare and has often attracted a considerable following as being a particularly potent field of merit. Ironically, today as in the past, the man who most seeks to realize the teachings of the Buddha by rejecting the world is likely to be the most sought after by people remaining in the world. Many more permanent monks have always devoted themselves to study of religious texts than have become adept at meditation.

In premodern Siam, an especially learned monk, who could read the scriptures and certain influential commentaries in Pali, was often recognized by a distinctive title. Although such titles were often conferred by the lay followers of a monk, the rulers of traditional Siam, like their counterparts in other Buddhist states, occasionally conferred titles, especially to very learned monks or those connected with monasteries supported by royalty. The kings thereby demonstrated their recognition of the significance of the sangha in their society while, at the same time, they asserted their authority over the sangha. In Siam the tension between popular and royal recognition of learned monks persisted until the late nineteenth century when reforms gave the royal government the sole right to confer clerical ranks.

Buddhist Kingship and Traditional Kingdoms

Kings and lords also appointed monks as abbots of the major *wat*s within their domains. These abbots typically came, not from the ordinary sangha, that is, the sangha that emerged from rural society, but from elite families. Although the kings of Siam, like their counterparts in other Buddhist societies in Southeast Asia, sought to incorporate all members of the sangha in their societies within a hierarchical order headed by royally appointed monks, these hierarchies never had the social significance that the Catholic hierarchy had in Europe. Buddhism could be perpetuated through local congregations without much reference to higher sangha authorities. Again, it was not until the reforms instituted at the end of the nineteenth century that an effective sangha hierarchy, encompassing all the monks in the country, was finally created.

The failure of kings in premodern Siam to assert their authority over all of the sangha within their domains indicates that Buddhism was not a religion of the elite but a popular religion that was well established in rural communities as well as in the towns. This fact had marked implications for the way in which the rulers, as well as the lords of the semiautonomous *myang*, established their legitimacy. Rituals in which kings and lords symbolically ordered their domains with reference to the sacred cosmos continued to be important and to impress at least those people who participated in them. But of at least equal importance was the notion that a person who had the right to rule, whether as king or lord, was one who "had merit" (*mi bun*), that is, was one who could be viewed as possessing extraordinary positive moral effectiveness of action as a consequence of previous positive *kamma*. Any man who successfully ascended a throne or became a lord was presumed to be a man possessing merit. It was necessary, however, for a king or lord continually to revalidate his charisma through conspicuous religious acts: making a pilgrimage to an important shrine, erecting a new religious edifice, and, above all, supporting the sangha.

That both ruler and populace adhered to Buddhism did not preclude a ruler's use of violence to gain his ends or those of the state. Kings and lords commonly employed torture and capital punishment as instruments of state. Because kings could not be held accountable to any law, they sometimes inflicted capital punishment on people who had committed quite petty infractions, but ones that had offended the ruler. Many kings in Siam, although not as many as in Burma, were deposed by their successors in violent palace coups. Wars were almost endemic. Not only were there numerous wars between Ayutthaya and the several kingdoms that existed in Burma, but there were also wars among the Tai states of Ayutthaya, Lanna Thai (Chiang Mai), and Lan Chang (Laos). Both wars and internal violence served to underscore the salience of the Buddhist message that the world was a vale of woe and suffering. Monks, through their detachment from the world, gained in esteem relative to those who held even the highest worldly status.

While the Buddhism of Siam was fundamentally similar to that of the other Tai states, and indeed to that found among the dominant peoples of Burma and Cambodia as well, some differences became relevant when Siam incorporated outlying territories into its domain. The orthographic system employed for religious texts by Siamese monks in the inner *myang* of Ayutthaya was a Khmer one that the Siamese call *khǫm*. In the realm of Lanna Thai, in what is today northern Thailand, a different script based on Mon and called Yuan was employed. In the Lao areas of Lan Chang and also in some outer *myang* of Ayutthaya the dhammic script (*tua tham*) used for religious purposes was essentially the same as the one used in Lanna Thai. The differences between the religious literatures of Ayutthaya on the one hand and those of the Lao areas and of Lanna Thai on the other tended to inhibit religious communication.

Within Siam proper, that is, within the inner *myang* of Ayutthaya, there were also some religious differences. Mon and Khmer continued to follow their own traditions. Muslim peoples who became subject to the king of Siam either lived in semiautonomous domains under their own lords or in separate enclaves within Siam proper. From about the seventeenth century on, there were small Christian communities in Ayutthaya, made up almost entirely of foreigners (Japanese as well as Westerners) who were confined to "stranger" quarters within the capital city. The tribal peoples of Siam, who maintained animistic beliefs, lived mainly in inaccessible border regions where the influence of the court was very weak. They were often ruled by their own chiefs, who, in turn, recognized the nominal overlordship of the king. So long as peoples who followed traditions different from those of the Siamese accepted the fact that the king was the source of sacral power, however they might have viewed that power, these differences did not become the basis for internal conflict.

ROOTS OF CHANGE IN THE EARLY CHAKRI PERIOD

In 1767, Burmese forces succeeded, after a siege lasting a year and a half, in conquering Ayutthaya. The Burmese invaders, as was typical in Southeast Asian warfare at the time, pillaged the city and took away to Burma the Siamese king, other members of the ruling family, and much of the populace that had not already fled. The destruction of the capital and the removal of the king plunged Siam into a turmoil that was to last for much of the following decade. Many people were attracted to would-be kings who claimed to have extraordinary *barami* (Pali, *parami*), or virtue in a Buddhist sense, or even claimed to be bodhisattvas, future Buddhas. One such man, Taksin, a half-Chinese former general under the last Ayutthayan king, was able to capitalize on his apparent charismatic potency and successful military prowess to make good his claim to the throne and to reunite the kingdom in 1776.

Since the old capital of Ayutthaya had been destroyed, it was assumed that it no longer embodied positive cosmic influences. Taksin therefore chose a new site for his capital: Thonburi, on the lower Cao Phraya River, situated across the river from where Bangkok stands today. Taksin succeeded not only in reuniting the kingdom of Siam but also in extending his sway over Chiang Mai, which had previously been a vassal of Burma. Taksin viewed his military success as evidence of his extraordinary virtue. Before long, he began to claim that he was a bodhisattva and insisted that he be so recognized by members of the Buddhist clergy. Claiming that their actions were justified because Taksin was deluded by a vision of his divinity, a group of officials staged a palace coup and placed another military leader, known to history as Chakri, on the throne.

The ascension of King Chakri to the throne in 1782 marked the beginning of the dynasty that has ruled Siam (later Thailand) to the present day. Although the first three kings of the Chakri dynasty are known in Thai by reign names (Yotfa, Loetla, and Nang Klao), they are usually designated in Western writings as Rama I, Rama II, and Rama III. Subsequent kings are referred to both by their names and the designation Rama followed by a roman numeral. King Bhumibol Adulyadej, the present king, is also known as Rama IX. The dynastic period initiated by Chakri is usually known as the Ratanakosin era, the era of the Emerald Buddha, since Chakri installed an image of that name, which he had taken from Laos, as the palladium, or sacred talisman, of the kingdom.

Rama I moved the capital from Thonburi across the Cao Phraya River to Bangkok where it has remained to the present day. As a port city, Bangkok was more oriented toward the outside world than was Ayutthaya and thus in a better position to become involved in the growth of international trade that was to become a feature of Southeast Asian life as the Europeans came to play an increasing role in the area from the early nineteenth century on.

Rama I, also known by the reign name of Phra Phutthayotfa (reigned 1782–1809) was one of the most influential kings ever to sit on the throne of Siam. During his reign, Siamese overlordship was established not only over the peoples living within the area of Siam proper but also over Lanna Thai; the Lao principalities of Luang Prabang, Vientiane, and Champasak, which were the successors to Lan Chang; parts of Cambodia; and several Malay sultanates in the south. To this day, some Thai hold that the rightful boundaries of their country should be those first established by Rama I. If this were the case, then all of what is today Laos, part of the Shan State of Burma, Siemreap and Battambang provinces in Cambodia, and Perlis and Kedah provinces in Malaysia would be part of Thailand. During World War II, Thailand used its alliance with Japan to reclaim these areas, only to lose them again in the wake of the Japanese defeat. But even without these territories, Thailand's present-day boundaries owe much to Rama I. If he had been less successful as a military leader, most of northern and northeastern Thailand as well as the Malay-speaking provinces of Pattani, Narathiwat, Yala, and Satun in southern Thailand might have been incorporated into neighboring countries whose boundaries were later fixed by their colonial rulers.

Rama I sought not only to establish effective political control over an enlarged realm but also to resurrect Siamese civilization from the ashes of Ayutthaya. During his reign, scribes were set to work copying the most important religious, literary, and legal texts of the past; leading members of the sangha were convened to record and correct the *Tripitaka*, the Buddhist scriptures as written in the Pali language; and poets and writers were supported to compose new works. Rama I himself is credited with having composed a new version of the *Ramakian*, that is, a Thai version of the Indian epic, the *Ramayana*. He also undertook a purge of the sangha, ridding it of members who had supported Taksin's messianic claims as well as those who were deemed to be in violation of the discipline (*vinaya*) incumbent on members of the order. He proscribed many animistic practices as being inappropriate for Buddhists, thereby laying the groundwork for the Buddhist reformation that was to follow in the mid- and late nineteenth century. Rama I and the other early Chakri kings did more than "restore" Siamese civilization following the fall of Ayutthaya. They began a new historical era, one that was significantly different from that of Ayutthaya.[13]

King Rama II, also known as Phra Phutthaloetla (reigned 1809–1824), and King Rama III, or Phra Nangklao (reigned 1824–1851), both encouraged the literary and artistic renascence begun by Rama I. During their reigns, Sunthon Phu, perhaps Siam's greatest poet, wrote most of his work. Rama II and Rama III pursued the same forward policies as Rama I toward peripheral areas, seeking to consolidate Siamese control over them. The Anglo-Burmese War of 1824–1826 introduced a new element in the international relations of Siam, one that Rama II and Rama III appear not to have understood fully. Nonetheless, the Burney Treaty, which Siam signed with Great Britain in 1826, a treaty that dealt with trade as well as border problems, foreshadowed a major shift in the role Siam would play on the international stage. It was also during the first half of the nineteenth century that Christian missionaries from Western countries began to appear in Siam in significant numbers, and through them, a young monk of princely blood was introduced to new realms of knowledge. Prince Mongkut, who in 1851 was to leave the monkhood and ascend the throne, gained from his interactions with missionaries and other Westerners insights into Western ways of thinking that were to make him radically different not only from his predecessors but also from most of the ministers and other ranking nobles of the court.

During his nearly three decades in the monkhood, Mongkut undertook a major reform movement within Siamese Buddhism. He believed that many accretions had grown up around the religion that obscured the true message of the Buddha. He studied the Pali scriptures in depth and learned all he could about sangha traditions in countries other than Siam. His conversations with Christian missionaries also stimulated him to reflect on the nature and essence of Buddhism. Before long, he had gathered round him a small coterie of monks who shared his desire for a purified sangha. When Mongkut became king, his associates in the sangha became the vanguard of a new fraternity (*nikaya*), the Thammayutnikai (Pali, Dhammayuti-nikaya), meaning those monks who adhered strictly to the *dhamma*, as contrasted with the Mahanikai (Pali, Maha-nikaya), the "large" (*maha*) fraternity of monks who continued to follow traditional practices.

When Mongkut assumed the throne in 1851, Siam was on the threshold of a new era. During his reign (1851–1868) and that of his son Chulalongkorn (1868–1910), Siam was forced to confront the challenge of Western colonial expansion. The process of meeting this challenge led ultimately to the transformation of Siam from a traditional into a modern nation-state. Although both kings were to make use of Western ideas in instituting this process, they also drew on the Siamese tradition that had been revitalized under Rama I and given new direction through the Buddhist reformation initiated by Mongkut.

NOTES

1. Because of the ambiguity in the meaning of the traditional word *ban*, which also means "house," it has been replaced in twentieth-century administrative usage by *muban*, literally, "collection of houses." In central Thailand, the Mon-derived term *bang* is sometimes found as a designation for village instead of *ban*. Thus, for example, the Thai village perhaps best known to Westerners because of the long period of ethnographic research carried out there—Bang Chan—has the *bang* designation whereas the village in northeastern Thailand in which I carried out fieldwork—Ban Noong Tyn—has, like other villages in northeastern and northern Thailand, the *ban* term.

2. David K. Wyatt, *Thailand: A Short History* (New Haven: Yale University Press, 1984), p. 7.

3. The term "Indianized state" was introduced by the famous historian, Georges Coedès—see his *The Indianized States of Southeast Asia* (Honolulu: East-West Center Press, 1968). Although this term conveys (even more so in the French term *les états hindouisés* from which it is translated) the idea that such states were shaped by Hindu ideas, Buddhist notions were often of at least equal significance for many states. For a discussion of the Indianized state as a microcosm of a sacred cosmos, see Robert Heine-Geldern, *Conceptions of State and Kingship in Southeast Asia*, Data Paper 18 (Ithaca, N.Y.: Cornell University Southeast Asia Program, 1956), and O. W. Wolters, *History, Culture, and Region in Southeast Asian Perspectives* (Singapore: Institute of Southeast Asian Studies, 1982), chap. 2. Stanley J. Tambiah and Clifford Geertz have seen in the Indianized state a more general model of statecraft, one that Tambiah terms the "galactic polity" and Geertz the "theatre state" (see Stanley J. Tambiah, *World Conqueror and World Renouncer: A Study of Buddhism and Polity in Thailand Against a Historical Background* [Cambridge: Cambridge University Press, 1976], esp. chap. 7; Tambiah, "The Galactic Polity: The Structure of Traditional Kingdoms in

Southeast Asia," *Annals of the New York Academy of Sciences* 293 [1977], pp. 60–97; and Clifford Geertz, *Negara: The Theatre State in Nineteenth Century Bali* [Princeton: Princeton University Press, 1980]). H.G. Quaritch Wales's *Ancient Siamese Government and Administration* (London: Bernard Quaritch, 1934; reprint, New York: Paragon, 1965), although dated, remains a useful source for understanding the Siamese form of the Indianized state. Charnvit Kasetsiri in *The Rise of Ayudhya: A History of Siam in the Fourteenth and Fifteenth Centuries* (Kuala Lumpur: Oxford University Press, 1976) and Tambiah in *World Conqueror and World Renouncer* offer more sophisticated interpretations.

4. The quotation is taken from the *Thai-English Dictionary*, comp. George Bradley McFarland (Stanford: Stanford University Press, 1944), p. 792. See also Wales, *Ancient Siamese Government*, esp. pp. 49ff.; Akin Rabibhadana, *The Organization of Thai Society in the Early Bangkok Period, 1782–1873*, Data Paper 74 (Ithaca, N.Y.: Cornell University Southeast Asia Program, 1969), pp. 21–23 et passim; and Tej Bunnag, *The Provincial Administration of Siam, 1892–1915* (Kuala Lumpur: Oxford University Press, 1977), pp. 7–8. On the traditional Siamese order, also see Richard A. O'Connor, "Law as Indigenous Social Theory: A Siamese Thai Case," *American Ethnologist* 8:2 (1981), pp. 223–237.

5. Wales, *Ancient Siamese Government*, pp. 49–50.

6. Ibid., p. 50.

7. This debate has been well reviewed by Craig J. Reynolds and Hong Lysa in "Marxism in Thai Historical Studies," *Journal of Asian Studies* 43:1 (1983), pp. 77–104.

8. Ibid., p. 85.

9. See, in this regard, H.G. Quaritch Wales, *Siamese State Ceremonies: Their History and Function* (London: Bernard Quaritch, 1931).

10. In Charles F. Keyes, *The Golden Peninsula: Culture and Adaptation in Mainland Southeast Asia* (New York: Macmillan, 1977), pp. 65–78, I provide a summary discussion of the "cosmological" religion as found in mainland Southeast Asia and the relationship of the Tai to this religion.

11. In Theravada Buddhism, the only bodhisattva who receives any attention is Maitreya (Pali, Mettaya; Thai, Phra Si An), the future Buddha who will come, according to legend, 5,000 years after Gotama Buddha, the Buddha who lived in India some 2,500 years ago.

12. See Charles F. Keyes, "Ambiguous Gender: Male Initiation in a Buddhist Society," in *Gender and Religion: On the Complexity of Symbols*, ed. Caroline Bynum, Stevan Harrell, and Paula Richman (Boston: Beacon Press, 1986).

13. Ben Anderson, drawing on the work of Nidhi Aeusrivongse, has said that "the rise of the present Jakri [Chakri] . . . dynasty at the end of the 18th century marked a decisive historical break from the high aristocratic civilization of the Ayutthayan era. (The early Jakri thus stand as Louis Philippe to Ayutthaya's Rois Soleil.)" See Ben Anderson, "Politics and Their Study in Southeast Asia," in *Southeast Asian Studies: Options for the Future*, ed. Ronald A. Morse (Lanham, Md: University Press of America, 1985), p. 47. Anderson refers to two papers in Thai by Nidhi Aeusrivongse on "Sunthǫn Phu, Bourgeois Poet Laureate" and "Bourgeois Culture and the Literature of the Early Rattanakosin Period."

3

Formation of the Thai Nation-State

In 1855, the British envoy Sir John Bowring went to Bangkok to persuade the Siamese court to open the country for trade. Following a period of intense negotiations, he persuaded the government of King Mongkut to sign a treaty. The Bowring Treaty provided not only for British authorities to have extraterritorial rights over British subjects, including those from the colonial dependencies of Burma, Malaya, and India, but for the removal of all restrictions on trade and for the fixing of very low export and import duties. The Bowring Treaty represented a watershed in Thai history: From the time of the treaty on, Siam was increasingly integrated into an international order dominated by Western powers. This process of integration led to Siam's transformation into a modern nation-state.

GROWTH OF AN EXPORT ECONOMY AND EMERGENCE OF A PLURAL SOCIETY

The Bowring Treaty

The extraterritoriality provision first laid down in the Bowring Treaty was to be included in subsequent treaties negotiated during the last half of the nineteenth century with other European countries, with the United States and, at the end of the century, with Japan. In these treaties, Siam was forced to surrender a considerable degree of sovereignty. Despite its loss of sovereignty, Siam was able to retain its independence while all the other countries of Southeast and South Asia were incorporated into Western-dominated colonial empires. Ultimately, the extraterritoriality provisions of the Bowring and subsequent treaties were to stimulate less change in Thai society than were the economic clauses of these treaties.

44

The Siamese crown had long derived a portion of its revenues from the control of trade. Internally, it had imposed taxes on commerce carried out in the territories under its control; externally, it had fixed duties on goods flowing through the main port of the country. By agreeing to the removal of restrictions on trade and to the fixing of very low duties on exports and imports, the Siamese government was forced to radically restructure the fiscal basis of the state. Bowring himself said that the treaty "involved a total revolution in all the financial machinery of the government."[1]

This revolution entailed a transformation in the sources of revenues for the Siamese government. Prior to the Bowring Treaty, a major portion of government revenues had been derived from royal trading monopolies, but under provisions of the treaty, these were abolished. The government was constrained, thus, to look to other sources to replace the lost revenues. Although direct taxes were increased and more efficiently collected, by the end of the century a number of indirect taxes, paid primarily by a growing Chinese population, were generating the largest proportion of revenues for the government. The taxes levied on opium, spirits, gambling, and lotteries, which were consumed or participated in almost exclusively by Chinese, provided up to half of all government revenues in the latter part of the nineteenth century. As G. William Skinner has said in his history of the Chinese community in Thailand: "It is not unfair to state that while the country depended on Chinese virtues for the expansion of commerce and industry, the government relied on Chinese vices for the expansion of public revenue."[2]

The expansion of international trade after the Bowring Treaty was signed not only attracted a large number of Chinese workers to construct the many new facilities or to work as stevedores, it also drew an increasing number of Siamese peasants into the commercial economy. Until the middle of the nineteenth century, peasants had rarely used currency, carrying on trade primarily through barter and paying taxes in kind or in labor. The governments of King Mongkut and especially of Chulalongkorn began to demand that the steadily increasing taxes be paid in cash. Moreover, the Bowring Treaty also stimulated the introduction of foreign products into Siamese markets, and these products could be purchased only with money. Siamese peasants began, particularly from the 1870s on, to generate cash income primarily through the production of crops for export.

Rice and Other Exports

Rice soon became the major export product of the country, and that commodity continues to generate a significant proportion of foreign exchange for Thailand even today. Between 1850 and 1907, rice exports rose from about 5 percent of the total crop produced to about 50 percent.[3] Peasants living in the central plains of Thailand were initially the primary producers of rice for export. Rather than intensifying production on existing fields in order to produce more than they needed for home consumption, peasants brought an increasing amount of acreage under cultivation. By the end of the century, and especially after the opening of the railway to Khorat (Nakhǫn Ratchasima) in 1900, peasants in northeastern Thailand also began to produce rice for the international market. Subsequently, villagers living in the Chiang Mai valley in northern Thailand also joined the ranks of those producing rice for export, although Northern Thai peasants never committed themselves so single-mindedly to rice cultivation as did peasants in the central plains and the northeast.

Rice was not the only export from Siam. In addition, rubber, tin, and teak generated significant amounts of foreign exchange for the country. As these commodities were produced in highly localized industries, tin and rubber in the peninsular south and teak in the northern region, they never had the degree of impact on the economy of rural Siam the expanded rice production did. From the latter part of the nineteenth century until well after World War II, most rural people generated cash income by producing a rice surplus, which was sold to local middlemen who in turn would sell the rice to the mainly Chinese-owned major firms that were part of an international network of rice dealers.

As villagers, predominantly those in central Thailand, devoted an increasing amount of their time to rice production, they spent less time on producing handicrafts and began to buy cloth and other Western goods in the market.[4] There was a sharp decline in local textile production in Siam, as there was in many other countries in Asia once they became a part of the global economy. Some villagers, especially in northeastern Thailand where peasants were only marginally involved in a cash economy, continued, however, to produce silk. In the early part of the twentieth century, the government even attempted, with Japanese assistance, to promote sericulture in northeastern Thailand. The effort was, however, a failure, and it was not until after World War II, and then with Western assistance, that silk began to be produced commercially in Thailand in significant quantities.

Although rice remained the country's major export for over a century after the Bowring Treaty, successive governments did very little to encourage improvements in rice production or to promote agricultural diversification. David Feeny, an economic historian, has concluded that these governments did not explore ways to increase agricultural productivity.[5] In part, the governments did not invest in projects that would stimulate agricultural development because it was felt that it was more important to use government revenues to bolster the country's security in view of the threat of colonial expansion. Thus, successive governments invested in railways to improve access to outlying parts of the kingdom and pursued conservative fiscal policies to avoid giving foreign powers any impression that the Thai could not manage the country's economy. In addition, the elite believed they would gain little from government investment in agriculture. Since most productive land was owned by individual farmers rather than by large landlords and since more money could be made through investments in urban areas than in farmland, the Siamese elite had little direct interest in raising productivity. Moreover, most members of the elite derived their incomes from the government, which in turn acquired the bulk of its revenues from taxes on opium, spirits, gambling, and lotteries rather than from taxes on agricultural production. For their part, peasants had no way to make their interests felt by the political leadership of the country.

Chinese Migration and the New Society of Bangkok

It was in Bangkok that the most radical transformations took place as a consequence of the opening of the country to the world economy. Even prior to the Bowring Treaty, Bangkok had become the major trading center of the kingdom, and once the treaty had come into effect, a rapid expansion of port and warehouse facilities, rice mills, commercial offices, and financial institutions took place. The proliferation of trade-related firms spurred the government to improve the city's infrastructure. New canals and then roads were built to facilitate transportation. The first road to be built was one Westerners called "new road" (*thanon caroen krung* in Thai, "prosperous city road"). Wooden bridges were replaced by concrete ones; a tramline was established; and early in the twentieth century a water-supply system was constructed. Both public works and privately owned firms required a considerable labor force. The new firms and expanding government agencies that dealt with the firms also created a demand for clerks who could not only read and write Thai but were also literate in other languages (most notably English or Chinese) and could handle accounts.

The new jobs created in Bangkok were filled overwhelmingly by Chinese migrants, mainly from southeastern China. Few Thai peasants were motivated to move from the countryside into Bangkok, in part because those closest to the city were able to generate significant cash incomes by remaining on their farms and raising rice for the export market. Chinese migrants had settled in Siam since Ayutthayan times (and probably even earlier) but had begun to immigrate in large numbers only after the founding of the Chakri dynasty. Most of the early-nineteenth-century migrants had found their way into the internal trade sector of the Siamese economy, and the Chinese controlled much of it by 1850. In part because of their role in internal trade, the government in the latter part of the nineteenth century contracted with some Chinese middlemen to collect taxes. Chinese also controlled many of the pre-1855 firms engaged in export and were well situated to participate in the growth of the export economy following the signing of the Bowring Treaty. One of the most significant roles played by local Siamese Chinese in the latter part of the nineteenth century was as recruiters of labor in the poorer regions of southeastern China.

Chinese migration increased rapidly after the Bowring Treaty and did not come to an end until the late 1930s. By the 1870s, the population of Bangkok had become overwhelmingly Chinese, and it remained so until after World War II. Because of restrictive laws (for example, the law prohibiting "aliens" from owning land) and because Chinese migrants were most likely to find work in jobs controlled by local Chinese, most immigrants ended up as unskilled construction workers or stevedores. Second-generation Chinese, as well as a few migrants with good connections or with some education, also found jobs as clerks or in retailing, including retailing outside of Bangkok.

The immigration of large numbers of Chinese in response to growing demands for labor in Siam led to the emergence of an ethnic division of labor that approximated what for Southeast Asian colonial dependencies of the Western powers has been termed a "plural society."[6] In Siam, the ethnic division of labor was most pronounced in Bangkok where the preponderant Chinese community (or, more precisely, communities, since the Chinese were divided by speech group and by province of origin), the dominant Siamese elite, and Western traders, diplomats, and missionaries all had very different interests and images of the future of Siam and their role in that future. The ethnic cleavages in Siam did not, however, become as marked as they were elsewhere in Southeast Asia for a very important reason. Whereas in the Dutch East Indies, the British colonies in Malaya, or French Indochina Western colonial domination, especially after Western schools were created, led immigrant Chinese (and also Indians in Malaya) to orient themselves toward Dutch, British, or French language, culture, and society, in Siam, which retained its independence, Chinese migrants felt constrained to orient themselves more toward Thai language, culture, and society. Although Siamese society, with its large Chinese migrant population, was in some ways similar to the societies of other Southeast Asian nations because of its incorporation into an international economic system, in other fundamental ways it evolved differently because, unlike those other societies, it was transformed politically by an indigenous elite rather than by Western colonial rulers.

NATIONAL INTEGRATION AND
THE REVOLUTION FROM ABOVE

King Mongkut and Early Western Influences

When Mongkut succeeded to the throne in 1851, he had about him a small number of advisers who had begun to perceive the growing role Western powers were playing in neighboring areas. In the mid-nineteenth century, the British appeared to the Siamese to be the most significant imperial power. In the latter part of the eighteenth and early part of the nineteenth century, Penang, Singapore, and Malacca—the Straits Settlements—came under British rule. As a consequence of the 1824–1826 war with Burma, the British had incorporated a part of lower Burma into their empire, and in 1852, a year after Mongkut came to the throne, the British took the rest of lower Burma in another war with the Burmese. The British conquest of lower Burma led to the formation of an Anglo-Siamese border commission to determine the boundaries between the two polities. For the first time in their history, Siamese rulers had to think in terms of territorial boundaries rather than in terms of vassals and subjects.

During Mongkut's reign, France also emerged as a power to be reckoned with. In the late 1850s, the French took over the southern part of Annam in what is today Vietnam and created the colony of Cochin China. Shortly thereafter, in 1863, the king of Cambodia was persuaded to allow the French to make his country a protectorate. Mongkut and his court were incensed by this idea as they considered Cambodia to be a Siamese vassal state. Although the compliant king of Cambodia signed an agreement with the Siamese attesting to his vassal status, the French forced him to renege on the agreement, and the Siamese found themselves with little choice other than to allow the French to assume effective control of the Khmer kingdom.

The expansion of the colonial dominions on the borders of Siam served as a goad to the Siamese to agree to some of the less palatable provisions of the Bowring Treaty. It also stimulated Mongkut to encourage the education of certain members of the royal family and the nobility so that they might be better equipped to deal with Westerners. Such education included not only language (especially English, which from that time to the present has been the most important Western language in Thailand) but also the rudiments of Western science and technology. Mongkut thus paved the way for Siamese to go abroad to acquire a Western education that could be put to good use in Siam. Mongkut's concern for education, including the education of women in the palace, also laid the foundation for the modernization of education that was to take place under King Chulalongkorn.

Mongkut's sponsorship of Western education among certain members of his palace entourage has been described in somewhat exaggerated and self-serving books by Anna Leonowens, an Englishwoman employed by Mongkut as a teacher. These books and later the musical and movie based on Margaret Landon's novel, *Anna and the King of Siam* created the false image of Mongkut as a romantic buffoon. The popularity of the movie in the West has created an unfortunate impression there of a man who was unquestionably one of the most acute and learned of any of the people who have shaped the destiny of Thailand.

Mongkut's interest in Western science led, ironically, to his untimely death. In August 1869, he organized an expedition to southern Thailand where, together with a French astronomer and other Westerners, he set out to demonstrate to a select group of royalty and nobility that eclipses could be predicted using modern scientific methods. In rejecting the mythical interpretation of eclipses as the sun's being consumed by the evil god Rahu, Mongkut continued his efforts to root out superstition that he had first begun while still a monk. Unfortunately, both Mongkut and his son and heir, Chulalongkorn, then fifteen years old, and many others on the expedition became seriously ill with malaria. Neither Western medical science nor traditional Siamese practice was able to combat this illness, and although the young Chulalongkorn recovered, his father died.

The Reforms of King Chulalongkorn

The transition from Mongkut's reign to that of Chulalongkorn was fraught with danger. Mongkut had feared that the British might take over the country after his death, especially if a succession crisis should occur. Those few members of the royalty and nobility who held effective power might well have come into conflict with one another over the succession, given that the heir apparent was still a minor. The succession of Chulalongkorn was assured, however, when Cao Phraya Srisuriyawong, a member of the Bunnag family (by far the most influential noble family in nineteenth-century Siam) and at the time the most powerful man in the kingdom after Mongkut, agreed to support the young prince, in part because he feared that if anyone else were placed on the throne, the British, who assumed that Chulalongkorn would succeed, would use the act as a pretext to annex Siam. In return for his support of Chulalongkorn, Srisuriyawong was named regent, a highly unusual step given that he was not a member of the royal family, even though married to one.

As a minor, Chulalongkorn had little influence on policy, and even after the end of the regency in 1873 he remained in a rather weak position relative to Srisuriyawong. This weakness may have prompted Prince Wichaichan, an older cousin of the king and a man who had some claim on the throne, to entertain a plan in 1874 to seize the throne. As *uparat*, the second-ranking member of the royal family, Wichaichan had built up a small army. He also had good contacts among the foreign community, especially the British. His plan, however, was unsuccessful, and he was forced to take refuge in the British consultate. This incident might again have prompted British intervention in Siamese affairs, but Srisuriyawong was able to defuse the situation. Wichaichan returned to his palace as *uparat*, although he played little part in public affairs from then on until his death. Chulalongkorn, for his part, was forced to recognize that, although technically ruler of the country, he was not yet fully in control of the affairs of state.

It was not until the 1880s, after Srisuriyawong had reached old age and Chulalongkorn's brothers—on whom he came to rely greatly—had come of age and could assume significant roles that Chulalongkorn began to institute the changes that were to transform Siam. Chulalongkorn and his advisers were keenly concerned with asserting effective authority over the various parts of the Siamese domain. They had already seen peripheral parts of this territory—some of the Malay vassal states in the south in addition to Cambodia—taken over by the colonial powers. A number of other areas were vulnerable to similar actions: the vassal *myang* in northern Thailand, of which Chiang Mai was the most important; the tributary principality of Luang Prabang in what is today Laos; the smaller Lao *myang* lying both to the east and to the west of the Mekong River; those parts of Cambodia—Battambang and Siemreap, the latter including the old capital of Angkor—still under Siamese control; and the remaining Malay vassal sultanates.

In the early 1870s, Chiang Mai was a difficult vassal. In 1874, in order to ensure that the new ruler of Chiang Mai, who had just come to power, would prove easier to deal with than his predecessor, the Siamese court appointed a commissioner and gave him a small force to provide on-the-spot advice to the Chiang Mai prince as to what Bangkok would see as appropriate types of actions.

The sending of a Siamese commissioner to Chiang Mai in 1874 anticipated the major reforms of 1892 in the administration of outlying areas. These reforms were devised by King Chulalongkorn and his brother, Prince Damrong Rajanubhab, who was appointed by the king to head the newly created Ministry of Interior. The provincial reforms of 1892 entailed the arrogation to the central government in Bangkok of almost all powers originally vested in vassal rulers and local lords.

Although the former lords were often given offices as "governors" or "district officers" in the new system of provincial administration or were made "advisers," they soon came to be replaced by officials appointed directly by Bangkok.

The provincial reforms involved a total restructuring of the bureaucracy in Siam. Prior to 1892, the structure of government still reflected the cosmological notions inherited from Ayutthayan times. The king was believed to reside at the center of a sacred space, with power emanating outward and downward from him. Officials' positions were defined with reference to where they were situated in this space. For example, the two preeminent "ministers" in traditional Siam—those who headed the *krom* ("departments") of Mahatthai (literally, "the great Thai") and Kalahom (literally, "meeting place for soldiers")—were defined respectively as the right- and left-hand ministers of the king. They had essentially the same functions, namely, administration and taxation of the populace, but they exercised these functions in two different parts of the kingdom. *Krom* Mahatthai was responsible for peoples living in the northern part of the kingdom, and *krom* Kalahom did the same for those living in the southern part. Under the reforms of 1892, these and other traditional *krom* were redefined as functional ministries (*krasuang*); Mahatthai became the Ministry of Interior, and Kalahom became the Ministry of Defense. Other new ministries, also defined in functional terms, were created. The redefinition of segments of the government according to function reflected a desire not only to make ministries and departments responsible for particular tasks but also to expand radically the scope of government in its relationship with the populace.

The development of a greatly enlarged bureaucracy necessitated the raising of even higher revenues than had been required during the reign of Mongkut. To obtain such revenues, Chulalongkorn reorganized the tax system to ensure that more tax revenues came to the central government. Local lords and rulers, who had hitherto believed they had the prerogative "to eat the land" (*kin myang*), that is, to retain part of the taxes they collected, were now no longer permitted to do so. Near the end of Chulalongkorn's reign, the tax farming system, whereby private individuals, usually Chinese, were sold the right to collect taxes for a certain amount less than that which would be realized if all taxes were actually paid, was eliminated. From this time on, all taxes were to be paid in money, not in kind. This latter requirement, together with the greater efficiency of the central government's tax collectors, imposed a considerable degree of hardship on those peasants who had little cash income.

Chulalongkorn's freeing of the slaves must be seen in the light of the need for increased revenues.[7] To speak of "freeing the slaves" in English is to conjure up an image of Abraham Lincoln and the black slaves of the U.S. South. Slaves in Siam were not, however, like the blacks; most were members of the personal retinues of members of the royalty, nobles, and provincial aristocrats. By being bound to a particular person, a slave was either exempt from corvée or the tax equivalent or else subject to a much lower tax obligation than was a freeman. Bondsmen also were not free to work their own land, and, therefore, were not subject to taxes on land and produce. When Chulalongkorn came to the throne and first began to consider the idea of ending slavery (he succeeded to the throne shortly after the end of the American Civil War), he was probably influenced in part by a concern that slavery in Siam would be seen as barbaric by Westerners. There was, however, no great pressure within Siamese society—including from slaves themselves—for emancipation. When he finally succeeded in bringing slavery to an end, after a succession of promulgations beginning in the 1870s, doing so was in the interest of the state, even though against the interests of many people who wished to have their own independent coteries of followers.

The abolition of slavery also contributed to a redefinition of the relationship of subjects to king. Prior to the reforms, peasants were on the lowest rung of a hierarchy that extended downward from the king through the heads of *krom* to the rulers, lords, and governors under a ministry to the subordinate nobility under these men. The reforms of the 1890s eliminated this traditional hierarchy and replaced it with a much simplified one in which the relationship between king and subject was mediated by only one type of intervening status holder, the *kharatchakan*. A *kharatchakan* could play many different functional roles, but all were, as the name indicates, "servants of the king." Although many members of the royalty and nobility retained power in the new system, and although the older hierarchical ideas continued to influence the way in which people thought about their place in the kingdom (for example, district officers—*nai amphoe*—were often treated by peasants and acted themselves as though they were "land-eating" lords), the reforms initiated a process that was to lead the general populace to see themselves as having a direct relationship to the king.

The reforms of 1892 have been referred to as a "silent revolution,"[8] but they were received with anything but calm in at least some parts of the kingdom. Even before the reforms went into effect, Siam was facing its most serious crisis yet as a consequence of threats posed by the imperial powers. This double crisis—the one internal, the other external—contributed to the sense that many peasants, especially those in the Lao-speaking areas of northeastern Thailand, had that their world was in chaos.

The Colonial Threat and Revolts in the Provinces

During the 1880s, both the British and the French extended their control over additional territories in Burma and Indochina respectively. A succession crisis after the death of King Mindon in Burma, followed by palace intrigues and unrest in the kingdom, provided the British with an excuse for invading upper Burma. By 1886, the British had brought all the former domains of the Burmese king under British rule. At the same time, France extended its "protectorate" over central and northern Vietnam and by 1888 was indicating that it intended to advance further into Lao areas, which the French claimed were subordinate to the Vietnamese court. Siam, however, also claimed these territories. With British and French forces now on the borders of Siam, the king and members of his court were faced with the unpalatable dilemma foreseen by King Mongkut when he had written in 1867 to his envoy in France about having to choose "whether to swim up-river to make friends with the crocodile or to swim out to sea and hang on to the whale."[9] As it turned out, the crocodile (France) came upriver, and not with the intention of making friends with Siam. The whale (Britain) meanwhile stayed out at sea and offered no tail for Siam to catch onto.[10]

After French forces pushed Siamese forces out of what is today northwestern Laos in 1888, the French envoy in Bangkok demanded that the Siamese recognize French suzerainty over the whole of the area east of the Mekong River, which would have entailed Siam's giving up an area it had controlled since the time of Rama I. The Siamese refused to accede to the French demand but agreed to the setting up of a border commission. This commission reached no conclusion, and, following a series of incidents, the French sent several gunboats up the Cao Phraya River to Bangkok in July 1893. The king counted on recent improvements in the military to prevent the boats from making their way to the capital. The French succeeded, however, in getting past the Siamese defenses, and with three gunboats facing them from the banks below the French consulate, the Siamese had little option but to agree to the French ultimatum.

In retrospect, Siam may be seen as fortunate in having escaped with only having had to accede to a relatively limited set of demands. The court was forced to give up territories east of the Mekong, to withdraw Siamese forces from Siemreap and Battambang and from within twenty-five kilometers of the Mekong River in northeastern Siam, to pay indemnities for the damages inflicted during the Cao Phraya battle, and to punish the people responsible for manning the Siamese defense. The circumstances were such that the French might well have insisted on establishing a protectorate over the whole of Siam or at least on taking over all of the Lao-speaking areas within Siam's domain, including those in what is today northeastern Thailand. The consequences of the 1893 confrontation were, nonetheless, extremely painful to Chulalongkorn. The king became seriously ill, and many people feared he would die. Although he did not, he remained depressed and did not resume a fully active role for almost three years.

The crisis spurred Prince Damrong, as minister of the interior, to implement rapidly the provincial reforms of 1892 to assure that the remaining outlying areas of Siam could not be claimed by Britain or France owing to the weakness of Siamese authority over them. In addition to placing Siamese officials in areas that had previously enjoyed relative autonomy, Siamese troops, newly reorganized along Western lines and equipped with Western weapons such as the Gatling gun, were also posted up-country (although not in the twenty-five-kilometer zone proscribed by the agreement with France).

The rapid transformation of the political system of the outer provincial areas precipitated a crisis of a different order, namely, resistance to Siamese authority by segments of the indigenous population. The first resistance antedated the 1892 reforms as hundreds of peasants in the Chiang Mai area protested against new taxes in 1889. The protest escalated into a full-scale rebellion by peasants of Khün descent (the Khün are a Tai-speaking people who originated in the Kengtung area of Burma) led by Phaya Phap, a local headman. The decision of the Chiang Mai court to support the Siamese sealed the fate of the rebels, many of whom were put to death. Another effort by Phaya Phap, who had escaped to Kengtung, to stage a rebellion in 1890 also was quickly suppressed by Siamese and Chiang Mai forces.[11]

The Phaya Phap rebellion of 1889–1890 proved to be a relatively minor incident compared to the large-scale uprising that took place in northeastern Thailand in 1901–1902. The peoples of northeastern Thailand had, prior to the reforms of 1892, been only indirectly ruled by the Siamese court. The order they knew was one in which the most important power holders were Lao lords (*cao*) of relatively small *myang*. When the reforms of 1892 were implemented, this order was suddenly destroyed. Siamese officials, many of them demanding taxes in cash, now replaced the Lao lords. The incorporation of Lao-speaking areas on the left bank of the Mekong River into French Indochina further contributed to feelings on the part of many peasants in northeastern Thailand that their world had been turned upside down. Messianic leaders, called "men-having-merit" (*phu mi bun*), emerged and proclaimed that an apocalyptic catastrophe was imminent. These leaders encouraged their followers to make attacks on Siamese posts. One such group succeeded in taking over the small Mekong River town of Khemmarat, thereby attracting many more people to the movement. Within a short time, several thousand people had become involved in this millenarian rebellion, and many thousands more had become convinced of the truth of the messages purveyed by the "men-having-merit." Again, superior Siamese force was triumphant, but not before many peasants had been killed in battle or as a consequence of the trials held in the aftermath of the rebellion.[12]

A rebellion by Shans in the northern town of Phrae and the potential of a rebellion by Malay rulers in southern Siam in 1902 also had their roots in the implementation of the 1892 reforms.[13] Although Siamese authority was reasserted in both instances with the backing of military force, Prince Damrong, the king himself, and others in the court recognized that it would be unwise and perhaps impossible to rule the outlying areas by military force alone. They were therefore to turn their attention over the next two decades to promoting a national culture that would legitimize Siamese rule.

Despite the rebellions at the turn of the century, France and Britain did not attempt to capitalize on internal Siamese weaknesses. This restraint was less out of respect for Siamese sovereignty than because a Franco-British agreement had been reached to maintain Siam as a buffer state between the two colonial dominions. What this buffer state was to include was not specified, however. By the end of Chulalongkorn's reign in 1910, Siam had been forced to cede parts of what are today Laos and Cambodia to France and some border *myang* in the north to Britain, as well as to recognize British control over several Malay sultanates that had once been Siamese vassals. The modern state of Siam retained the Siamese heartland of central Thailand, the Lanna Thai principalities of what is today northern Thailand, the Lao and some Khmer and Khmer-related domains in northeastern Thailand, and the sultanate of Pattani as well as some other Malay-speaking areas in southern Thailand. The peoples of these disparate areas had not only been brought under the control of a centralized state but also were to be made to feel that they belonged to a common nation.

FOUNDATIONS OF A NATIONAL CULTURE

The Religious Basis of National Culture

As King Chulalongkorn moved to create a new type of state, one defined with reference to territorial boundaries in which all subjects were linked directly to the king through a bureaucracy organized along functional lines, he found himself forced to abandon the older notion of the state as having an "exemplary center"[14] in which authority was dramatically asserted by the king in the capital. Somewhat paradoxically, Chulalongkorn had followed his father's lead in restoring many of the royal Brahmanical rituals of the Ayutthayan period, rituals that even given the Buddhist elements added to them seemed to be associated more with a model of the Indianized "theater state" than with the modern state Chulalongkorn seemed intent on creating. Even as late as 1930, Quaritch Wales, who had studied the rites of the Siamese court and who had observed the funeral rites held in 1925 for King Vajiravudh, wrote that the populace had "an innate love and respect for all forms of royal pageantry, and it is the magnificence of the state procession, the splendour of the Urn enthroned upon the catafalque, or the brilliantly illuminated Brah Meru [the funerary pyre that is constructed in imitation of the sacred mountain, Meru], that impresses them that their King is a great King."[15] Although such pageantry, even today, perpetuates an archaic idea that through imitation of the cosmic order, an order in the human world can be ensured, it no longer suffices, as Chulalongkorn was aware, to legitimize the authority of the monarchy throughout the populace. Within the new state of Siam there were many people— including a large proportion of the Chinese population living in Bangkok— for whom such ritual was mere display and many others—those living in the distant parts of the kingdom—for whom such acts by the king were too remote to be of significance. For the modern state of Siam to be accepted as legitimate among a large proportion of the populace, it had to be seen as promoting a "national" interest.

Although Chulalongkorn's son and successor, Vajiravudh (1910–1925), has been said to have fathered modern Thai nationalism, his nationalism was built on foundations created during Chulalongkorn's reign and had its roots in Mongkut's. Thai nationalism represents a selective reinterpretation of tradition and the promotion of this reinterpretation as being the tradition of all "Thai" in common. The reinterpretation began with Mongkut's reform of Buddhism.

As a monk, Mongkut was very aware of the fact that Buddhist practice in Siam incorporated many local customs that were not traceable to early Buddhism as found in the scriptures. The Thammayut order that emerged from Mongkut's reforms spurned most such accretions and sought to institute a practice of the religion that was in keeping with scriptural precedents. The Buddhism of the Thammayut order was not linked with any of the different forms of Buddhism found among the various Tai peoples of Siam, but this strict Buddhism was used as the basis for a reform of the entire sangha—including non-Thammayut monks—during the reign of King Chulalongkorn.

The man to be credited with the creation of what might be termed "Thai Buddhism" (as distinct from the Buddhism of the Siamese of central Thailand, the Lao of northeastern Thailand, the Khon Myang of northern Thailand, or other non-Tai groups such as the Mon and Khmer) was a son of Mongkut and a brother of Chulalongkorn—Prince Vajirañana. This prince had entered the monkhood as a young man and soon rose to become abbot of the very important Wat Bowǫnniwet in Bangkok and subsequently the head of the Thammayut order. By the early 1890s, he was one of Chulalongkorn's closest advisers, one who shared the king's and Prince Damrong's vision of creating a modern Thai nation-state.

From the 1890s on, Prince Vajirañana began to work toward bringing monks in the country into a unified sangha in which the same (reformed) Buddhist tradition would be practiced and communicated to the laity. The initial step in this direction came in 1898 when he cooperated with Prince Damrong in setting up a standard system of education to be taught by monks in monastery schools throughout the country. Although Prince Vajirañana later decided that monks should not be secular teachers, this experience led him to create a standard curriculum for the education of novices and monks. This curriculum, written in what must be called "standard Thai," presented Buddhist doctrines and history with reference to canonical works, commentaries, and accepted historical sources rather than with reference to any of the popular texts previously employed by the monks in local monasteries.

In 1902, the king promulgated a law that created a unified sangha under the supreme patriarch (*sangharat*; literally, "king"—*raja*—of the sangha, a man appointed by the king). Prince Vajirañana, although not to become patriarch until 1910, was given responsibility for implementing this law. In order to ensure that local members of the sangha would begin to conform to the dictates of the 1902 law, he appointed provincial sangha heads who were given roles rather similar to those of the governors and commissioners appointed by Prince Damrong to implement the Provincial Reform Act of 1892. Perhaps the most important element in the sangha organization act of 1902 was the provision that no monk could ordain other men into the sangha unless he were vested with the authority to do so by the patriarch. Whereas in the past, any monk who had been in the order for ten years was qualified by tradition to perform ordination, now it was possible only for monks who recognized the authority of the sangha's equivalent of the king. The control of the patriarch and high sangha authorities over local members of the monkhood was also asserted through the requirement that all monks must be registered on entering the order.

It took some time for people living in outlying areas to realize the implications of the sangha organization act of 1902, in part because in the villages, religious practices went on much as before. Considerable resentment began to build up, especially in northern Thailand, because of the efforts being made to replace many local practices by ones prescribed by the Thai sangha authorities. This resentment developed into a serious crisis in the early 1930s when a very highly respected northern Thai monk—Khruba Srivijaya—refused to respect the Thai sangha's authority that denied him the right to ordain other monks and novices. The crisis reached a head in 1935 after disciplinary actions had failed to cow Khruba Srivijaya, and his followers appeared ready to support him in open resistance to the Thai sangha and perhaps to the state itself. Finally, a compromise was reached whereby the sangha authorities allowed Northern Thai customary practices to be continued in local temples and, in turn, Khruba Srivijaya accepted the authority of the Thai sangha to determine who would be allowed to perform ordinations.[16]

When, during the reign of King Vajiravudh, Buddhism was designated as one of the three pillars of Thai nationalism—the others being the Thai nation or people and the monarchy—it was not Buddhism in general that was being referred to; rather, it was the Buddhism contained in the religious curriculum devised by Prince Vajirañana and practiced and taught by monks who recognized the authority of the legally constituted sangha. Regional and ethnic traditions, such as those of the Northern Thai and the Lao in northeastern Thailand, while tolerated to some degree, became suspect both for perpetuating "superstitions" and for contributing to a sense of regional or ethnic distinctiveness.

In addition to creating a state-controlled Buddhism, thus making possible a Buddhist nationalism, King Chulalongkorn, Prince Damrong, and Prince Vajirañana also laid the foundations for a state-controlled system of education in which all children throughout the country would study the same "national" language (standard Thai), study the same "national" history (one that accentuated the role of the Siamese monarch and deemphasized the roles of local lords and rulers), and learn the same "national" songs (especially those dealing with the monarchy and with the Thai people). Schools would also teach the rudiments of mathematics and science to prepare the citizens of the nation to help develop the country. During the reign of Chulalongkorn, only the foundations of a statewide system of education were established. Although primary education became compulsory during the reign of Vajiravudh, it was not until the mid-1930s, after the revolution of 1932 and after schools had been established in most rural communities, that the educational system became the instrument of Thai nationalism that Chulalongkorn and his brothers had envisioned.

Kingship and Thai Nationalism

Although King Chulalongkorn perpetuated many court practices that were rooted in a notion of the king as a godlike being at the center of a cosmological system, he also initiated some changes that were to lead to the monarch being seen as the embodiment of the Thai nation. He abolished the requirement that people prostrate themselves before the king, and he began to appear in a greater variety of public functions than had any of his predecessors. It was his son and successor, King Vajiravudh, however, who explicitly undertook the task of reshaping the role of the monarch to suit a nationalist purpose.

Vajiravudh preferred a literary and artistic life to a political one. He had spent much of his youth and young adulthood studying in England and was therefore far less bound by court traditions than previous Siamese rulers. In striking contrast to his father and grandfather, who had followed traditional practice in taking many wives and consorts, Vajiravudh preferred the company of other males and remained unmarried until nearly the end of his reign. By any standard, whether it be that of the traditional Siamese monarch of Ayutthayan times or that of the modern king represented by Mongkut and Chulalongkorn, Vajiravudh was an unconventional king of Siam. He was also a rather ineffectual one. These qualities spurred some members of the growing military and civil bureaucracy to look toward a type of government that was not based on an absolute monarch.

Vajiravudh's wish to create a new type of kingship that was more in line with his own experience and interests led him to institute practices that provided a more direct relationship with the populace. He created the paramilitary Wild Tiger Corps (sυa pa), whose members could come from any segment of Thai society provided they were deemed to be "good citizens." Members were not distinguished in the corps by their status in the larger society: prince and commoner, high official and clerk, old and young, all wore the same uniform. Although members of this corps actually came from only a small proportion of the populace and were overwhelmingly members of the elite, the publicity the corps received accentuated the notion that the king was a companion of people who were ordinary Thai citizens. Moreover, by appearing himself in the same uniform as other members of the corps—and the sυa pa uniform was the king's preferred form of public dress—he presented himself not as the occupier of a throne at the center of a sacred space but as a citizen king. Vajiravudh's model of popular kingship has been emulated by subsequent kings, most notably by the present king, Bhumibol

Adulyadej. The Village Scouts (*luk sya chaoban;* literally, "village tiger cubs") movement, which gained a very large membership among villagers and people from all walks of life during the late 1970s, has a direct prototype in the Wild Tiger Corps. The Village Scouts, like the Wild Tiger Corps, is an elite-promoted movement that accentuates a nationalism centered on the monarch.

Vajiravudh was not, in fact, a citizen king; he was still an absolute monarch. The fact that he held absolute power while at the same time presenting himself as a citizen king was perceived by some people who were close to the court at the time as contradictory. There were those among the royalty who would have preferred that he act more like his father; others in the growing civil and military services began to conceive of a state in which absolute power was not vested in an absolute monarch. In 1911, certain members of the officer corps had planned a coup d'état, but their plans were aborted before they could act. Despite their failure, these early plotters were the forerunners of others who would ultimately succeed in bringing the absolute monarchy to an end.

THE 1932 REVOLUTION AND A NEW POLITICAL ORDER

The End of the Absolute Monarchy

The reforms of the 1890s led to a rapid expansion in the number and types of jobs available in government service. Positions multiplied in the bureaucracy, and a new modernized military also opened new job possibilities for yet other people. Many who were recruited into government service as *kharatchakan* came, not from the royalty or from the rather small nobility, but from urban commercial or clerical backgrounds; some even came from rural families, primarily from central Thailand. Recruitment into the bureaucracy or the military was based less on family connections than on the ability to acquire the necessary education required for a position, that is, on merit rather than blood. Not a few of these "new" men (and almost all were males) were of Sino-Thai origin. Many forged their closest ties with others, not on the basis of their own or their family's prior connection to the court, but on the basis of having attended the same schools in Siam or abroad. The people who had been trained abroad—mainly in England and France, although some officers were trained in Germany—also had become acquainted at first hand with political systems that were very different from that of Siam. These men became aware that they had common interests that varied greatly from those of the king, members of the royal family, and the king's courtiers. That they should come to demand to share in the power of the state was inevitable, but the outcome of their making such a demand was not foreordained.

King Vajiravudh did not live to see any major challenge to the power of the throne. He died, still a relatively young man, in 1925, leaving no heir. He was succeeded by a half-brother Prajadhipok (1925–1935), who had also been educated in England. He had never expected to become king and was thus rather unprepared when he was elevated to the throne. Recognizing both his own limited knowledge of the affairs of state and the problems he had inherited from the previous reign, he turned to a group of now somewhat aging princes who had been close associates of Chulalongkorn and to other men in the royal family to help him in governing the country. Although his reliance on Prince Damrong and other princes seemed necessary to the inexperienced king, it appeared to the new civil officials and military officers to be a constriction of their power when they hoped for a broadening of it.

Shortly after his succession, Prajadhipok undertook a number of trips both within and outside the country. Because of the expansion of the railway system, especially to the north, Prajadhipok was able to visit parts of the kingdom never previously seen by a ruling monarch. These travels, which again have been emulated in modern times by King Bhumibol, were designed to bolster the king's image as a ruler of all the peoples in the realm. Prajadhipok's trips to neighboring countries—the Dutch East Indies, Indochina, Singapore—can be interpreted in part as an effort on the part of the king to assert Siam's equality with the colonial powers. His European manners and fluent English facilitated his task. It should be noted in this connection that Prajadhipok came to the throne at a time when many of the unequal treaties of the nineteenth century were being revised so as to return to Siam sovereignty over people living within its boundaries.

Prajadhipok, despite being unprepared for the throne, began to show himself to be a somewhat more effective ruler than his predecessor. And unlike any previous king since Mongkut, he no longer had to fear that Siam would fall under colonial rule. His reign was, however, seriously troubled by the world economic crisis of the 1930s. Rice prices plummeted, and with them government revenues. Despite the hardships the Great Depression created for the peasantry, especially in the central plains, it did not stimulate peasant unrest. Unlike their counterparts in Burma, few Thai peasants had to mortgage their land in order to expand production. They were able, thus, to maintain their farms and to grow most of the foodstuffs needed for their families. The citizens who were hardest hit came from the salaried middle class and comprised mainly those who had recently been recruited into the bureaucracy and the military. Their salaries were cut while taxes on salaries were increased.

Unlike members of the royal family and nobility who owned property, mainly in Bangkok, people in the new middle class rarely had sources of income other than their salaries. This class, whose members faced a deteriorating economic situation and harbored a sense of resentment toward the king for having restricted the exercise of power mainly to advisers chosen from members of the royal family, spawned the group, "the Promoters," which staged the successful revolution of 1932.

The Promoters consisted of a relatively small number of young men, mainly members of the civil service but also some in the military, who had received their education in France or England where they had begun to envision a Siam with a democratic system of government. On June 23, 1932, while the king was away at his summer palace in Hua Hin in the southern part of the kingdom, the Promoters quietly mobilized troops whose commanders had been persuaded to join them and cut off the telephone lines to the houses of the king's senior advisers. Early on June 24, these advisers, together with Prince Boriphat who was acting as the representative of the king in Bangkok, were arrested and brought to the throne hall. The Promoters—declaring themselves the vanguard of the People's party—issued a proclamation that announced to an unsuspecting populace that a radical change in government had been effected in Siam. This proclamation, written by Pridi Banomyong (then known by his royally given title and name as Luang Pradit Manutham), was strongly anti-royalist. It ended: "Let us understand that this country belongs to the people, not to the King as we have been deceived into believing. Whereas the ancestors of the common people fought the enemy to maintain national independence, the royalty just reaps the fruits which it does not deserve to have."[17]

Despite this statement, the monarchy was not abolished. Rather, the king was invited to become a constitutional monarch, and on his return to Bangkok two days later, Pridi formally apologized for the extreme position expressed in the proclamation. The other members of the Promoters also apologized to the king, who, in turn, signed a proclamation forgiving them for the illegal actions taken during the course of the coup. At the same time, he also agreed to accept the limits that had now been placed on his power and to become a constitutional monarch.

In Search of a New Political Structure

The agreement by the king and the Promoters to perpetuate the monarchy within a constitutional system probably prevented the outbreak of a civil war. It did not, however, satisfactorily resolve the question of what the role of the monarch should be in the new order. Indeed, the question of what the nature of that order should be also was not determined by the events of June 1932. Debate over these issues was to continue for the next year and a half.

The provisional government that assumed power after the 1932 Revolution comprised not only members of the Peoples' party but also people, members of royalty excepted, who had served the king in the previous government. Members of the People's party—a group formed originally in France, headed by Pridi, and including Luang Phibun Songkhram (whose original name was Plaek Khittasangkha), then a lieutenant-colonel—regarded themselves as the true revolutionary founders of the new order and intended to institute a type of government in which sovereignty would ultimately rest in the people. They were, however, dependent on senior military officers and older civil servants to effect a transition from the old to the new system without a violent upheaval. The compromised character of the new government was reflected in the choice of the conservative Phraya Mano Pakorn (better known as Mano) as the prime minister until elections could be held for a parliament to replace the provisional assembly.

The tensions in the transitional government came to a head over an economic plan proposed by Pridi. The plan was predicated on the government's assuming a central role in economic planning, and it also proposed that the populace be organized into cooperatives in which resources would be collectively owned and managed. To the conservatives in the government, the plan appeared "communist" in tenor. In order to eliminate pressure by supporters of Pridi in the government and assembly to institute the plan, Phraya Mano, with the backing of several senior military officers, prorogued the assembly, reorganized the government without Pridi and his supporters, and forced Pridi to go into exile. Mano also made public a memorandum by the king that was strongly critical of Pridi's plan. The newly reorganized government issued the first anticommunist act in Thai history, one that was in this instance to be used as a means to prevent the return of Pridi.

Phraya Mano's actions were strongly resented by many of the Promoters, including Phibun and his close military associate, General Phahon Phonphayuhasena (born Phot Phahonyothin). Some two and a half months after Mano had prorogued the assembly, Phibun led the first military coup of the constitutional period. This successful coup led to the installation of a new government under General Phahon and the reconvening of the assembly. A conservative reaction was not long in coming. In October 1933, Prince Bavoradej, who commanded forces in the northeast, led troops to the outskirts of Bangkok and demanded that the government resign. In the ensuing conflict, the king, who was once again at Hua Hin, assumed a neutral position. When Phibun led a successful counterattack against Bavoradej's forces, the king was placed in an extremely compromising position. He chose to leave Siam and went into exile in England, remaining there until his death in 1941. In 1935, he formally abdicated the throne, recognizing that he could no longer play an active role in shaping Siam's future. In so doing, he effectively removed the kingship from Thai political life.

Following Prajadhipok's abdication, the decision regarding the succession was made by a government that included almost no member of the royalty. The successor chosen was a young boy, Ananda Mahidol (who was on the throne from 1935 to 1946), a grandson of Chulalongkorn. At the time, Ananda was a schoolboy in Switzerland, and he did not return to Thailand until 1945. It was not until Bhumibol ascended the throne following the tragic death of his brother Ananda in 1946, and in reality not until Bhumibol began to become actively involved in public affairs in the 1950s, that the monarchy again became an important factor in Thai political life.

The governments formed by Phahon between 1933 and 1938 can be said to have sincerely worked to implement the aims of the 1932 Revolution. Although Phahon was himself a general, he did not rule as the head of a military government. Rather, he conferred with both the civilian faction of the government, led by Pridi after his return from exile and exoneration of the charges of being a communist, and the military faction, led by Phibun. Phahon assumed that his governments were responsible to an elected parliament (or National Assembly) and appointed upper house, and, although the parliaments elected during the period were hardly representative of the country as a whole, they did include many representatives from provincial areas who were thus able to voice their views at the highest levels of Thai government for the first time in the country's history.

The Phahon governments were hampered by the continuing effects of the Great Depression. That Siam experienced little economic development during the period was not, thus, a function of the government's being bound by special interests. Indeed, despite the government's need for revenues, taxes that most affected the peasantry were actually reduced—a policy decision that may well have averted a rural crisis comparable to those occurring in neighboring Burma and Vietnam.

The extension of primary education to the vast majority of Thai communities should be counted as perhaps the most notable accomplishment of the Phahon governments. This effort was predicated on the premise that for democracy to become established in Siam, it was essential that the citizens come to see themselves as part of a common nation. Under subsequent governments, however, this nascent nationalism came to be harnessed, not to democracy, but to new authoritarian forms of rule.

At the end of December 1938, following a government crisis that had led to the election of a new parliament in November, Phibun became prime minister. For the next six years, with the support of the military, he was to assume an increasingly authoritarian role—one that was facilitated by the outbreak of World War II and Phibun's alliance with Japan. Even before he became prime minister, Phibun and his followers had begun to be influenced by the ultranationalism rampant in Europe and especially in Japan. He favored the idea that the country needed a leader (*phunam*) who would not be like the kings of old but would be articulate, authoritative, and able to embody the aspirations of the nation. Phibun saw himself as such a leader, one who could unite all Thai. As an indication of the type of pan-Thai nationalism he sought to promote, Phibun, shortly after taking office, had a law enacted that changed the name of the country from Siam to Thailand. This change of name marked a new phase in the process, begun under King Mongkut, of transforming the traditional Siamese state into a modern Thai nation-state.

NOTES

1. Sir John Bowring, *The Kingdom and People of Siam*, 2 vols. (London: John W. Parker and Son, 1857; reprint, Kuala Lumpur: Oxford University Press, Oxford in Asia Historical Reprints, 1977), 2:227.

2. G. William Skinner, *Chinese Society in Thailand: An Analytical History* (Ithaca, N.Y.: Cornell University Press, 1957), p. 129.

3. James C. Ingram, *Economic Change in Thailand, 1850–1970* (Stanford: Stanford University Press, 1971), p. 41. On the expansion of rice cultivation, also see David B. Johnston, "Opening a Frontier: The Expansion of Rice Cultivation in Central Thailand in the 1890s," *Contributions to Asian Studies* 9 (1976), pp. 27–44.

4. See S. A. Resnick, "The Decline of Rural Industry Under Export Expansion: A Comparison Among Burma, Philippines, and Thailand, 1870–1938," *Journal of Economic History* 30:1 (1970), pp. 51–73.

5. See David Feeny, *The Political Economy of Productivity: Thai Agricultural Development, 1880–1975* (Vancouver: University of British Columbia Press, 1982).

6. J. S. Furnivall, who first proposed the notion in a study of the Netherlands East Indies, defined a plural society as one "comprising two or more elements or social orders which live side by side, yet without mingling, in one political unit" (Furnivall, *Netherlands India* [Cambridge: Cambridge University Press, 1939], p. 446). Also see Furnivall, *Colonial Policy and Practice* (1944; reprint, New York: New York University Press, 1956), esp. pp. 303–312.

7. On the system of slavery as it existed prior to the time of King Chulalongkorn, see B. Terwiel, "Bondage and Slavery in Early Nineteenth Century Siam," in *Slavery, Bondage, and Dependency in Southeast Asia*, ed. Anthony Reid (New York: St. Martin's Press, 1983), pp. 118–137.

8. The characterization is that of Fred W. Riggs in *Thailand: The Modernization of a Bureaucratic Polity* (Honolulu: East-West Center Press, 1966), p. 111.

9. Quoted in Abbot L. Moffat, *Mongkut: The King of Siam* (Ithaca, N.Y.: Cornell University Press, 1961), p. 124.

10. The competition between France and Britain over territories belonging to Siam and the ultimate resolution of the crisis of the 1890s are discussed by Jeshurun Chandran, *The Contest for Siam 1889-1902: A Study in Diplomatic Rivalry* (Kuala Lumpur: Pererbit Universiti Kebangsaan Malaysia, 1977). On the particular role of the French, see Pensri (Suvanij) Duke, *Les relations entre la France et la Thailande (Siam) au XIXe siècle d'après les archives étrangères* (Bangkok: Chalermnit, 1962).

11. Shigeharu Tanabe has analyzed the Phaya Phap rebellion on the basis of both historical documents and oral history in his "Ideological Practice in Peasant Rebellions: Siam at the Turn of the Twentieth Century," in *History and Peasant Consciousness in South East Asia*, ed. Andrew Turton and Shigeharu Tanabe, Senri Ethnological Studies, 13 (Osaka: National Museum of Ethnology, 1984), pp. 75-110. Also see J. Ansil Ramsay, "Modernization and Reactionary Rebellions in Northern Siam," *Journal of Asian Studies* 38:2 (1979), pp. 283-297.

12. On the millenarian uprisings in northeastern Thailand in 1901-1902, see Charles F. Keyes, "Millennialism, Theravāda Buddhism, and Thai Society," *Journal of Asian Studies* 36:2 (1977), pp. 283-302; Yoneo Ishii, "A Note on Buddhistic Millenarian Revolts in Northeastern Siam," *Journal of Southeast Asian Studies* 6:2 (1975), pp. 121-126; and Chatthip Nartsupha, "The Ideology of 'Holy Men' Revolts in North East Thailand," in Turton and Tanabe, *History and Peasant Consciousness*, pp. 111-134. These uprisings were not limited to northeastern Thailand but also took place in what had become French Laos; see John B. Murdoch, "The 1901-1902 'Holy Man's' Rebellion," *Journal of the Siam Society* 62:1 (1974), pp. 47-66.

13. The best accounts of the Shan and Malay rebellions, or would-be rebellions, exist only in Thai; see Tej Bunnag, *Khabot R. S. 121* [1902 Rebellions] (Bangkok: Foundation for Promotion of Social Science and Humanities Texts, 2524 [1982]).

14. The notion of the state as an "exemplary center" is taken from Clifford Geertz, *Islam Observed* (Chicago: University of Chicago Press, 1968), p. 36; also see Geertz, *Negara: The Theatre State in Bali* (Princeton: Princeton University Press, 1980).

15. H. G. Quaritch Wales, *Siamese State Ceremonies: Their History and Function* (London: Bernard Quaritch, 1931), p. 166.

16. On Khruba Srivijaya's resistance to the establishment of Thai Buddhism in northern Thailand, see Charles F. Keyes, "Buddhism and National Integration in Thailand," *Journal of Asian Studies* 30:3 (1971), pp. 551-568. That article discusses the more general question of the establishment of Thai Buddhism following the promulgation of the 1902 act.

17. Thawatt Mokarapong, *History of the Thai Revolution: A Study in Political Behavior* (Bangkok: Chalermnit, 1972), p. 245.

4

Military Politics in Thailand

Although Phibun Songkhram assumed the prime ministership in 1938 in accord with constitutional provisions, he clearly based his power largely on his control of the military, and the military was to be further strengthened as World War II approached. In late 1940 and early 1941, Thailand provoked a number of incidents on the border with French Indochina, which was at a disadvantage because of the German victory in France and creation of the Vichy regime. These incidents escalated to the point where Thailand was effectively brought into war with French Indochina. Through Japanese mediation, the French colonial government agreed to return to Thailand the portions of Laos and Cambodia that had been ceded by Siam to France in the late nineteenth century. The war with France not only provided the Thai military with its first experience of actual combat, but the successful outcome of the conflict also made Phibun very popular. To commemorate the success of the venture, Phibun had a victory monument erected in Bangkok; to this day it stands as a symbol of Thailand's form of anticolonialism.

The move to reclaim territories previously lost to the colonial powers was but one aspect of the irredentist policy that Phibun began to promote. Naming the country Thailand indicated his intention to unite all the Tai-speaking peoples, including not only those who lived in Thailand but also those in Laos, Burma, and southern China. Phibun's irredentist foreign policy had its ultranationalistic domestic counterpart. To be "Thai" now was not only to speak a Tai language and be born of parents who were also Thai but also to be Buddhist. Luang Wichit Wadthakarn, a close associate of Phibun and a member of his cabinet, began to produce a number of revisionist works on Thai history and foreign relations that expressed the new ideology in a stridently chauvinistic manner. Some of Luang Wichit's most pointed attacks were directed toward the Chinese in Thailand. Phibun's government adopted policies in keeping with this ideology, restricting Chinese immigration to Thailand, forbidding aliens access to many types of occupations, and establishing state enterprises to assume roles previously performed by Chinese-owned private firms.

WORLD WAR II AND THE DEMOCRATIC TRANSITION

Thailand as an Ally of Japan

Events soon enabled Phibun to realize some of his expansionist goals abroad. On December 8, 1941, Japanese troops landed in southern Thailand, and the Japanese government demanded that they be accorded the right of passage on their way through to attack Malaya and Burma. Although Thai troops initially resisted the Japanese forces, within several days Phibun had agreed to the Japanese ultimatum; indeed, it is believed that he had concluded a prior agreement with the Japanese to allow them this right. Within a month, Thailand had signed a mutual defense pact with Japan and joined with Japan in declaring war on the Allies.

Pridi, who had been finance minister in the Phibun government, resigned in the wake of the agreement with the Japanese. Phibun did not, however, force Pridi to leave the political scene but appointed him to the Regency Council, which represented the monarchy in the absence of King Ananda. Although first sharing the regency with another man, Pridi effectively served throughout the war as the sole regent of the country.[1] Somewhat paradoxically, given his strongly antimonarchical views at the time of the 1932 Revolution, Pridi's insistence as regent that the monarchy, which he now represented, was independent of the government helped lay the groundwork for a more influential monarchy in the postwar period.

Toward the end of the war, Pridi, in his position as regent, supported the clandestine anti-Japanese Free Thai movement. This movement was founded in the United States and England following the Thai declaration of war on the Allies. Seni Pramoj, then Thailand's ambassador to the United States, refused to deliver this declaration to the U.S. government, and that government reciprocated by not declaring war on Thailand and later by providing support for the Free Thai movement. The movement drew many of its members from Thai students in the United States and England who had been stranded there when war broke out and had been unable to return home. After training, some were smuggled into Thailand where they met up with local Free Thai who had been organized under Pridi. The Free Thai movement not only helped the Allied cause during the war but also used links with the Allies, especially the United States, to gain support for muting demands that Thailand be treated as an enemy country at the end of the war. The Free Thai also established links with Southeast Asian nationalist movements, especially those in Indochina. Such links were to have significant repercussions for Thailand's foreign policy in the immediate postwar period. The members of the Free Thai were, in addition, to provide support for an important postwar political movement.

Initially, Phibun's alliance with the Japanese seemed to be advantageous to Thailand. In line with provisions in a secret protocol to the treaty of alliance with Japan, Thailand took over territories in Burma and Malaya that had been ceded to the British in the late nineteenth century. Although the war brought an end to trade with Western countries, the greatly expanded trade with Japan at first seemed to make up for this loss. Many Thai profited from supplying provisions to the large number of Japanese soldiers stationed in Thailand. As the war progressed, however, the economic situation rapidly deteriorated. Not only was the government forced to expend large amounts of money on maintaining its army in the newly acquired territories and on other functions related to the war, but it also was forced to extend increasingly large amounts of credit to the hard-pressed Japanese. The resulting inflation and scarcity of goods on the market began to erode Phibun's popularity. As it finally became evident that the Allies would win the war, many of Phibun's original supporters turned against him. Phibun recognized that Thailand's alliance with Japan was going to prove a serious problem for the country following an Allied victory. He thus began to provide tacit support to the Free Thai.

Ostensibly for defense reasons, but also because Phibun wished to found a memorial to himself as the founder of a new Thailand, he proposed to build a new capital in the north central part of the kingdom at Phetchabun. The Phetchabun scheme proved, however, to be very unpopular. Lacking sufficient money to hire laborers, the government recruited them through a new version of the old corvée system. Villagers recruited to work on the new city not only resented having to work for no pay but also often fell ill from the malaria that was endemic in the area. Whatever popularity Phibun had gained through his promotion of Thai nationalism was now seriously compromised by the hardships people experienced both from the demands placed on them by the government and by the worsening economic situation. In 1944, Phibun resigned when parliament voted not to support the Phetchabun scheme.

Pridi might have been the choice of many people to succeed Phibun, but he was unacceptable to the Japanese. Instead the conservative Khuang Aphaiwong formed a new government, one that was, however, seen only as transitional for the remaining months of the war. Once Japan surrendered, a new government was formed under Seni Pramoj who, as head of the Free Thai outside Thailand, was viewed by Pridi and others to be in the best position to deal with the Allies, especially Great Britain and France, which considered Thailand to be at war with them.

Postwar Political Crisis

After the war, Britain and France demanded that Thailand return all territories taken during the war and, in addition, those taken during the 1940–1941 conflict with France. Thailand was also to pay very large reparations and to punish those who had been "war criminals." The United States, having never recognized Thailand's declaration of war, did not join in these demands. On the contrary, it used its good offices to help Thailand in its negotiations with Britain and France. The role played by the United States during this immediate postwar period proved to be the beginning of a "special relationship" between Thailand and the United States—one that would lead to marked changes in Thai society from the mid-1950s through the mid-1970s.

The election of January 6, 1946, appeared to usher in a new era of parliamentary democracy. Pridi, who had stepped down as regent following the return to Thailand of King Ananda Mahidol, assumed the premiership. He was faced with increasing fractiousness among political groups as new alliances were forged in the aftermath of Phibun's departure from the political scene. Such infighting, not altogether unexpected given the radically changed political circumstances, might not have been of serious concern if it had not been for a tragic event that seriously compromised Pridi's reputation.

On June 9, 1946, King Ananda was found dead in the palace from a bullet wound in his head. The circumstances of his death were not clear from the beginning, and no one in the royal family who may be presumed to know anything about the situation has ever discussed it. The death was first reported to have been an accident, caused by King Ananda's playing with a gun. This interpretation, made public by Pridi's government, was met with considerable skepticism. A commission of inquiry appointed by Pridi issued a report that cast even further doubts on the situation when it ruled out accident as the cause of death. Several years later, when Phibun had returned to power and Pridi was in exile, a judicial investigation concluded that the death had been regicide and that it had occurred with Pridi's knowledge. Three men who had been on the palace staff at the time of the death were charged with conspiracy. Although they were convicted and executed, many people felt they had been made scapegoats and were not convinced of Pridi's guilt. To the end of his life, Pridi insisted that he had had absolutely no role in the matter. On the contrary, he reiterated time and again that he had been a strong supporter of the king and the royal family. For many Thai to this day, a serious question hangs over the death. Whatever the actual circumstances, there is little question but that it led to Pridi's fall from power.[2]

On November 8, 1947, the army, led by several officers who had been retired after the end of the war as well as a few still on active duty, staged a successful coup d'état. Although plans had called for the arrest of Pridi and Admiral Thamrong Navasawat, Pridi's close associate and then prime minister, they both escaped and made their way into exile. Although the success of the coup may have been ensured by public dissatisfaction at the government's inability to provide a satisfactory explanation for the death of King Ananda, most of the people who participated in it were motivated by a desire to reestablish the prestige and influence of the military, which had been discredited following the war. Many in the military—including such coup leaders as Phin Chunnahawan, Phao Sriyanonda, and Sarit Thanarat—felt they and other high-ranking army officers had served their country well in the military campaigns against the French and in the Shan State in Burma but that these campaigns now counted for nothing since Thailand had been forced to give up the conquered lands following the end of World War II. Many senior officers had been forced to retire from active duty following the war and were excluded from any significant role in society. The coup leaders also seized upon the current economic crisis in the country, caused primarily by the strain of meeting the reparation demands imposed by Britain and France, as justification for the coup.

The 1947 coup marked the beginning of a period in which the Thai military, and more specifically the army, assumed the role of determining the character of the governments that rule Thailand even to the present day. Although the military had been involved in the 1932 Revolution and military men, most particularly Phibun, had participated in the governments between 1932 and 1947, the role played by the military had been a supporting rather than a preeminent one. The coup of 1947 changed the parameters of Thai political life.

THE RETURN OF PHIBUN AND THE RISE OF THE ARMY

In part in consideration of how the coup might be viewed by the United States, Great Britain, and France, the leaders of the 1947 coup first installed a civilian government under Khuang Aphaiwong. Although Khuang succeeded in attracting to his government a number of able people, he was allowed to remain in office only four months. In April 1948, the coup leaders forced Khuang to resign in order to make way for the formation of a new government under Phibun.

Although Phibun was to be prime minister for a decade, he was far less powerful in this role after the war than he had been during his previous period in office. At the outset he faced an unstable political situation. Conflicts still remained within the coup group itself, and Pridi and his supporters among former members of the Free Thai still sought to return to power. In February 1949, with naval support and with the backing of former Free Thai still in the country, Pridi attempted to stage a coup and return to power. Although previously Pridi had advocated using democratic means to effect political change, he now contributed to the legitimation of force as a means for such change by attempting to return to power through a coup. His effort failed, and in the aftermath Pridi was forced once more to go into exile. This time he never returned, and after spending twenty years in China moved to France where he remained for the rest of his life. The navy, for its role in the attempted coup, was deprived for many years to come of the level of budgetary support given to the army, and senior naval officers were forced to resign. Many of the remaining Free Thai leaders in the country were arrested, and several prominent members, including four who had been ministers in earlier administrations, were murdered by police. Several of those killed were from northeastern Thailand, where they were highly respected among the local Lao peoples. Their deaths contributed to the growing sense among northeasterners of alienation from the central government.[3]

Political infighting among the military leaders who had come to power in 1947 continued throughout the next several years. In June 1951, the navy made an attempt to recoup its power by taking Phibun hostage. The air force launched an attack on the navy ship where Phibun was held, and though Phibun survived, the incident revealed clearly that he was not considered indispensable even by those people who had made him prime minister.

The real power figures to emerge in the post-1951 period were General (later Field Marshal) Sarit Thanarat, who came to exercise preeminent control over the army, and General Phao Sriyanonda, who gained control of the police. Both men were to develop their respective institutions with considerable financial support from the United States. Aid from that country enabled both institutions to become much more professional and efficient than before; at the same time, they also became powerful instruments of state that both Phao and Sarit could use for their own ends. Phao turned the police into agents of coercive power. During his years in power, they were often used to suppress dissent; at the same time, they became known for an increasing tendency to extract wealth for their own benefit from the populace. During the 1950s, the police became heavily involved in the opium trade in northern

Thailand as well as in other forms of corruption. Although recent governments in Thailand have attempted to reform the police, that institution still carries a marked legacy from the Phao era. Sarit's army was not as blatantly coercive, in part because it had little role in extending state power directly over the populace. It did, however, assume the special role of "protecting the nation," which in practical terms meant backing the authority of the government when challenged by opponents such as Pridi and his supporters. The notion that the army has a unique responsibility to protect the nation also continues as a legacy today. Sarit, like Phao, also used his powerful position for personal gain.

Phibun was able to govern the country in part because he played Phao and Sarit off against each other. At the same time, he also sought to establish an independent power base among the populace at large. Ever since he had joined the Promoters in 1932, Phibun had espoused the idea of popular participation in politics, and unlike the leaders who succeeded him, he never considered governing without a parliament. During World War II he had tried to establish a popular image of himself as the embodiment of Thai nationalism. In the mid-1960s he returned to a similar approach, seeking through the promotion of certain aspects of Thai culture, and especially through the patronage of Buddhism, to generate nationalist sentiments of which he would be the beneficiary. But his efforts to promote and embody a spirit of Thai nationalism must be considered to have failed, for Phibun sought unsuccessfully to substitute himself as an alternative to the monarchy as the basis for engendering in the populace a sense of Thai national identity.

Phibun also faced increasing economic problems, a consequence in no small part of the very policy of economic nationalism he promoted. In keeping with this policy, his government set up a number of state enterprises, almost all of which proved to be unprofitable. He also continued his earlier practice of placing restrictions on private enterprises owned by aliens, which involved mainly those owned by Chinese. A new generation of owner-managers of these enterprises sought allies among some high-ranking members of the government by naming them to the boards of their companies, thereby getting around legal restrictions on the economic activities of aliens. The result was both politically corrupting and economically inefficient.

In 1955–1957, Phibun pushed through parliament new democratic reforms to enable a wider sector of the populace to participate in the political life of the country. Although his intentions may have been commendable, his democratic experiment failed. The Thai bureaucracy, like all bureaucracies, was structured along hierarchical lines. In the Thai case, the members of the bureaucracy assumed that their superior status entitled them to determine what was best for the populace without being held accountable to representatives of the people. The bureaucracy thus resisted Phibun's democratic reforms. Moreover, Phibun's government was too closely linked with Phao's corrupt and coercive police to make the move toward democracy either feasible or credible. Phao's patent manipulation of the February 1957 elections led to a public outcry against the government and to the army's dissassociating itself from support of the election results. In September 1957, Field Marshal Sarit Thanarat, Phibun's erstwhile supporter, overthrew the government. He had at least the tacit support of the royal family and was popular among many people in the country. Phibun was forced to go into permanent exile, like his former colleague and political enemy, Pridi. Phibun died in exile in Japan in 1964. General Phao also fled the country, and he, too, died in exile in the same year.

The September 1957 coup appeared initially to usher in a new democratic era. Sarit installed a civilian, Pote Sarasin, as interim prime minister and promised new elections within ninety days. The elections of December 1957 are considered to have been the fairest since those of January 1946. Had political parties been well established at this point, it is possible that a democratic system might have been initiated by the 1957 coup. With the partial exception of the Democrat party, which in the immediate postwar period had developed something of a constituency among conservatives in Bangkok, however, political parties in Thailand at the time were not based on popular support. Rather, they consisted of cliques associated with particular leaders, and as the fortunes of these leaders waxed or waned, the cliques expanded or contracted. In the absence of a clearly defined and well-organized party system, Sarit and his lieutenants, Generals Thanom Kittikachorn and Praphat Charusathien, organized a majority of the members of parliament in a coalition supporting the military-based government.

Sarit did not immediately assume the premiership; because of ill health he left the country for treatment in the United States. In January 1958, Thanom Kittikachorn formed a government with Praphat Charusathien as his vice-premier and minister of interior. Thanom's efforts to combine the effective authority of the military with the nominal power of a democratically elected parliament created problems from the very beginning. In October 1958, Sarit returned suddenly from abroad and with the complicity of Thanom and Praphat and the backing of the military brought this hybrid form of government to an end. From the time of this coup—or, as Sarit himself termed it, the "revolution" (patiwat)—of October 1958 until the student-led revolution of October 1973, Thailand was under the rule of an authoritarian regime.

MILITARY DICTATORSHIP, ECONOMIC DEVELOPMENT, AND REEMERGENCE OF THE MONARCHY

During the period of authoritarian rule from 1957 to 1973, first under Sarit and then, after his death, under his protégés, Thanom and Praphat, the army arrogated to itself the right to define national interests and to institute measures to realize those interests. The Sarit and Thanom-Praphat governments made development (*phatthana*) both an economic goal to be pursued and an ideology on which the legitimacy of the government was based. This economic development policy promoted by the military-led governments contributed, especially after the stimulus of involvement in the U.S. war in Vietnam in the 1960s, to the rapid expansion of the business sector. The people belonging to this sector began, by the end of the period, to feel excluded from policymaking and sought a greater role in the government. As a legitimating ideology, development proved to have far less appeal than nationalism associated with the monarchy. As the king and queen assumed an increasingly active role in defining the relationship between the monarchy and nationalism, so they became increasingly in a position to withdraw support from the military government and to precipitate an end to military rule. This event was not to occur, however, until well after the death in 1963 of Sarit Thanarat, the man responsible for establishing military rule in the first place.

The Rule of Sarit Thanarat

Sarit represented a new type of leader in Thailand, for unlike Phibun and many others who had participated in the 1932 Revolution, he had not studied abroad and did not share the ideals of those people who sought to transform Thailand into a Western-style parliamentary democracy. Sarit looked for his political models, not to the democratic West, but to the patriarchal system of premodern Siam. In a 1959 speech he said:

> In this modern age, no matter how much progress is made in political science, one principle in the traditional form of Thai government which still has utility and must be constantly used, is the principle of *phoban phomuang* [father of the family and father of the nation]. The nation is like a large family—provincial governors, vice-governors, and district officers are like the heads of various families. Local administrators must keep in mind that the people under their jurisdiction are not strangers, but are sons and daughters, brothers and sisters, nieces and nephews of a large family.[4]

In the system instituted under Sarit, paternalistic leadership was provided by the army and legitimated by the king. The bureaucracy became the instrument for the implementation of policies the leadership determined were best for the populace. No provision was made for any sector of the society outside of the bureaucracy and the military to articulate its own interests or to seek to influence the formation of policies that would promote such interests.

Sarit abolished political parties; they were not to be allowed to organize again until 1965. He governed without a parliament, and although a constituent assembly was appointed in 1958 with a mandate to write a new constitution, it was ten years before any constitution was produced. Sarit also moved to end the relative autonomy that the Buddhist sangha had acquired since the reforms of 1902. Not only did he take action against several senior monks who resisted government efforts to constrain their activities,[5] but in 1962, he promulgated a law that brought the entire sangha under much closer control by the government. During the years of the Sarit regime and those of his successors, the sangha was increasingly co-opted into working to promote national goals set by the government. Sarit also placed restrictions on the mass media. Newspapers and other periodicals were subject to censorship, and educational and cultural organizations could organize only under strict constraints.

Economic Development and the Rise of a Middle Class

Sarit's efforts to bring all sectors of the society under the control of a highly authoritarian government did not, however, extend to the business sector. On the contrary, during the period of military dictatorship this sector expanded greatly and spawned many new institutions. Sarit encouraged the growth of this sector because such growth was in line with his policy of promoting economic development. For Sarit, development (*phatthana*) meant more than just a rising gross national product; it also included striving toward material improvements in the lives of the populace because Sarit hoped such improvements would be seen as indicative of the moral effectiveness of the government. Development in Sarit's terms was rooted in the old Thai idea that prosperity and well-being reflected the merit of the ruler. This traditional idea was harnessed to modern economic programs by the technocrats that Sarit and his successors increasingly employed.

Led by the advice of Western-trained economists and by a mission sent in 1957–1958 by the World Bank, Sarit turned away from Phibun's program of creating state-owned enterprises and instead promulgated laws that made investment of capital in private enterprises attractive to both internal and external investors. During these years, many companies and individuals, both inside and outside the country, took advantage of the favorable investment climate promoted by the government and of what was perceived to be a stable political situation compared with other countries in the region. Some investors were attracted by the prospect of being able to employ workers who could not, because of prohibitions on the forming of unions and the staging of strikes, demand high wages. Moreover, Thailand was seen not only as having expanding markets for many goods and services but, from the mid-1960s on, as an ideal location for the many firms that began to provide the specialized goods and services associated with the war in Indochina. During the 1960s, according to a handbook produced for the U.S. army, "gross domestic product (GDP) [in Thailand] grew at an average annual rate of 8.3 percent."[6] Although the agricultural sector also grew during this period, averaging, according to the same source, 5.7 percent a year during the 1960s, investments were made primarily in the nonagricultural sector. In 1951, agriculture had accounted for 50.1 percent of the GDP while industry had accounted for 18.3 percent and commerce 18.0 percent. By 1960, agriculture accounted for only 39.8 percent and by 1970 had dropped to 28.3 percent; industry, meanwhile, had risen to 26.2 percent in 1960 and 31.6 percent in 1970, and commerce, which first declined to 15.2 percent in 1960, rose to 19.1 percent in 1970.[7] Although the percentage of the labor force employed in agriculture dropped only a few percentage points from 82.4 percent in 1960 to 79.3 percent in 1970, the absolute numbers of people employed in the new industries grew substantially. Most of those working in the new industries were located in Bangkok.[8]

The proliferation of new firms and the marked expansion of the business sector during the period from 1957 to 1973 began to create pressure for a change in the relationship between the business sector and the ruling elite. Prior to World War II, Chinese businessmen in Thailand had faced serious problems because few held Thai citizenship. To ensure that their firms would not suffer from restrictive legislation, many Chinese business leaders bought protection from whomever in the government or bureaucracy they thought could help them. In the post–World War II period, such ad hoc arrangements evolved into a more sophisticated pattern whereby leading Chinese businessmen enlisted "the permanent support of influential Thai officials by effecting formal business alliances with them."[9] Those who benefited most from the new arrangements were close associates in the two major political cliques that emerged during the period from 1948 to 1957 when Phibun was prime minister. Although Phibun appears to have become a board member of only one major business, members of the clique associated with Phao and his father-in-law, Phin Chunnahawan, held an average of 11.8 memberships on boards, and people in the Sarit faction held an average of 7.3.[10]

Although General Phao and some (but not all) members of the clique associated with him had lost many of their board memberships in the wake of the 1957 coup, Sarit, Praphat, Thanom, and others in their faction profited greatly during the period they controlled the government. An investigation following Sarit's death revealed that he had an estate amounting to 2.9 billion baht (approximately $145 million at the rate of exchange prevalent in the mid-1960s).[11] While their wealth does not appear to have approached that of Sarit, it was revealed after the 1973 coup that both Praphat and Thanom (through his wife) had benefited greatly from their period in office. As Fred Riggs points out, the involvement of high government officials in the business sector was "a consequence, not a cause, of their power position."[12]

During the 1960s, the business sector in Thailand underwent a marked change. No longer was it the province of what Riggs has called "pariah entrepreneurship."[13] Not only did alliances by members of Chinese business firms with members of the Thai elite begin to bring forward ethnic Thai (often sons of members of the board) who saw themselves as headed for business careers in these companies, but people of Chinese descent who still dominated the business sector became less Chinese. The older generation of Chinese businessmen who did not hold Thai citizenship, who had Chinese names, who often had been educated in China, and who spoke mainly Chinese languages gave way to a new generation of Sino-Thai who were Thai citizens with Thai names, who had been educated in Thai-medium schools, and who more often than not spoke Thai as their primary language.

At the same time, members of many new firms that emerged during this period lacked access to the ruling elite, whose members tended to sit on the boards of only long-established firms. Many new-generation Sino-Thai businessmen began to feel that they lacked any means of influencing policies that directly affected their business activities. This sense of alienation from the political system contributed significantly to the downfall of the Thanom-Praphat government in 1973.

King Bhumibol, an Activist King

Another major actor in the demise of the Thanom-Praphat government was the king. During the period of military dictatorship, the monarchy reemerged as a significant institution in its own right for the first time since 1932. Although the people who had staged the 1932 coup had backed away from declaring Siam a republic, they had viewed the monarchy as an institution that should be without significant power. Pridi had used his role as regent to advance what he, not the young

King Ananda, considered to be in the best interests of the country. Phibun had also sought to use the monarchy for his own ends. The judicial inquiry that he set up to look into the death of Ananda was carried out not so much to get at the truth of the tragedy as to discredit his former rival, Pridi. During the mid-1950s, when Phibun attempted once again to promote a popular nationalism, he set himself up as the patron of the Buddhist religion, a role previously played only by kings. In the celebrations in 1956 and 1957 that Phibun ordered for the 2500th anniversary of the death of the Buddha, the king was conspicuously absent. The king's quick support for Sarit's coup in 1957 suggests that he was not altogether unhappy with Phibun's overthrow.

In 1950, after King Bhumibol returned from his studies in Switzerland, he and his wife, Queen Sirikit, began to tour the country and to give regular radio broadcasts. The enthusiastic response to the royal trips up-country and to the broadcasts encouraged the king and queen to assume more active roles in national life. When Sarit came to power, he "turned to the throne for support and legitimacy."[14] Sarit, as Thak Chaloemtiarana, the major student of the Sarit period has pointed out, lacked the legitimacy that had been claimed by the people who had staged the 1932 coup. In a very real sense, he turned back the clock and sought to renegotiate the relationship between monarchy and government on a basis different from that established by the Promoters who led the 1932 coup. The king (and queen) tacitly entered into this process of renegotiation.

During 1959–1961, the king and queen, at Sarit's suggestion, made many trips abroad to help build a positive image of the country, which otherwise might have been ill viewed in light of Sarit's authoritarian actions. Sarit, for his part, restored many traditional rites and ceremonies in order to allow the king to be seen in his royal role among the populace. Sarit also encouraged the royal couple to make frequent trips to different parts of Thailand, and such trips were increased following Sarit's death. They provided the king with an opportunity to advance his own view of Thai nationalism, one centered on the monarchy. By the late 1960s, the royal couple had clearly succeeded in restoring to the monarchy an independent role in the Thai polity. By assuming this role, the king found himself able to gain popular support, which proved central in the ending of the period of military dictatorship.

The Legacy of Sarit

Sarit was a very strong leader who epitomized what in Thailand is known as a *nakleng*. A *nakleng*, according to Thak Chaloemtiarana, is "a person who was not afraid to take risks, a person who 'lived dangerously,' [who was] kind to his friends but cruel to his enemies, a compassionate person, a gambler, a heavy drinker, and a lady killer. In short, the kind of person who represented one central model of Thai masculinity."[15] Sarit showed himself as a *nakleng* not only in his decisive manner in determining policy but even more in his direct use of government power. Such use was nowhere more evident than in his ordering the summary execution of several men charged with arson and with fomenting communist rebellion. His stable of mistresses rivaled the harems of the premodern kings, whom, in fact, he may have been emulating, and he often chose as one of his mistresses a member of a family or group he wished to control politically. His heavy drinking led eventually to his early death from cirrhosis of the liver. Although Thanom and Praphat, who also had many *nakleng* characteristics, were to head the government for ten years after Sarit's death, neither ever succeeded fully in emerging from the shadow of Sarit. When Sarit died in 1963, he was accorded a funeral sponsored by the king. Although the revelations about the sources of his great wealth and his use of power for his own ends have somewhat diminished his reputation, he continues to be acclaimed by many Thai as the model for the strong leadership they believe their country needs.

The government of Thanom and Praphat continued most of Sarit's policies, many of which they financed with huge amounts of U.S. military and economic aid provided during the Vietnam War. In part because of Thailand's role in that war, the economy grew rapidly during the 1960s. The effects of this growth were manifest mainly in Bangkok, where the middle class grew rapidly. Members of this class began to exert increasing pressure on the Thanom-Praphat government to open up the political system to wider participation. In 1968, after ten years of deliberation, the constituent assembly finally drew up a new constitution that had the apparent approval of Thanom and Praphat. After promulgation of the constitution by the king, elections were held in 1969. Even the limited participation of a parliament controlled mainly by supporters of the government proved, however, to be an irritation to Thanom and Praphat. Only two years later, they staged a coup against their own constitution and prorogued the National Assembly.

Efforts to return the country to strict authoritarian rule merely intensified popular resistance to military dictatorship. In October 1973, following large popularly supported demonstrations by students, Thanom, Praphat, and Narong Kittikachorn—Thanom's son and Praphat's son-in-law who had been brought into the ruling triumvirate—found they could no longer control the instruments of power, nor could they depend on the legitimation provided by the throne. All three were forced to flee the country. In the wake of their departure and with it the military dictatorship in Thailand, a quite different type of political order was to be established.

THE STUDENT MOVEMENT AND THE REVOLUTION OF OCTOBER 14, 1973

The crisis that precipitated the end of military dictatorship in 1973 was generated by increasingly vociferous demands by students calling for a return to constitutional rule in Thailand. The student movement, which emerged in the early 1970s, had its roots in social discontents that were increasingly felt by members of urban Thai society. Although some students were also influenced by radical ideology, they initially had very little contact with the Communist party of Thailand (CPT), whose support came primarily from peasants, especially those in northeastern Thailand. It was not until after 1973 that a significant alliance was formed between the urban-based student movement and the rural-based CPT.

The student movement that was to be instrumental in bringing about the overthrow of the military dictatorship in 1973 emerged both in the major universities in Bangkok and in the newer universities and teacher colleges up-country. Ever since the 1932 Revolution, universities in Thailand, but not the vocational schools or the military academy, had fostered some of the democratic ideals of the Promoters. As early as 1957, student leaders who championed democratic ideals had protested the corruption of the elections held in February of that year. These protests had helped provide a popular rationale for Sarit's coup. After Sarit became prime minister, however, he clamped down on student activities, and many student leaders were arrested.

During the 1960s, the absolute number of students attending universities jumped dramatically even though the percentage of adult Thai who had any tertiary education remained below 1 percent. The demand for higher education was greatest among the children of the growing middle class of Bangkok. The number of students graduating from universities during the 1960s was greater than the capacity of the bureaucracy to absorb them, and an increasing number of people with a university education began to look for employment in the professions or commerce. That the making of policy decisions should remain in the hands of a very small military-bureaucratic elite proved highly galling to those with university educations who would never have the opportunity to become part of that elite.

University and college students were often exposed to new interpretations of Thai society offered by young teachers who had been trained abroad, especially in the United States. Through them, Thai students also learned about the student-based antiwar movement in the United States, while the war in nearby Vietnam, Laos, and Cambodia exposed students to its many ambiguities in closer and more intimate ways as well. The Thanom-Praphat government sent a small contingent of Thai troops to join the U.S. war effort, and the presence of U.S. soldiers on "rest and recreation" resulted in whole sections of Bangkok and parts of a number of up-country towns being transformed into strings of gaudy nightclubs and brothels thinly disguised as massage parlors.

The Thanom-Praphat government, while still keeping the country under martial law, was more permissive than Sarit had been regarding student activities as well as about what was published in the press and in books. In 1963, the journal *Social Science Review* was founded by an English-educated intellectual, Sulak Sivaraksa, and for the next decade, under Sulak and subsequent editors, the journal served as a major forum for critical reflections about Thai society, especially among the growing number of politically conscious students. By the early 1970s, such students and other intellectuals were publishing criticisms of the government and visions of a new order in Thailand in a number of different journals as well as in cheaply produced pamphlets and books.

Many of these publications were sponsored by the National Student Center of Thailand (NSCT), an organization founded in 1965. With the elections of 1969, the NSCT began to assume leadership of the student movement through coordination of the many other student organizations located on campuses throughout the country, and the NSCT acquired an even more significant role in 1971 after Thanom and Praphat conducted a coup against their own government, suspending the constitution and abolishing the National Assembly. With the banning of political parties, the NSCT became the only organization outside the government and the bureaucracy able to express public dissatisfaction with government policies.

By late 1972, the government began to perceive student protests as threatening. In November 1972, a major campaign was begun under NSCT leadership to boycott Japanese goods in an effort to focus attention on the increasing number and rapid growth of Japanese firms in Thailand and on the government's encouragement of Japan's expanding role in Thailand's economic life. During 1973, protests were aimed directly at the government itself. The decision to extend the term of military office for Field Marshal Thanom beyond the retirement age of sixty was criticized, as were the promotion of the unpopular Narong Kittikachorn to be heir apparent and the unwillingness of the government to promulgate a new constitution. The arrest in early October of thirteen student leaders and several university faculty members under charges of being party to a communist plot to overthrow the government sparked massive student protests. It has been estimated that on October 13, 1973, "400,000 people gathered in the area around Thammasat University and then marched to the Democracy Monument [commemorating the 1932 Revolution], carrying the national flag and portraits of the king and queen."[16]

October 14, 1973, was a day unlike any other in modern Thai history. Student protests turned violent as thousands of demonstrators attacked and burned government buildings—including the lottery office, which, because lottery profits had been skimmed off for political purposes by the rulers, symbolized the corruption of the military dictatorship. More than a hundred students were killed in clashes with riot police. Although it was announced that evening that Thanom had ordered the armed forces to suppress the uprising, in fact he had lost control of those forces. General Krit Sivara, the army commander in chief who effectively controlled the armed forces, refused to send troops out against the students. Without this support, Thanom, Praphat, and Narong— who, apparently, were ready to kill thousands of students if necessary— could no longer maintain themselves in power.

The crisis did not end, however, with General Krit, like Sarit in 1957, capitalizing on student protests and forming a new military government. The students, for their part, were neither sufficiently organized nor provided with a secure enough base of power to determine the shape of a new government. Rather, the king brought the crisis to an end. By so doing, he acquired a pivotal role in determining the future of the Thai political order. Determined to avoid anarchy and further bloodshed, the king asked Thanom, Praphat, and Narong to leave the country, and they had no choice but to accede to his request. The king then went on the radio to announce the departure of the triumvirate, to inform the country that there would be a return to constitutional government, and to ask students and others to return to home. The king was heard, and the 1973 Revolution ended. Although the king's action forced the military from then on to share power with civilian politicians, including representatives from the vocal urban middle classes, its most significant effect was to reverse the relationship between monarch and government that had existed since the 1932 Revolution. The king was now no longer a mere symbol to be manipulated by the government in power; he had become a significant center of authority in his own right.

NOTES

1. Originally there were two members of the Regency Council. In 1944, Lieutenant-General Prince Athit, the second council member, resigned, and the parliament made Pridi sole regent.

2. The only systematic account of King Ananda's death is that of the journalist Rayne Kruger in *The Devil's Discus* (London: Cassell, 1964). Kruger concluded that King Ananda had been shot accidentally by his brother, the present King Bhumibol. Kruger's book has never been commented on publicly by anyone in the royal family, and it has long been banned in Thailand.

3. See Charles F. Keyes, *Isan: Regionalism in Northeastern Thailand*, Data Paper, 65 (Ithaca, N.Y.: Cornell University Southeast Asia Program, 1967), pp. 34–35.

4. Translated and quoted in Thak Chaloemtiarana, *Thailand: The Politics of Despotic Paternalism* (Bangkok: Social Science Association of Thailand and Thai Khadi Institute, Thammasat University, 1979), p. 165.

5. On Sarit's conflict with and domination of the sangha, see Somboon Suksamran, *Political Buddhism in Southeast Asia: The Role of the Sangha in the Modernization of Thailand* (New York: St. Martin's Press, 1976).

6. Frederica M. Bunge, ed., *Thailand: A Country Study* (Washington, D.C.: Government Printing Office, 1981), p. 122. This study was prepared by the American University, Foreign Area Studies, under contract with the U.S. Army.

7. Statistics given in Saneh Chamarik, *Problems of Development in the Thai Political Setting*, Paper no. 14 (Bangkok: Thai Khadi Research Institute, Thammasat University, 1983), p. 13.

8. Ibid., p. 14. These figures are somewhat misleading because in the 1960s, there was a marked increase in seasonal migration from the rural areas, especially from the northeastern region, to Bangkok. Most of these seasonal migrants would have shown up in the census data as being employed in the agricultural sector.

9. G. William Skinner, *Leadership and Power in the Chinese Community of Thailand* (Ithaca, N.Y.: Cornell University Press, 1958), p. 191.

10. Figures from Fred W. Riggs, *Thailand: The Modernization of a Bureaucratic Polity* (Honolulu: East-West Center Press, 1966), pp. 256, 269, and 288. The fact that Phibun held only one such membership may represent a continuation of the anti-Chinese attitude he had espoused during his previous tenure as prime minister from 1938 to 1944.

11. Thak, *Thailand: Politics of Despotic Paternalism*, p. 337.

12. Riggs, *Thailand: Modernization of a Bureaucratic Polity*, p. 297.

13. Ibid., p. 251.

14. Thak, *Thailand: Politics of Despotic Paternalism*, p. 311.

15. Ibid., p. 339.

16. David Morell and Chai-anan Samudavanija, *Political Conflict in Thailand: Reform, Reaction, Revolution* (Cambridge, Mass.: Oelgeschlager, Crunn and Hain, 1981), p. 147.

5

The Thai Polity After the 1973 Revolution

Following the October 1973 Revolution, the army went into a temporary eclipse. The corruption of the former ruling triumvirate—Thanom Kittikachorn, Praphat Charusathien, and Narong Kittikachorn—and many of their associates was exposed and strongly criticized in the press. General Krit Sivara, now the senior military figure, did not seem to wish to assume a direct role in governing the country, and the army was thus excluded for the most part from the initial planning stages of the creation of a new political order. Trying to set up a government that did not include high-ranking members of the military proved, however, as foredoomed to failure as the similar effort in 1945 had been. Not only military officers but also many civilians came to insist that a government that did not include strong military leadership would result in political chaos. It took, however, three years before the military once again reasserted its assumed right to lead the country. In the interim, a number of new political organizations emerged.

QUEST FOR A NEW POLITICAL ORDER

A New Constitution and National Elections

Following the downfall of the old government, the king played the preeminent political role. He personally selected as interim prime minister a man of unquestioned loyalty to the throne. Not only was Sanya Thammasak a member of the Privy Council, but he was also acceptable to a wide sector of the populace. As former rector of Thammasat University, he had gained the respect of many students. He was, moreover, a former chief justice with a record of incorruptibility and a highly respected leader of the lay Buddhist Association of Thailand.

86

In addition to appointing Sanya as prime minister, the king also developed a unique mechanism for replacing the discredited National Assembly appointed by the old government with a new interim parliament. With the advice of a small number of people whom the king felt he could trust, he appointed 2,436 members to a national convention and charged them with selecting the 299 members of an interim National Assembly. Unlike any previous body, the National Convention included a significant number of local leaders—mainly commune (*tambon*) headmen—from rural society while at the same time the numbers of military and police officers and civil servants appointed to the convention were considerably lower than those in any previous assemblies. Although the low percentage of military and police officers in the convention (14 percent) was replicated in the National Assembly (13 percent), an indication of the temporary decline of the military, the percentages of local leaders and civil servants in the two bodies was reversed. In the convention 27 percent of the seats were filled by local, mainly rural, leaders; in the assembly they accounted for only 6 percent. In contrast, whereas civil servants constituted 13 percent of the convention members, they made up 37 percent of the assembly. Clearly, many members of the convention (especially local leaders) felt constrained to support those members from the bureaucracy who had long been accustomed to exercising authority over the country.[1]

Prime Minister Sanya also appointed an eighteen-member constitutional drafting committee whose members were drawn primarily from the upper echelons of the bureaucracy and business elite but also included several political leaders and a number of university professors. Although the process of drafting a constitution took longer than Sanya had allowed for, and although the conservative assembly altered many of the provisions included by the more liberal drafting committee, the constitution approved in October 1974 still stands as the most democratic constitution in Thai history.

The passage and promulgation of this constitution made possible the holding of an election for a new National Assembly. Competition for seats in this assembly was carried out by political parties that came closer to being actual parties than had their predecessors in previous elections. The 1932 Revolution had been staged by a very small group of bureaucrats and military men who were without any popular base of support. Although a parliament was created after that revolution, the people who stood for election in the 1930s were affiliated, not with parties, but with whatever faction in the ruling elite they had established patron-client relations. In the rather open political situation that followed the end of World War II, there was some movement toward the formation of popularly based parties. The most successful of these efforts resulted in the founding in 1946 of the Democrat (Prachatipat) party, a party that gained some support among the Bangkok middle class. The leaders of the Free Thai movement, who might have been able to capitalize on the grassroots network they had built up during the war to form a significant political party, were, however, forced from the political stage by the coup of 1947. The people elected to assemblies after 1947 typically had very tenuous party affiliations, and most were persuaded either before or after an election to join a coalition supporting whatever government was in power.

By 1973–1974 the situation was very different. The government of Sanya Thammasak had been appointed only as a transitional arrangement, and he had no intention of developing a party following with an eye toward remaining in power after elections were held. The military was divided. The student movement had taken the initiative in promoting popular participation in politics but had little practical experience of political life. But while many of the parties that emerged in 1974 remained little more than elite cliques, they had to pay more serious attention to the concerns of prospective voters than had most parties in previous elections.

After legislation permitting the registration of political parties was passed in 1974, a veritable proliferation of political parties took place. Only a few of these parties proved to be significant. Several sought to perpetuate the role of the formerly dominant military-bureaucratic factions. The most important of these were the Thai Nation (Chat Thai) party, which, headed by Major-General (retired) Pramarn Adireksan, had close ties to the military faction that had been associated with the late General Phao, Pramarn's father-in-law, and the Social Justice (Thamma Sangkhom) party, which, headed by a rich businessman, Thawit Klin-prathum, had close ties to General Krit. Two smaller parties, the Social Nationalist (Sangkhom Chatniyom) party and the Social Agrarian (Kaset Sangkhom) party, like the two other right-wing parties, also drew their support from the old military-bureaucratic cliques. All four parties, and especially Thai Nation and Social Justice, had strong financial backing from businessmen who had been closely aligned with these cliques. Abundant funding made it possible for these parties to finance the very expensive campaigns run by many of their candidates.

The new leftist parties, by contrast, were seriously hampered by limited financing. Some former leftist assembly members, mainly from northeastern Thailand, joined in the United Socialist Front (Naeo Ruam Sangkhomniyom). The front was handicapped at the outset of the election campaign not only by limited resources but also by the death in 1974 of its well-known leader Thep Chotinuchit. The front was joined by two new leftist parties, the Socialist party of Thailand (Sangkhom Niyom haeng Prathet Thai) and New Force (Phlang Mai), both of which were associated with the student movement. The Socialist party was headed by two former assembly members, Somkit Srisangkhom and Khaisaeng Suksai, and its secretary-general was Dr. Boonsanong Punyodyana, a former sociology professor at Thammasat University. The New Force party was headed by Dr. Krasae Chanyawong, who had been awarded the Magsaysay Award for his medical services among rural peoples. Dr. Pramote Nakhonthap, another Thammasat academic, became the secretary-general of the New Force party.

Situated between the parties that sought to create a new, more just social order and those committed to a restoration of something like the ancien régime were the Democrat (Prachatipat) and Social Action (Kit Sangkhom) parties. The Democrat, the oldest established party in Thailand, adopted a reformist approach, one that appealed primarily to the urban middle class in Bangkok and townspeople up-country. The Social Action party, with close ties to the new business elite of the country, also adopted a reformist position, in part with the intent of bringing the business sector more directly into policy formation. The Social Action party was headed by Kukrit Pramoj, the brother of Seni Pramoj who had long headed the Democrat Party. These two parties differed, however, in their second level of leaders. Both Chuan Leekpai and Phichai Rattakun, who were deputies of Seni in the Democrat party, were experienced politicians with strong commitments to parliamentary government. Boonchu Rojanasathien, who was to become the second most well-known leader of the Social Action party, was a former vice-chairman of the Bangkok Bank. Boonchu epitomized the commitment of the Social Action party to promoting dynamic capitalism.

When elections took place in January 1975, the electorate had to choose from among a plethora of parties, many of which aggressively competed for votes. Perhaps because the new situation was confusing, the turnout was relatively light. Votes were spread among a large number of parties, and no one party gained a majority of the 269 seats in the assembly. The Democrats won the most seats (72), and Seni was finally able to put together an unstable coalition government with support from the leftist parties, the Social Action party, and the opportunistic Social Agrarian party. Even with this support, and that of three members of minor parties, the Seni government only held 133 out of the 269 seats in parliament.[2]

Seni quickly found it impossible to maintain this minority-supported coalition, and less than two months after he had formed his government, a no-confidence vote was passed in the assembly, forcing Seni's government to resign. Kukrit Pramoj, Seni's brother and the head of the Social Action party, shifted alliances and, with the support of the right-wing parties, was able to form a new government. The center and leftist parties that had supported Seni now formed the opposition. Kukrit's government was also relatively short-lived. When a no-confidence vote proposed by the opposition for debate in mid-January 1976 seemed likely to succeed, army leaders became seriously concerned about what a center-left alliance might do if it proved able to form a government. They gave Kukrit an ultimatum: call new elections or allow the army to take control of the government. Committed to democratic government, Kukrit called for new elections.

Labor and Farmer Movements

The army was concerned not only about what might take place if a Democrat-leftist coalition government came to power but also about the recent growth of new labor and farmer organizations. These groups, supported by the student movement, demanded radical changes in the Thai political and economic systems. The 1973 Revolution had brought students into politics in a significant way, and even though some attached themselves to particular parties, primarily the New Force and Socialist parties, many felt that parties alone were inadequate to channel the concerns of people facing serious social problems. These students turned their attention to developing and assisting new labor and farmer organizations that became the vehicles through which attention could be focused on the inequities in Thai society.

The growing economy of Bangkok had resulted in the recruitment of hundreds of thousands of people into the urban labor force. Between 1960 and 1970, the nonagricultural labor force increased by more than 1 million, or from 2.2 million to 3.19 million people,[3] most of this growth occurring in Bangkok. Whereas prior to World War II urban workers had been primarily of Chinese descent, by the mid-1960s the labor force had become overwhelmingly Thai. Most of the new workers came from rural areas in the provinces near Bangkok or from the northeast, the poorest and most underdeveloped part of the country. Many new workers, and especially those from the northeast, were only temporary sojourners in Bangkok, coming to work for a few months or years in unskilled jobs and then returning to settle in their home communities. A significant percentage—exact information on their numbers is difficult to find—stayed on, however, often moving into skilled or semiskilled jobs in the growing manufacturing sector of the economy.

For most of the period from 1958 to 1973 labor unions were prohibited, and salaries were determined by managers and owners of firms who wished to keep wages low. A few illegal strikes occurred, averaging 17 a year between 1966 and 1971, but few laborers felt brave enough to challenge the government's ban on unionization. In 1972, the Thanom-Praphat government reluctantly permitted the forming of labor associations, but only under strict, regulated conditions. Although this more permissive stance toward labor stimulated some increase in labor activities—there were 34 strikes in 1972—it was the challenge that the student movement posed to the government that encouraged workers to organize. From the beginning of 1973 to October 14, 134 strikes broke out, and between the revolution of October 14 and the end of the year there were 367. Labor agitation remained high throughout the next three years.[4] These strikes were not merely a function, however, of a more open political system; they also represented efforts by labor to deal with the economic recession of 1973. The textile industry, in particular, suffered a sharp decline as demand for Thai textiles dropped sharply during the oil crisis of 1974.

In mid-1974, some 20,000 textile workers from about 600 factories located in or near Bangkok went on strike, supported by the National Student Center of Thailand. The strike ended a week later when the Sanya government agreed to help the workers in their negotiations with their companies and to raise the minimum wage to 20 baht (less than $1) per day.[5] Continuing strike activity and the organization of an increasing number of workers into unions led to the passage of the Labor Relations Act of 1975. Although the governments of Sanya and subsequently of Seni and Kukrit showed themselves willing to respond to pressures by organized labor, the military looked on the numerous strikes as evidence of growing chaos. This fear was exacerbated by the radical rhetoric of the leaders of the Labor Coordination Center of Thailand (LCCT). It seemed to matter little to those in the military who were concerned about the LCCT that the group represented only a very small number of workers compared with the more moderate Federation of Labor Unions of Thailand or that the LCCT collapsed in mid-1975 when Prasit Chaiyo, the head of the union, led a long and unsuccessful strike against the Dusit Thani Hotel.

The emergence of groups representing farmers' interests was also viewed with alarm by many people in the military. During the Sarit and the Thanom-Praphat regimes, a policy of unbalanced development had been promoted; that is, the governments had laid primary emphasis on the development of the nonagricultural private sector. Although programs promoting agricultural development had also been established, their primary purpose had been national security rather than the economic growth of the agricultural sector. As a result of those policies, the agricultural sector had fallen significantly behind the nonagricultural sector in its contribution to the gross domestic product. This shift had not been associated with a commensurate movement of labor out of agriculture and into industry. Workers employed in agriculture still accounted for nearly 80 percent of the labor force in 1970 as compared with 82 percent in 1960 while those employed in industry accounted for only a little more than 4 percent in 1970 as compared with about 3.5 percent in 1960. Meanwhile, differences in per capita income not only between individual families but also between different parts of the country had also increased. In 1960, the average per capita income in northeastern Thailand, the poorest and most underdeveloped region, was 19.2 percent of the average per capita income in Bangkok. By 1970, the same figure was 16.2 percent. Even in the much more prosperous central region of Thailand, the average per capita income in the region relative to that of Bangkok declined from 45.5 percent in 1960 to 41.5 percent in 1970.[6]

Although most farmers in Thailand, today as in the 1960s and 1970s, own and operate their own land-holdings, by 1970 tenancy and landlessness had begun to become serious problems in certain areas of the central plains and in the Chiang Mai valley in northern Thailand. Throughout the country, farmers found it very difficult to obtain credit for agricultural activities from either government or commercial sources. They often felt that government regulations interfered with rather than facilitated their efforts to realize profits. Many farmers also had experienced the use of arbitrary power by the police and sometimes by other provincial officials. Finally, while villagers throughout the country were being pushed into programs the government claimed were designed to bring about development or to ensure their security, villagers themselves were not permitted by the government to participate in the shaping of these programs.[7]

After the 1973 Revolution, a number of students went into the countryside to spread democratic ideas among the people. These students, many of whom had never even visited rural areas, soon began to realize that it would be more helpful to listen to villagers telling them their problems instead of attempting to instill them with somewhat impractical philosophical principles. This shift caused the National Student Center of Thailand to support the first large-scale protest by farmers in March 1974. The Sanya government proved sympathetic to the protestors' request for higher rice prices and earmarked some 300 million baht to meet farmers' demands. This positive response encouraged other villagers to organize their own petitions to the government for help with tenancy problems or for redress of other grievances.

As the petitions and protests of farmers multiplied in mid-1974, the Sanya government came to recognize that it needed some means to respond. In early June, the government created an extraordinary committee "empowered to reallocate land and investigate grievances of landless farmers. This new committee was given unprecedented authority to arrest and detain uncooperative land owners."[8] The government clearly did not anticipate the level of response farmers would make to the establishment of this committee. Between June and September, the committee received 53,650 petitions; it was so overwhelmed by the sheer number it was able to act on only 1,635 of them.[9]

Recognizing that discontent in the countryside could be channeled to political advantage, the more radical factions of the student movement—the Federation of Independent Students of Thailand (FIST) and the People for Democracy Group (PDG)—began working with certain farmer leaders to keep up pressure on the government. These efforts culminated in a demonstration of about 50,000 people in Bangkok in November 1974. The demonstration had an electrifying effect not only because of the large numbers involved but even more because upwards of fifty monks participated. The procession that marched toward Government House was led by a number of monks associated with what was called the Young Buddhist Monks group.[10] Never before in twentieth-century Thailand had monks engaged in such an overt political act. The monks who participated were sharply attacked in many newspapers, especially those expressing the views of military and right-wing groups, and public opinion, led by these newspaper articles, began to shift away from support of popular protest.

Both the Sanya government and that of Kukrit, which took office after the brief Seni interlude, introduced programs designed to eliminate at least some of the problems faced by farmers. Under Sanya, the National Assembly passed one law that specifically earmarked money for the welfare of farmers and another that established rent controls. In 1975, Kukrit's government introduced and pushed through the National Assembly an act transferring 2,500 million baht of revenue from the central government to *tambon* councils, that is, subdistrict or commune councils, to be spent on public works projects. This act was the first significant move in the direction of decentralization made since the reforms of Chulalongkorn in the 1890s. The projects were supposed to be selected not, as in the past, by officials of the Ministry of Interior posted up-country but by the *tambon* councils themselves. Although the fact that the projects were much the same throughout the country— consisting primarily of the digging of water storage tanks—indicates that there was a strong central government hand in guiding the decisions made by the *tambon* councils, the program did give villagers some control over significant amounts of government money (425,000 baht, or over $20,000, per *tambon* per year). Since 1975, this program in one form or another has been sponsored by every government, save that of Thanin Kraivichien in 1976–1977.

Although the Tambon Development Program (or Work Generation Program as it later came to be called) and the land reform laws instituted by the Sanya government were welcomed by many people in the rural areas, they did not eliminate many of the problems faced by villagers. Moreover, the fact that the government had responded to direct pressure suggested to some leaders that rural interests could best be realized through an organization that directly represented farmers. In December 1974, the Farmers' Federation of Thailand (FFT) was established, again with the support of some student organizations. The FFT was based primarily in the Chiang Mai valley and was headed by a former village headman from that area, Intha Sibunruang. Although the FFT continued throughout its existence to press for land reforms that would be of particular help to the large landless population in the Chiang Mai valley and some areas in the central plains, it also espoused a broad enough program to attract in 1975 and 1976 thousands of members from areas in the country where land issues were not the main concern of farmers.

The phenomenal growth of the FFT, the proliferation of strikes by urban workers, and the support of both labor and farmer movements by radical factions of the student movement frightened many urban middle-class people and even many villagers who began to wish for a return to a more ordered, authoritarian system. The communist victories in neighboring Laos, Cambodia, and Vietnam in April 1975 intensified fears among urban middle and upper classes and conservative peasants that the student, labor, and farmers' movements could be the vanguard of a communist revolution in Thailand. These fears contributed to the atmosphere in which radical right-wing movements emerged in 1975 and 1976 and ultimately provided a rationale for yet another military takeover of the government.

THE RADICAL RIGHT AND THE RETURN OF THE MILITARY

Right-Wing Groups

The success of the popular demonstrations by students and the organization of labor and farmer groups outside the control of the government had changed the parameters of Thai politics.[11] Fearing the growth of those new elements, right-wing members of the military as well as some former military officers countered by sponsoring or supporting rightist movements. Some of the rightist groups had only limited followings, but others had wide popular support among the middle and lower-middle classes[12] and can be seen as part of the latters' desire for and push toward greater participation in politics comparable to that also sought by the leftist movements. This impetus was aborted, however, by violent confrontations between leftist and rightist groups and by the coup of October 6, 1976, which brought the military back to the center of the political system.

Of the right-wing groups that emerged in 1975 and 1976, the Red Gaurs (*krathing daeng*) was probably the one with the most clearly defined military backing. It was organized by officers connected with the Internal Security Operations Command, and more specifically with a certain Colonel (later Major-General) Sudsai Hasdin. The Red Gaurs became essentially a paramilitary group, drawing its membership from former mercenaries who had fought for the United States in Laos and from vocational students in Bangkok. Although the latter had joined with university students in the 1973 Revolution, they separated themselves from leftist student organizations thereafter. Unlike most of the university students, vocational students came primarily from lower-middle- rather than middle-class backgrounds, and during the economic recession of the mid-1970s, many were having considerable difficulty in finding jobs after graduation. By joining the Red Gaurs or other paramilitary groups, these students or former students acquired both status and some income.

A second group, known as Nawaphon,[13] although also established by active and retired military officers of rightist orientation, had more of the character of a popular movement. Its leader, Wattana Kiewvimol, was a flamboyant speaker whose meetings sometimes resembled those of religious revivalists. At them he appealed to the audience for a commitment to king, nation, and religion comparable in some ways to the commitment to Christ demanded by charismatic Christian preachers. Wattana's followers were primarily up-country townspeople, not villagers or Bangkok urban dwellers. Closely linked to Nawaphon, and providing it with an intense ideological dimension, was the charismatic monk Kittivuddho Bhikkhu. Over the previous decade, Kittivuddho had built a vast network of monks throughout the country in association with his Chittaphawan College in central Thailand. This network gave him access to the populace in a way that could not be duplicated by any military-backed group. In mid-June 1976, he gave a sermon in which he said that killing communists was not sinful but meritorious because communists were bestial types and agents of the devil (Mara) who threatened the nation, the religion, and the monarchy. Although Kittivuddho was strongly criticized by many leading laymen (but few senior monks) for such sentiments, his militant Buddhism provided an ideological rationale for rightists, especially those in Nawaphon, to engage in violent action against presumed communists.[14]

The most lasting of the right-wing groups to become prominent in the 1975–1976 period was the *luk sya chaoban* (literally, "village tiger cubs"), known in English as the Village Scouts. This group had been founded in 1971 by the Border Patrol Police with the support of the Ministry of Interior as a government-sponsored program to mobilize villagers in security-sensitive areas in support of the state and against communism. In 1973, the king and queen became patrons of the Village Scouts, and the organization was redefined to make membership open to people throughout the country, in towns as well as in villages. After the revolution of October 14, 1973, the Village Scouts became identified as a royalist rather than as a government movement, although recruitment was still primarily the responsibility of local officials and the movement still received the support of the Border Patrol Police, which, in turn, had very close relations with the royal family. During the five-day initiation sessions held for new scouts, the themes of nation, religion, and monarchy were given expression in many of the activities such as songs, games, and plays. People from many different backgrounds were instilled with the belief tht they shared a common cause, that of Thai nationalism and anticommunism. The submersion of social differences in the nationalist cause also was symbolized by the common uniform worn by members no matter what their background. Signifying their role in the movement, King Bhumibol and Queen Sirikit appeared from time to time in scout uniform.[15]

Although large numbers of people became members of the Village Scouts—some observers have claimed that by 1978 some 5 percent of the total population had been initiated[16]—only a very small proportion of the total actually could be mobilized for any concerted political action. Most people who joined, especially after the October 6, 1976, coup, were motivated primarily by the desire to show publicly their loyalty to the monarchy. The activist element, linked closely with the sponsoring Border Patrol Police, assumed, however, a significant role in the confrontation with leftist groups that intensified during 1976.

Although never clearly identified, there was in the Border Patrol Police, in the Internal Security Operation Command which was in charge of counterinsurgency, and elsewhere in the military a small coterie of military and police officers who were willing to use any means to eliminate the growing political influence of the student, labor, and farmer movements and the leftist political parties. This coterie sanctioned, if it did not order, the assassination of almost all the major leaders of the farmer movements as well as several politicians associated with the leftist parties. Between March 1974 and August 1975, twenty-one leaders of the farmers' movement, including Intha Sibunruang, the head of the Farmers' Federation of Thailand, were killed. This systematic destruction of the leadership of the farmers' movement resulted in its elimination as a means for the expression of rural interests and grievances.[17]

Although some labor union leaders also became the object of assassination attempts, there was less of a concerted effort to destroy the labor movement through coercive means than there was to crush the farmers' movements. The labor unions were already assuming a lower profile. The leftist Labor Coordination Center of Thailand had declined markedly in influence following its unsuccessful strike against the Dusit Thani Hotel in 1975, and another organization with reputed army backing, the Federation of Labor Unions of Thailand (FLUT), assumed dominance of the labor movement. The FLUT survived, albeit unofficially, and even became allied with General Kriangsak Chomanan, who was to become prime minister in 1977.

Having effectively eliminated the farmers' movement, the death squads next turned their attention to the leftist parties. During the election campaign between mid-January and mid-April 1976, some thirty or more supporters of leftist parties were killed. They included a New Force party member of the National Assembly and, most notably, Dr. Boonsanong Punyodyana, the secretary-general of the Socialist party of Thailand. Supporters of leftist parties were frequently intimidated. In the election, the leftist parties captured only six seats compared to the thirty-seven they had won in the 1975 election. Although genuine concern on the part of the populace at what had happened in neighboring Indochina in 1975 contributed to the turning away of the electorate from the leftist parties, the violence directed at these parties, together with the incessant effort in the press and on the military-run radio stations to link the leftist parties with communism, must be seen as the major causes of the decline of support for the left-wing movement.

Political Crisis and the October 1976 Coup

The April 1976 election for 279 seats in the National Assembly initially appeared to have produced a stable center-right government. The new government proved, however, unable to gain and hold the backing of the military. Instead of the political fragmentation produced by the 1975 election, the 1976 election was dominated by four parties— the Democrat, which won 114 seats; Social Action, which won 45; Thai Nation, 56; and Social Justice, 25. Not only were the leftist parties effectively eliminated from parliament, but Kukrit Pramoj himself, while seeing a substantial gain for his Social Action party, lost his seat to Samak Sunthornwej, an extremely outspoken right-wing member of the Democrat party who had strong army backing. With Kukrit gone and the Democrats now holding the largest number of seats in parliament, Seni Pramoj, the Democrat party leader, became the obvious choice to form a new government.

Seni formed a center-right coalition government, which controlled 206 of the 279 seats in parliament. Recognizing that military support was essential to the success of the coalition, Seni asked General Krit Sivara, the former army commander generally regarded as the strongest leader in the military, to become minister of defense. Unfortunately, General Krit died just two days after he was asked to assume this post, and after his death, nobody remained in the military who could control the actions of the several factions. Those closest to Krit—including General Kriangsak Chomanan, later himself to become prime minister— were in a structurally weak position in relation to other military cliques, which included officers formerly associated with General Phao—notably General Chalad Hiranyasiri and the two retired major-generals, Pramarn Adireksan and Chatchai Chunhawan, who now headed the Thai Nation party and a strong group, associated with General Yot Thephasadin na Ayutthaya, which was loyal to General Praphat.

This latter group pressed for Thanom and Praphat to be allowed to return to the country. In mid-August, the government was put to a severe test when Praphat, testing the extent of this support, returned from exile. Students immediately organized demonstrations to protest his return, and the Seni government also sought to persuade Praphat to leave. After being in the country for ten days, during which time he had an audience with the king and queen, Praphat agreed that the time was not yet propitious for his return and left the country once more. He had been gone scarcely three weeks when Thanom returned.

Thanom had taken much better care to ensure that he would be permitted to remain. After arriving from Singapore, he went directly to Wat Bowǫnniwet and was ordained as a monk. His ordination was calculated to enable people to interpret his return in a traditionally acceptable Thai way, whereby a temporary stay in the monkhood is seen as a way of leaving the mundane world so that one can return to it as a new man now tempered by the moral discipline of the order. The fact that the king and queen visited the temple to offer alms to Thanom after he became a monk also signified their public acceptance of him despite his past actions.

The leaders of the student associations reacted strongly to the return of a man they had forced out of office as a "tyrant," and the large-scale student demonstrations that followed Thanom's return put the Seni government in a dilemma. Most members of the Democrat party also wished to see Thanom leave the country, but a small number of Democrats together with the various right-wing parties supported his return. When Seni attempted to reorganize the government without the right-wing parties or the right-wing members of his own government, the king refused to approve the new cabinet; high-ranking members of the military also refused to support it. Division over Thanom's return was fast making the continuation of a parliamentary-based government untenable.

On September 25, 1976, two students who had been distributing posters demanding the expulsion of Thanom were stopped by police in Nakhon Pathom Province near Bangkok; shortly afterward they were found hanged, having first been strangled. The danger of further violence increased as students organized large-scale protests in Bangkok while rightist movements—in particular Nawaphon—demonstrated in support of Thanom. The army radio station and right-wing newspapers launched a strident attack on the student protestors, charging them with posing a danger to nation, religion, and the monarchy.

On October 5, an incident occurred that precipitated a violent climax to the confrontation. At Thammasat University, a group of students staged a mock hanging to call attention to the murder of the two students ten days before. A photograph of the student action published in a right-wing newspaper appeared to show one of the students made up to look like the crown prince. Although the picture was later found to have been altered, it was used at the time by right-wing newspapers, the army radio station, and the rightist groups as evidence of lèse-majesté on the part of the students. On the evening of the fifth, Village Scouts, Red Gaurs, members of Nawaphon, and others joined units of the Border Patrol Police outside Thammasat University where some 4,000 students were lodged. The following day, on what many subsequently came to call "bloody October 6th," an assault was launched on the university. Forty-six students by government count, and many more according to unofficial estimates, were killed. Many were brutally murdered and their bodies burned on the spot. Hundreds more were wounded, and some 1,300 were arrested. The police also scoured Bangkok, arresting hundreds of other students and political activists throughout the city.

On the evening of October 6, a military group calling itself the National Administrative Reform Council announced over the radio that it had seized power "in order to restore stability and law and order to the kingdom."[18] Martial law was instituted, parliament was abolished, and the constitution, which had taken so long to write, was set aside. It appeared that there was to be a return to some type of military dictatorship like that which had existed prior to 1973.

The government that emerged in the wake of the October 6 coup did not, however, represent a return to the ancien régime. The military officers who staged the coup—Admiral Sangad Chaloryu, General Serm Na Nakhon, General Kriangsak Chomanan, and Air Chief Marshal Kamol Dechatunka—had associated themselves with General Krit in not backing Thanom and Praphat in October 1973. This group also preempted any move by the resurgent Phao faction, which had links to the Thai Nation party. Moreover, the National Administrative Reform Council did not install as prime minister either a military leader or a compliant politician but a man who was clearly the choice of the royal family, Thanin Kraivichien.

ALL THE KING'S MEN AND MILITARY-CIVILIAN RULE

Right-Wing Failure and Its Aftermath

Two months after the October 6 coup, the king said in an address to the nation that "at a time when our country is being continually threatened with aggression by the enemy, our very freedom and existence as Thais may be destroyed if Thai people fail to realize their patriotism and their solidarity in resisting the enemy. . . . Accordingly, the Thai military has the most important role in defense of our country at all times, ready always to carry out its duty to protect the country."[19] The king clearly viewed the openness of Thai politics in the period from 1973 to 1976 as threatening to the solidarity of the nation and had, thus, chosen to identify himself with and provide legitimation for a particular type of government, one in which the military would play a preeminent role. The monarchy (including the queen, who was to become very influential in her own right) went even further in assuming a direct role in determining who should head the government. Thanin Kraivichien—a former Supreme Court Justice, a member of the Privy Council, and an arch anticommunist—became prime minister after the October 6 coup because he was the king's (or, some people believe, the queen's) choice.

Many observers regard the government of Thanin as the most repressive in Thai history, surpassing in its authoritarian control of the populace even the governments of the various military dictators. Thanin was an ideological rightist who believed that almost any dissent represented a threat to the state. People were arrested not only for acts clearly aimed at undermining the state or for being communists but also for endangering society (*phai sangkhom*). This last category gave local officials, police, and even ordinary citizens with grievances against their neighbors license to have thousands of people throughout the country arrested and detained. Political parties and student groups were banned, strikes were made illegal, and strict censorship was imposed on the press. The October 6 coup and the subsequent harsh reactionary policies implemented by the Thanin government convinced thousands that a radical revolution was the only alternative to a right-wing authoritarian regime. Many people left their homes to join the Communist party of Thailand in order to work for a revolutionary change in the Thai political system.

Thanin did not, however, have the full support of the military leadership. In March 1977, General Chalad Hiranyasiri, the leader of the Phao faction in the military, attempted a coup. The coup failed, and because Chalad had personally killed another general, he was not allowed to go into exile as previous leaders of failed coups had done but was executed. But by October 1977, the military leaders who had staged the October 1976 coup decided that Thanin must go. They were led in this opinion not only by their assessment of what Thanin's government was doing internally to Thai society but also by their recognition that the U.S. government was becoming increasingly unhappy with Thanin. The members of the National Administrative Reform Council forced Thanin and his government to resign, and in their stead, a new government was formed under General Kriangsak Chomanan. Although the October 1977 coup was prompted by a number of concerns on the part of the military, the fear that if Thanin remained the society would soon face, not a relatively small-scale communist-led insurrection, but a major civil war was perhaps the primary factor.

The Kriangsak government made possible a return to a more open political system, although not one as open as in the 1973–1976 period. Some degree of participation in politics has been permitted in Thailand since October 1977, mainly through the institution of an elected lower house, while at the same time a number of restrictions on freedom of speech and assembly have been lifted with the removal of press censorship. Since about 1979, the government has allowed labor, student, and farmer groups to organize, albeit on a restricted basis. Nevertheless, the military has continued to reserve to itself the right to ensure "political stability" and to provide the leadership of the government, and the monarchy has continued to intrude itself directly in determining the composition as well as the legitimacy of any government.

The Kriangsak government reinstituted a constitution, although the 1979 constitution proved to be closer to the 1932 model than to the 1974 one. Under the provisions of this constitution, an elected National Assembly shared legislative responsibility with an appointed Senate. Kriangsak chose the vast majority of members of the Senate and packed it with members of the military. Elections were held in April 1979, but they were viewed with considerable skepticism by large sectors of the populace. Only 24 percent of the eligible electorate voted, as compared with 47 percent in April 1976. The extremely low turnout in Bangkok— 19.5 percent—was a factor in the major loss of seats experienced by the Democrats in Bangkok constituencies. The election left the Social

Action party, led by Kukrit Pramoj, the single biggest party, holding a total of 79 out of 301 seats. The Democrats saw a marked decline in their support, from 114 seats in 1976 to 30 in 1979. Most of these losses were picked up by the Peoples' party (Prachakọn Thai), led by the right-wing leader and erstwhile Democrat, Samak Sunthornwej. Samak's party won nearly all Bangkok seats, most of which had been held previously by Democrats. The right-wing Thai Nation party also lost seats, dropping from 56 in 1976 to 37 in 1979. The only party on the left to win any seats was the New Force, which gained 8 seats in 1979 as compared with 3 in 1976. Most of the other seats were won by independents and by members of small parties that had little cohesiveness. Following the elections, some 30 members of the National Assembly from these other small parties were brought together in the Mass Line party headed by Major-General Sudsai Hasdin, the military officer who had gained dubious fame as the "godfather" of the Red Gaurs.[20]

Kriangsak did not hold membership in any party, and although he sought support for his policies from a majority of those elected to the lower house, he looked more for support to the appointed members of the Senate. He gained popular support as a welcome change from the repressive Thanin regime, but his power base was quite narrow. He was more the de facto than the preferred candidate of the military, and he appears to have had only grudging support from the monarchy, especially since he had replaced Thanin, whom the king quickly appointed to the Privy Council. The fact that Kriangsak was unable to retain the premiership is not surprising, but his voluntarily stepping down in March 1980 in favor of Prem Tinsulanonda was highly unusual. No previous military prime minister had ever willingly given up power. Kriangsak appears to have done so primarily because he lacked both popular and military support. In particular, the influential Young Turks, mainly colonels who had at first supported Kriangsak in both the army and the upper house, had turned away from him. Kriangsak probably realized that if he tried to hold on to power, a coup would have been inevitable. Such a coup might well have led to the return of a more authoritarian form of government.

The Government of the Resilient Prem Tinsulanonda

General Prem Tinsulanonda, the commander in chief of the army who replaced General Kriangsak as prime minister, had acquired a reputation as a capable professional soldier who showed no interest in using his position for personal gain, a stance that was credible in that he has been a lifelong bachelor and has not been enmeshed in family politics. He had had considerable combat experience in fighting communist-led forces, mainly in the rural northeast where he had served as commander of the Second Army Area. From this experience, he had acquired a strong sense that socioeconomic problems in the rural areas led villagers to turn toward supporting or joining a CPT-led insurgency. He shared with Kriangsak the conviction that the major way to fight insurgency was through programs to alleviate the problems of the rural poor rather than through military action. In 1978, Kriangsak had elevated General Prem to commander in chief of the army. As head of the army, Prem somewhat reluctantly acceded to the request of other army officers that he succeed Kriangsak. In addition, Prem had the strong backing of the king. Although Prem apparently had no wish to become prime minister, he has retained the office for the longest of any incumbent since 1973.

Prem's major support in the military initially came from a group of young army officers, mostly graduates of the same military academy class (Class 7, which graduated in 1960), known as the Young Turks. In the wake of the October 6, 1976, coup, in which these officers apparently played a passive role, the Young Turks had emerged as the most cohesive faction in the army. They had first supported Kriangsak and as a consequence had seen many among their numbers appointed to the upper house. Although retaining the long-held belief that the military had primary responsibility for preserving the nation and ensuring the stability of the government, they differed markedly from the older-style military elite that had emerged after the 1947 coup. The Young Turk officers were conscious of living in a different society from that which their superiors had known. Many had seen poverty firsthand in those parts of rural Thailand where they had been sent to combat insurgency, and they had contacts among urban intellectuals who were critical of the maldistribution of wealth and power in the society. Also, at least one of the leaders had been strongly influenced by modernist Buddhist thought that stresses personal detachment while remaining active in the world.[21]

Initially, the Young Turks found General Prem an ideal leader, but within a year of his assuming the premiership they came to feel he was not attending sufficiently to their ideas about how the country should be governed. After becoming prime minister, Prem sought to broaden his power base by gaining the support of a coalition of parties in the National Assembly. The coalition between the Democrats, the Social Action party, and the Thai Nation was, however, a very uneasy one. In particular, leaders of the Social Action party and the Thai Nation party had different ideas about the role the government should play in promoting economic development. Prem had appointed the banker and deputy head of the Social Action party, Boonchu Rojansathien, as deputy prime minister in charge of economic affairs. In this role, Boonchu pursued economic policies, which he labeled "Thailand, Inc.," that favored industrialization and the promotion of exports. By implementing these policies, he directly threatened the commercial interests of some leaders of the Thai Nation party. Conflicts between the leaders of the two parties led finally to the withdrawal of the Social Action party from the coalition in March 1981.

When Prem formed a new government in mid-March, he brought in leaders of two other parties that had been formed from among independents and members of smaller parties. In making Major-General Sudsai Hasdin, the leader of the Mass Line party, minister attached to the office of the prime minister, Prem stirred up considerable controversy because of Sudsai's role in the leadership of the Red Gaurs who had played such a brutal role in the October 6 coup. This justification in 1981 of the role the Red Gaurs had played in 1976 seemed to indicate that Prem might also support similarly coercive actions if he deemed that circumstances justified them. The second man Prem brought into the government was General Prachuab Suntharangkura, the head of the United party. The Young Turks strongly disliked both Prachuab and Sudsai, viewing them as "political opportunists." They were also dismayed by Prem's links with the leadership of the Thai Nation party and other senior military men who appeared to the Young Turks to view political office as a means to enhance their own clique's commercial interests.

Early on the morning of April 1, 1981, the Young Turks staged a military coup. As they controlled most of the critical military units in and around Bangkok, they soon secured control of the key military, government, and communication centers in Bangkok. Yet, despite such advantages, the coup failed because it lacked one absolutely essential element—legitimation by the king. On hearing news of the impending coup, the king, the queen, the rest of the royal family, and Prem left Bangkok by helicopter and flew to the northeastern town of Khorat. There Prem, backed by the king and with the support of Major-General Arthit Kamlangek, indicated that he would resist the coup attempt by force if necessary. It was not force, however, that brought the coup to an end only three days later. When the coup was denounced by the king and queen, the coup leaders accepted the fact that they had failed and negotiated their surrender to Prem and Arthit. As Chai-anan Samudavanija, a leading Thai political scientist, has written: "The April 1981 coup group had in fact captured the state power by having control over Bangkok but its power lacked legitimacy due to the group's failure to seek audience with the King as it was the King alone who could give tacit consent to their action."[22]

In the wake of the failed coup, not only did the king's man, Prem, continue in power but the military leader who had stood by the royal family, Major-General Arthit, quickly rose above other more senior officers to become head of the army. From having been only a division commander in 1980, he became commander in chief of the army in 1982. The Young Turks, although accorded clemency by Prem and pardoned by the king for staging the coup, were purged from the army. Thirty-eight officers, including the most successful members of the military academy's Class 7, were discharged. Without the Young Turks, the military became more fragmented than ever.

The failed coup had the unintended consequence of making the National Assembly somewhat more significant than it had been before. Many of the Young Turks had been members of the upper house, and with them gone, its influence was now weakened. In recognition of the new importance of the National Assembly, former Prime Minister Kriangsak decided to form a political party and run for parliament himself. In August 1981, he won a by-election in Roi-et in northeastern Thailand by a huge landslide. Following the election, he formed the National Democratic party, comprising mainly members of smaller parties. From his position in parliament, Kriangsak began to reemerge as a significant political leader.

Elections held in April 1983 saw a significant gain in the number of seats held by the Thai Nation party, which had made use of the considerable support provided it by wealthy backers to campaign more successfully in the countryside. The party won 73 out of 324 seats in the lower house and, with support from independents and other members, could count on 108 votes in that house. This amount of control seemed sufficient to mount an effort to make the party's leader, General Pramarn Adireksan, prime minister instead of Prem. Prem himself had not affiliated with any political party and, following the election, announced his intention to step down. This announcement has been viewed by some people as a political ploy, for within twenty-four hours of making the announcement, he was persuaded by the leaders of the other major parties in parliament to remain in power, at which point the Thai Nation party withdrew its challenge. The 1983 election also saw the continued growth of the Social Action party, which captured 93 seats as compared with 79 in the 1979 election. The Social Action party and the Thai Nation party have emerged, for the time being, as the two major contenders for political influence in parliament, although neither is in any position to name a prime minister.

On September 9, 1985, a small contingent of troops led by Manoon Rupekachorn, one of the Young Turks who had been sacked from the army after the abortive coup of April 1, 1981, attempted another coup.

Although this effort was no more successful than the 1981 attempt, it was considerably more bloody. At least five people, including two Western journalists, were killed, and scores were injured by rebel fire. Although Manoon was allowed to flee the country as part of a deal to end the coup attempt, several retired high-ranking military officers were arrested in the aftermath. Most prominent among these were General Kriangsak Chomanan, the former prime minister; General Serm na Nakhorn, former supreme commander; Air Chief Marshal Krasae Intharat, former deputy supreme commander; and General Yot Thephasadin na Ayutthaya, former deputy army commander. Most observers believe that Manoon had also anticipated support from a number of still-active senior officers. The fact that the coup was attempted at a time when there was something of a power vacuum in Bangkok—Prem was in Indonesia on an official visit, General Arthit and the crown prince were both in Europe, and the king and queen were at their palace in southern Thailand—suggests that if there had been wide support for the coup among the military it might well have been successful.

Although the coup leaders claimed that the deteriorating economic situation was justification for their action, the causes were more complex. Prem's government had recently moved to end several illegal investment funds that had drawn their clientele primarily from military officers. Many, including a number of high-ranking officers and former officers, had lost heavily as a result and were attracted to the coup in reaction to the position adopted by Prem. It is also clear that the attempted coup of September 1985 indicated continued factionalism within the military, with at least two factions competing for royal support for their right to provide leadership of the nation.

In a situation in which no one military faction has been strong enough to stage a coup, Prem has been able to remain in power for an unexpectedly long time. The apparent stability of his government masks, to some extent, an underlying uncertainty about the future of the Thai political system. This uncertainty was exacerbated in the late 1970s and early 1980s by widespread concern about the changing role of the royal family.

In 1972, Prince Vajiralongkorn, who had been educated in part in England and in part at a military academy in Australia, was invested as crown prince. Although heir to the respect felt by many Thai toward members of the royal family, his reputation suffered from his apparent lack of interest in public affairs and rumors concerning his greater interest in his mistress and other women than in his official wife. There was, therefore, widespread popular approval when, in 1977, Princess Sirindhorn was raised by the king to become crown princess, placing her next in line to her brother in succession to the throne. Since being elevated to this position, Princess Sirindhorn has played a much more active public role than her brother, leading many people to think, and some even to hope, that she might be chosen to succeed her father on the throne.

The succession question became a major issue in 1982 when the king became seriously ill. Even though Princess Sirindhorn's actions suggest that she would make a very popular sovereign should she ever succeed to the throne, Prince Vajiralongkorn's close links with the military—he has been trained as a pilot—suggest that he might align himself with military rule if he were to become king. Since 1983, the prince, possibly sensitive to public feeling, has begun to play a role more like that performed by his father. He has become increasingly conspicuous at public functions and, especially, in showing concern for the plight of the urban poor. With this changed role, his possible succession to the throne has become more acceptable to many people who had previously been critical of his actions. Speculation about his relationship to the military continues, however, to cast a cloud over the role of the monarchy in the future of the Thai political system.

THE RISE AND DECLINE OF
THE COMMUNIST PARTY OF THAILAND

In the 1960s and 1970s, and especially after the coup of October 6, 1976, it appeared that the future might lie with a communist-led government brought to power through revolution. That possibility, however, receded markedly once the Thanin government was replaced by the governments headed by Generals Kriangsak and Prem.

Formation of the CPT and Its Expansion Into Rural Areas

The Communist party of Thailand was founded in 1942, a quite recent date compared to most other Communist parties in Asian countries. It has its roots in a branch of the Chinese Communist party that existed in Thailand prior to World War II, and to this day the CPT has remained closely linked to the Communist party of China. This linkage has been a major factor in the recent decline of the party's influence and support.

Although the party enjoyed a brief period of legal existence following World War II, because Thailand needed the Soviet Union's backing in order to enter the United Nations, it has been banned since 1947. After that time, the party, many of whose leaders were of Sino-Thai origin, shifted from being primarily an urban-based group to one whose supporters came mainly from rural communities. During the 1950s, it began to extend its support among villagers in northeastern Thailand, where repressive actions taken by the Phibun and Sarit governments against a number of former political leaders from the northeast coupled with ongoing conditions of poverty and a growing sense of alienation among many Lao-speaking northeasterners made the CPT program of radical change appealing.

Recruitment of members was, however, very slow. The CPT was not able to translate the very real discontents felt by rural people, especially in northeastern Thailand, into mass support for revolutionary change; moreover, it was hampered by the absence of legally recognized institutions through which it might work to promote its programs. Although the party apparently decided as early as 1961 to turn to armed revolt against the government following the execution of the northeastern former member of parliament, Krong Chandawong, it was not until 1965 that the first armed engagement between the CPT and government forces took place, and the CPT's Thai People's Liberation Army was not set up until 1967.

Even at a time when communist revolutions were succeeding in Vietnam, Laos, and Cambodia, the CPT was able to mount only a relatively small insurgency, not a full-scale revolution. As John Girling, a leading student of Thai politics has written: "It is an insurgency in terms of protracted, still fairly small-scale, guerilla-type operations: 'armed propaganda' in villages, attacks on police posts, blowing up bridges, ambushes of military convoys, and so on."[23] Prior to 1976, the CPT had only very limited success in convincing people that it understood the root causes of inequality and repression in Thai society and that it offered a realistic means to eliminate those causes. For the most part, the people who joined the CPT insurrection were motivated as much by ethnic as by class concerns. In northeastern Thailand, the concerns were those of the Lao or Isan ("northeastern") populace relative to the dominant Thai; in the north, they were those of the tribal peoples, especially the Hmong and Karen; and in the south, they were those of Malay Muslim peoples living in a Buddhist state. But while ethnicity has served as a basis for defining the interests of certain sectors of the populace as different from those of the state, it has not proved to be a basis for recruiting many people for an armed insurrection against the government.

In 1975, a decade after taking up arms against the government, the CPT had about 8,000–10,000 armed insurgents organized into relatively independent operational units. Most of these operated in northeastern Thailand in areas along the Mekong River, in the hills known as the Phuphan Mountains, and in hilly areas bordering Cambodia. In the far south of Thailand, CPT members constituted only a small proportion of the insurrectionaries, the majority belonging to Malay-Muslim secessionist organizations and to the Malaysian Communist party, which operated on the border between Malaysia and Thailand. CPT units were found in the mid south, near Nakhon Si Thammarat and Suratthani, and upper south, near Prachuap Khiri Khan. Tribal-supported CPT units were also to be found in Tak Province near the Burmese border as well as in the northeast near the Laotian border. Although the CPT had only limited success in establishing effective control over much of the populace (most of the areas they operated in were relatively underpopulated), they were able to resist constant military attacks by much larger and better-equipped units of the Thai army, air force, and Border Patrol Police.

The Political Crisis of the 1970s and the Turn Away from the CPT

The student uprising of 1973 appears not to have been influenced by communist ideology to any significant extent. After the uprising, however, many student leaders as well as some labor and farmer leaders, came to see themselves as having a common cause with the CPT. Up until October 1976, those leaders remained committed to working within the system, attempting to secure changes through open political means rather than through militant struggle. The assassination of farmer leaders and politicians, especially Dr. Boonsanong, and the violence of rightist groups sanctioned by certain army and Border Patrol Police leaders in the October 6, 1976 coup, however, prompted many leaders and members of student movements, as well as some leftist politicians and farmer and labor leaders, to believe that working within the system was doomed to failure. In the wake of the October 6 coup, some 2,000–3,000 people, approximately half of whom were students, "went to the jungle" to join the CPT-led armed insurrection.

The new recruits not only augmented the ranks of the insurrectionaries, but also gave the CPT a new degree of legitimacy. In 1977, the CPT seemed to represent the only reasonable alternative to a right-wing authoritarian government. By 1979, at the apogee of its power, the CPT had somewhere between 12,000 and 14,000 men under arms, and probably upwards of 2 million villagers were subject to some degree of communist influence. Even then, only about 200,000 or 300,000 villagers would have been under what the CPT refers to as "state power," that is under the direct control of the CPT and outside the control of the government.[24]

The students and others who joined the CPT in late 1976 and early 1977 also brought into the communist movement people with new ideas about how the struggle should be waged. These ideas did not accord entirely with the Maoist ideology to which the CPT had long been committed. Initially, the ideological differences were subordinated to the common goal of revolutionary change. A new united front organization, the Committee to Coordinate Democratic and Patriotic Groups, was formed, the leadership of which included representatives of all the groups and political parties whose members had fled into the jungle. This coalition of many different elements proved unwieldy, however, and never coalesced in a truly united front.

Many of the students gained their Marxist ideas not from Maoist texts but primarily from the works of Jit Poumisak, a brilliant student of Thai history, ethnography, and literature who had written a number of works in the 1950s in which he analyzed Thai society in Marxist terms. The importance of Jit's works lay in the fact that he had reworked Marxist notions in Thai intellectual terms, something the CPT had never succeeded in doing.[25] In addition, the students had read translations of some of Lenin's works by Western Marxist scholars. On the basis of the ideas they had drawn from their reading, they came up with a rather different analysis of Thai society than that offered by the CPT. In particular, they differed over the degree to which Thai society was shaped by premodern "feudal" (in Jit's terms, *sakdina*) patterns or by recently introduced capitalist ones. Transcending these differences regarding the appropriate mode of analysis to use for understanding Thai society was the question of how to weigh national versus class interests.

This question became a burning one following the Vietnamese invasion of Cambodia at the end of 1978. The growing tension between Vietnam and the Kampuchea of Pol Pot on the one hand and between Vietnam and China on the other had already created some problems for the CPT and its united front. With the Vietnamese invasion of Cambodia, however, the question of where the CPT stood with reference to Vietnam became a major issue. Many of the 1976 recruits were convinced that Vietnam and China were placing national interests above revolutionary ones and that the Thai should do the same. The older leaders of the CPT continued to maintain that the Chinese model (even though Maoism had begun to be discredited in China) remained the only valid one for revolutionary change. The pro-Chinese group was, however, undermined by the efforts of the Chinese government to improve relations with Thailand, which entailed a tacit agreement on the part of the Chinese to curtail support of the CPT. The Vietnamese, for their part, also withdrew support from the CPT and had Laos deny it sanctuary in that country because the CPT had sided with the Chinese in the Sino-Vietnamese dispute. A small group of the CPT, apparently made up primarily of newer members, sided with Vietnam and formed a splinter party. These divisions, and especially the withdrawal of outside support, effectively immobilized the insurrection. The collapse was evident when in mid-1979 the Voice of the People of Thailand, the clandestine radio station broadcasting CPT and united front programs, ceased broadcasting. More significant, increasing numbers of people who had joined the insurrection began to take advantage of an amnesty offered by the government of General Kriangsak.

Kriangsak presented this amnesty as a way of healing the breach created by the events of October 6, 1976, and of signifying that the government had clearly abandoned the coercive authoritarianism of Thanin. The first people to take advantage of the offer were mainly those who had gone to the jungle after October 6. By early 1980, some 400 had returned, leaving the CPT "in severe disarray."[26]

In the early 1980s, not only did most of the students and others who had joined the CPT after October 6, 1976, return but units of the Thai People's Liberation Army, which had been fighting since the 1960s, also began to accept the amnesty offer. The watershed apparently came in March 1982 at the CPT's fourth party congress—actually a number of separate meetings in different parts of the country coordinated through Morse code transmissions. As one leader of a unit that gave itself up said, "The result of the congress did not represent the voice of the Thai people."[27] The congress had seen efforts by some party members to effect a change from the long-standing Maoist line fail. This failure led many people to become alienated from the party, and large-scale defections, including defections by some high-ranking members of the party, followed. By late 1982, it was estimated that in northeastern Thailand "as few as 750 main-force guerrillas" remained, down from a probable high of 5,000 in the late 1970s. The same estimate placed the total number of insurgents nationwide at "no more than 4,000."[28]

Prem continued Kriangsak's program and after the 1983 elections reiterated the policy "which placed politics ahead of military action in combating communist insurgency."[29] The policy was opposed by at least one powerful faction in the military, a faction that was successful in arranging the arrest of a number of suspected high-ranking members of the CPT in 1984. These arrests were part of this faction's effort to reinstitute a more authoritarian government. Although the CPT currently appears to be on the verge of total disintegration, a renewal of repressive measures might, as after October 1976, revive its credibility.

EXTERNAL RELATIONS

Thailand's relations with foreign countries have, since the Bowring Treaty of the mid-nineteenth century, been shaped by two major concerns: the integrity of the nation-state and the development of international trade. These concerns have always led Thailand to orient itself toward those powers that were felt most likely to ensure the country's security and to provide markets for Thai products and sources for those goods Thailand wished to import.

The Special Relationship with the United States

During the colonial period, foreign policy was predicated primarily on Siam's relationship with Great Britain and the latter's dependencies in Asia. In the mid-1930s, Japan began to assume a much more important role in Siam's trade, and by the late 1930s it also was becoming a major influence on the government's security concerns. From 1941 to 1945, Thailand based its foreign policy almost exclusively on its relationship with Japan. After World War II, Thailand turned away not only from the defeated Japan but also from Great Britain, whose role as a colonial power was rapidly diminishing. Instead, it began to turn toward the United States, whose helpful role in enabling Thailand to become accepted by the Western powers after World War II had laid the basis of a special relationship between the two countries. This special relationship continued from the late 1940s and early 1950s until the end of the war in Indochina in the mid-1970s. Since then, Thailand's foreign policy has been shaped primarily with reference to the country's positive relations with members of the Association of Southeast Asian Nations (ASEAN) and its antagonistic relationships with Vietnam and, to a lesser extent, Laos and the People's Republic of Kampuchea.

From the U.S. point of view, Thailand in 1950 represented an important bastion against communist expansion. The success of the communist revolution in China in 1949 had led the U.S. government to develop a policy of containment of communism. In Southeast Asia, Thailand and the Philippines became the keys to the pursuit of this policy. The Phibun government in Thailand also was deeply concerned about what the coming to power of a communist government nearby might mean for Thailand, especially given the large Chinese community in the country. Moreover, the Thai government was already predisposed to accept a closer relationship with the United States because of the role the latter had played in attempting to dampen the demands leveled against Thailand by Great Britain and France following World War II. Perhaps of greatest significance, the Phibun government saw the relationship with the United States as a means for strengthening the Thai military and police.

In 1954, Thailand signed the U.S.-sponsored Southeast Asia Collective Defense Treaty (also known as the Manila Pact), a treaty that laid the foundations for the creation of the Southeast Asia Treaty Organization (SEATO)—which had, in fact, only two Southeast Asian members, Thailand and the Philippines (the other members being Australia, France, Great Britain, New Zealand, Pakistan, and the United

States). The organization proved to be ineffectual for realizing the purposes of the Manila Pact, namely collective defense. SEATO headquarters in Bangkok signified, nonetheless, Thailand's commitment to support the U.S. cause. Because of Thai concerns about whether or not SEATO could help Thailand in the event of a military conflict, the United States in 1962 committed itself in a joint communiqué by then-Secretary of State Dean Rusk and the Thai foreign minister, Thanat Khoman, to help Thailand in the event of aggression whether or not multilateral action under the Manila Pact agreement was forthcoming. Although SEATO became an anachronism after the end of the war in Indochina and was finally dissolved in 1977, the United States is still, in theory at least, bound by the Manila Pact and the Rusk-Thanat agreement to defend Thailand in the case of an external attack.

During the 1950s, the United States began to provide Thailand with large amounts of arms and training for Thai military and police forces. In the 1960s, as the United States became more and more involved in the war in Vietnam, military assistance to Thailand not only increased but Thailand itself was drawn into the war. As it had done in the Korean War, Thailand sent a small contingent of troops to fight alongside the anticommunist forces, this time in Vietnam. In addition, Thai soldiers were also hired to fight in what initially was a "secret war" in Laos. Of even greater significance, Thailand permitted the United States to create "a 'war infrastructure' in Thailand—airfields, logistical camps, communications systems, intelligence operations."[30]

The size of direct U.S. military aid and military investment in Thailand was enormous, totaling over $2 billion for the period between 1951 and 1971.[31] This money was not the only source of a marked skewing of the Thai economy that occurred during this period as a consequence of the government's commitment to help the United States in its communist containment policy. During the height of the Vietnam War, as many as 50,000 U.S. troops were stationed in Thailand, and thousands of Americans in Vietnam took their "rest and recreation" leaves there. The war helped create a new wealthy class in Thailand from among those people who held contracts for construction or services to the United States or the Thai military. It also contributed markedly to corruption in the military and police, as well as to a dramatic rise in prostitution, alcoholism, and drug use.

Although the U.S. government justified much of its direct military assistance to Thailand on the grounds that it improved the Thai military's capacity to resist foreign aggression, the Thai government used such aid primarily to strengthen the position of the military in its control of the government and to combat a growing rural insurgency. The U.S. government joined in support of Thailand's counterinsurgency program not only by providing military assistance but also by sending economic aid aimed at promoting development that would reduce or eliminate the causes of insurgency. Although U.S. economic aid to Thailand during these years was never as significant as the military aid, it still totaled $650 million for the period from 1950 to 1975.[32] Most of it went for construction of a road system, mainly in "security-sensitive" areas in northeastern and northern Thailand and to a lesser extent in similar areas in the far south, and for building hydroelectric and irrigation dams.

Relations with Japan, the EEC, and Middle Eastern Countries

The conspicuous U.S. presence in Thailand during the 1960s and 1970s disguised to a considerable degree the fact that Thailand was also developing a very significant relationship with Japan during the same period. Whereas the U.S.-Thai relationship was predicated primarily on security concerns, Thai relations with Japan were shaped almost exclusively by trade. From at least 1960, Japan became Thailand's foremost trade partner. As can be seen in Table 5.1, Japan's share of exports from Thailand ranged from about 18 percent in the 1960s to between 20 percent and 28 percent in the 1970s. The next biggest recipients of exports from Thailand were, collectively, the countries of the European Common Market (EEC). The United States dropped from second place in 1960 to third place in most subsequent years.

Japan has played an even larger role as a source of imports, accounting for approximately one-third of Thailand's total imports from 1965 on (see Table 5.2). Although in the 1960s the EEC was the source of about 28 percent of imports into Thailand, its percentage of the total dropped in the 1970s. The United States was the third major source throughout the 1960s and 1970s, but it rarely accounted for half the amount of imports that originated in Japan. The dominance of Japan in Thailand's trade relations became especially obvious in Bangkok in the late 1960s when many imported consumer goods were recognizably of Japanese origin. The first major demonstration organized by the student movement—one that would lead within a year to the downfall of the Thanom-Praphat government—was an anti-Japanese-goods campaign in 1972. The campaign not only contributed to the growth of the student movement but also made the government at that time and subsequent governments sensitive to the implications of becoming overly dependent on Japan in trade relations. Despite this fact, Japan's influence on the Thai economy has continued to grow; by the 1980s, the Japanese had replaced the Americans as the largest expatriate community in Bangkok.[33]

TABLE 5.1
Principal Recipients of Exports from Thailand for Selected Years, 1960-1978
(In Percentages)

	1960	1965	1970	1975	1978
Japan	17.7	18.2	25.5	27.6	20.3
EEC Countries[a]	13.2	18.1	18.3	15.9	26.3
United States	13.9	7.5	13.4	11.0	11.0
Singapore	11.2	6.1	6.9	9.0	8.1
Malaysia	17.1	14.6	5.6	4.7	5.2
Indonesia	4.0	2.0	2.3	1.9	1.7
Laos	1.1	2.2	2.9	0.6	0.4
Hong Kong	8.7	6.6	7.5	6.0	5.3
Taiwan	0.9	0.6	2.2	2.4	1.3
Saudi Arabia	2.1	1.4	2.2	1.4	1.4
Others	10.1	22.7	13.2	19.5	19.0
TOTAL	100.0	100.0	100.0	100.1	100.0

Source:
    Frederica M. Bunge, ed., Thailand: A Country Study (Washington, D.C.:
    Supt. of Documents, United States Government Printing Office, 1981),
    p. 291, Table.

Note:
    a. Netherlands, West Germany, France, Belgium, Italy, United Kingdom,
        and Denmark

TABLE 5.2
Principal Sources of Imports to Thailand for Selected Years, 1960-1978
(In Percentages)

	1960	1965	1970	1975	1978
Japan	25.6	33.3	37.4	31.5	30.7
EEC Countries[a]	28.0	27.8	22.3	16.1	14.3
United States	16.6	15.5	14.9	14.3	13.6
Saudi Arabia	0.2	0.1	2.0	9.0	5.6
Singapore	7.4	0.9	1.0	2.0	4.1
Others	22.2	22.4	22.4	27.1	31.7
TOTAL	100.0	100.0	100.0	100.0	100.0

Source:
    Frederica M. Bunge, ed., Thailand: A Country Study (Washington, D.C.:
    Supt. of Documents, United States Government Printing Office, 1981),
    p. 292, Table.

Note:
    a. West Germany, United Kingdom, France, Netherlands, Italy, Belgium,
        and Denmark

Trade relations with the European Common Market countries, although now second in economic significance only to those with Japan, have not had political implications comparable to those arising from Thailand's relations with Japan. The EEC relations, together with those with Japan and the United States, do, however, indicate clearly the commitment that all recent Thai governments have made to policies designed to promote capitalist development of the country.

The sudden leap in the percentage of Saudi Arabian imports into Thailand in the early 1970s reflects a growing use of petrochemicals in Thailand for an increasing number of industries, agriculture (especially in the manufacture of fertilizer), transport, and private consumption, especially automobiles. This growth made Thailand vulnerable to the oil crisis, and the consequences of that crisis contributed to the political unrest of the mid-1970s.

Relations with ASEAN and Indochinese Countries

Although Singapore and, to a lesser extent, Malaysia have been significant trading partners for Thailand, this relationship has been overshadowed by the membership that these three, together with Indonesia and the Philippines, share in the Association of Southeast Asian Nations. ASEAN, first founded in 1967, had little importance until after communist governments came to power in Vietnam, Laos, and Cambodia. Since 1975, and especially since the Vietnamese invasion of Cambodia at the end of 1978, ASEAN has been seen by its member states and by the world at large as a regional bloc. The policies that Thailand and the other member states have adopted toward Vietnam and especially toward the contending factions in Cambodia have been shaped by agreements reached in meetings of ASEAN foreign ministers. Although ASEAN remains predicated on relatively limited common interests, it still represents the first significant move toward regional cooperation in Southeast Asia.

The willingness of Thai governments to join with other ASEAN members in forging a common policy toward Indochina reflects the importance of Indochina today in Thailand's relations with other countries. Prior to 1972, Thailand supported a U.S. communist-containment policy that presupposed that a communist takeover in Vietnam would pose a threat to Thailand and that China was to be viewed as the prime mover in communist expansion in Southeast Asia. President Nixon's trip to China in 1972 together with the cease-fire agreement reached at the end of 1972 (and signed in 1973) with the Democratic Republic of Vietnam destroyed the premises on which Thailand had hitherto based its foreign policy. The need for a new orientation became pressing after the United States withdrew from Vietnam and the change of governments in Vietnam, Cambodia, and Laos in 1975. By that time, Thailand was already shifting its policy toward China, having lifted a trade ban with that country in 1974. In 1976, Thailand reversed its long-standing hostility toward the People's Republic of China by severing diplomatic relations with Taipei and opening relations with Beijing.

The stance taken toward the new governments in Vietnam, Cambodia, and Laos was initially cautious and then, during the Thanin regime, hostile, although diplomatic relations with Laos were maintained. After the October 1977 coup, General Kriangsak again changed Thai government policy, recognizing Vietnam and opening contacts with the Pol Pot government in Cambodia. Efforts to improve relations with Vietnam came to an abrupt end, however, following the Vietnamese invasion of Cambodia and its installation there in early 1979 of the Heng Samrin government. The flow of refugees from Cambodia, which had begun in 1975 and which the Thai government had thought it had contained, became overwhelming. Moreover, with Vietnamese troops moving through Cambodia to the border with Thailand, the Thai government began to fear a possible Vietnamese invasion of Thailand. The Chinese attack on Vietnam in 1979, for the purpose, at least in part, of diverting Vietnamese military attention away from the destruction of Khmer Rouge forces, also signaled to Thailand China's willingness to prevent a Vietnamese attack on Thailand.

Since 1979, Thailand's policy toward Indochina has remained essentially unchanged. It has provided sanctuary and semicovert support first for the Khmer Rouge forces and subsequently for the forces of the other two factions of the government of Democratic Kampuchea. Thailand, together with the other ASEAN countries, has worked successfully to prevent the replacement of Democratic Kampuchea by the Vietnamese-backed People's Republic of Kampuchea in the United Nations. Although the Thai foreign minister and other Thai officials have had periodic talks with their Vietnamese counterparts, as of early 1986 there had been no movement toward any compromise on the Cambodian issue that both governments would accept. The dry-season offensives launched each year by Vietnamese forces and small contingents of the army of the People's Republic of Kampuchea against the forces of Democratic Kampuchea have led to a number of border incidents and have stimulated continued Thai concern about a potential Vietnamese invasion. Although Thailand has not entered into a formal military agreement with China, the two countries continue to share a common view of the Indochinese situation.

The continuing conflict in Cambodia and the tension on the Khmer border with Thailand have provided justification for the Thai military to seek increased amounts of arms, including very sophisticated and very expensive U.S.-made fighter planes. The Thai military, especially the army, has also been able to gain public support for its role in government because of fears of potential invasion by Vietnam. In 1984, the external threat was once again linked, by at least some people in the military, with a potential internal threat. In July 1984, twenty-two communist suspects were arrested and charged with renewing ties with the Vietnamese and Laotian Communist parties in order to gain support for insurrection in Thailand.

External relations both constrain and are manipulated by internal elements in the process of shaping a Thai political order in the 1980s. So long as threats to Thailand's security are deemed important, the Thai military can justify its preeminent role in guarding the nation. Continued hostile relations with Vietnam (replacing the hostile relations with China in the 1950s and 1960s) serve the interests of some elements in the Thai military. On the other hand, it is in the interest of the business sector, and the parties that represent this sector, to seek improved relations with Vietnam in order to emphasize trade as the major concern in Thailand's external relations. Although security still outweighs trade in Thailand's orientation toward other countries, the effects of economic growth over the past thirty years in Thailand have created an ever-larger constituency for those who would like to see a shift in emphasis in both external affairs and internal politics.

NOTES

1. David Morell and Chai-anan Samudavanija, *Political Conflict in Thailand: Reform, Reaction, Revolution* (Cambridge, Mass.: Oelgeschlager, Gunn and Hain, 1981), p. 103.

2. Ibid., pp. 112–113.

3. Ibid., p. 262.

4. Statistics from ibid., p. 188, table.

5. Ibid., p. 190; also see John L.S. Girling, *Thailand: Society and Politics* (Ithaca, N.Y.: Cornell University Press, 1981), pp. 201–202.

6. Percentages from Saneh Chamarik, *Problems of Development in Thai Political Setting*, Paper no. 14, (Bangkok: Thai Khadi Research Institute, Thammasat University, 1983), pp. 13 and 15.

7. See Andrew Turton, "The Current Situation in the Thai Countryside," in *Thailand: Roots of Conflict*, ed. Andrew Turton, Jonathan Fast, and Malcolm Caldwell (Nottingham, Eng.: Spokesman, 1978), pp. 104–142.

8. Morell and Chai-anan, *Political Conflict in Thailand*, p. 215.

9. Ibid., p. 216.

10. See Somboon Suksamran, "Political Monks: Personalism and Ideology," in *Strategies and Structure in Thai Society*, ed. Han ten Burmmelhuis and Jeremy H. Kemp (Amsterdam: Universiteit van Amsterdam, Antropologisch-Sociologisch Centrum, 1984), p. 160.

11. See, in this regard, Prudhisan Jumbala, "Towards a Theory of Group Formation in Thai Society and Pressure Groups in Thailand After the October 1973 Uprising," *Asian Survey* 14:6 (1974), pp. 530–545.

12. See, in this regard, Ben Anderson, "Withdrawal Symptoms: Social and Cultural Aspects of the October 6 Coup," *Bulletin of Concerned Asian Scholars* 9:3 (1977), pp. 13–30. Also see Girling, *Thailand: Society and Politics*, p. 210, n. 45.

13. The name Nawaphon can be translated as "Ninth Power," perhaps an allusion to the present king's being the ninth of the dynasty, or "New Force," albeit with a very different connotation from the party (Phlang Mai) whose name also translates into English as "New Force."

14. See Charles F. Keyes, "Political Crisis and Militant Buddhism in Contemporary Thailand," in *Religion and Legitimation of Power in Thailand, Laos, and Burma*, ed. Bardwell L. Smith (Chambersburg, Penn.: Anima Books, 1978), pp. 147–164.

15. The most detailed account of recruitment and ritualized training of Village Scouts is Marjorie Muecke, "The Village Scouts of Thailand," *Asian Survey* 20:4 (1980), pp. 407–427. Muecke's account, it should be noted, is based on observations made in 1977–1978, a period in which the scouts played a somewhat different role than they had prior to the coup of October 1976. See also Morell and Chai-anan, *Political Conflict in Thailand*, pp. 242–246.

16. Muecke, "Village Scouts of Thailand," p. 407.

17. Morell and Chai-anan, *Political Conflict in Thailand*, p. 226. Andrew Turton in "Limits of Ideological Domination and the Formation of Social Consciousness," in *History and Peasant Consciousness in South East Asia*, ed. Andrew Turton and Shigeharu Tanabe, Senri Ethnological Studies, 13 (Osaka: National Museum of Ethnology, 1984), pp. 19–74, discusses at length the way in which coercive power was used to destroy popular movements. Although I agree with Turton that coercive power has been used to maintain state control in recent Thai history, I also would maintain that state authority has still been predicated primarily on ideological legitimation. I will return to this point in the last chapter of this book.

18. Quoted in Morell and Chai-anan, *Political Conflict in Thailand*, p. 275. On the October 6, 1976, coup and its aftermath, see William Bradley, David Morell, David Szanton, and Stephen Young, *Thailand, Domino by Default? The 1976 Coup and Implications for U.S. Policy*, Southeast Asia Series, no. 46 (Athens, Ohio: Ohio University Center for International Studies, 1978); E. Thadeus Flood, *The United States and the Military Coup in Thailand: A Background Study* (Washington, D.C.: Indochina Resource Center, 1976); and Robert F. Zimmerman, *Reflections on the Collapse of Democracy in Thailand*, Occasional Paper Series, no. 50 (Singapore: Institute of Southeast Asian Studies, 1978) in addition to relevant sections of Anderson, "Withdrawal Symptoms"; Girling, *Thailand: Society and Politics;* and Morell and Chai-anan, *Political Conflict in Thailand*.

19. Translated and quoted in Girling, *Thailand: Society and Politics*, p. 215. The original in Thai appeared in *Siam Chotmaihet*, December 2–8, 1976.

20. Different sources provide somewhat contradictory information on the party membership of the people elected in April 1979. Differences in the figures

are an indication of shifts in party membership made by some following the election. I here employ figures given by Chai-anan Samudavanija, *The Thai Young Turks* (Singapore: Institute of Southeast Asian Studies, 1982), p. 53n. Also see Frederica M. Bunge, ed., *Thailand: A Country Study* (Washington, D.C.: Government Printing Office for the American University, Foreign Area Studies, 1981), pp. 190–193.

21. Chai-anan, *Thai Young Turks*, has examined in detail the characteristics of the Young Turks. The Buddhist influence appears to have been strongest in the case of Major Chamlong Srimuang, whose friends, according to Chai-anan (p. 29), call him "half monk-half man." Chamlong, it should be noted, disassociated himself from the Young Turks before the abortive coup of April 1981. He remained in the military, rising to the rank of lieutenant-general, until 1985 when he retired in order to run for governor of Bangkok. In an account of the election, the *Far Eastern Economic Review* (November 28, 1985, p. 36) referred to Chamlong as "a populist figure, who wears farmer's garb and is a strict devotee of the eight Buddhist silas or moral principles" and as a "vegetarian celibate." Clearly, his image as a lay Buddhist ascetic contributed significantly to his unexpectedly large victory as a nonpartisan candidate against the nominee of the Democrat party, a party that has long had strong electoral support in Bangkok.

22. Chai-anan, *Thai Young Turks*, p. 66.

23. Girling, *Thailand: Society and Politics*, p. 257.

24. The figure of 12,000–14,000 insurrectionaries in 1979 comes from Girling, ibid. In the same work, Girling reports that in 1975, the government estimated that "communists in the Northeast have 'some' or 'growing' influence in about 2,700 villages, with a population of more than 1.5 million" (p. 262). My figure of 2 million is an extrapolation from this figure to the whole country. Morell and Chai-anan (*Political Conflict in Thailand*, p. 297) report that the students who fled into the jungle after October 6 were placed in "the 250 liberated villages where the CPT was in full control." See the map in Girling (p. 261) for the locations of the CPT strongholds as of 1977.

25. On Jit's philosophy and its influence on leftist thought, see Craig J. Reynolds and Hong Lysa, "Marxism in Thai Historical Studies," *Journal of Asian Studies* 43:1 (1983), pp. 77–104. Also see E. Thadeus Flood, "The Thai Left Wing in Historical Context," *Bulletin of Concerned Asian Scholars* 7:2 (1975), pp. 55–67, and Yuangrat Wedel, "The Communist Party of Thailand and Thai Radical Thought," *Southeast Asian Affairs, 1981* (Singapore: Institute of Southeast Asian Affairs, 1981), pp. 325–339.

26. Morell and Chai-anan, *Political Conflict in Thailand*, p. 303.

27. *Far Eastern Economic Review*, December 10, 1982, p. 16.

28. Ibid.

29. *Far Eastern Economic Review*, June 2, 1983, p. 16.

30. Girling, *Thailand: Society and Politics*, pp. 237–238.

31. Estimate based on data provided by J. Alexander Caldwell, in his *American Economic Aid to Thailand* (Lexington, Mass.: Lexington Books, 1974), pp. 171–172, table.

32. Girling, *Thailand: Society and Politics*, p. 235.

33. Many of these expatriates not only promote trade between Thailand and Japan but also manage the large investments Japanese firms have made in the country; see Sura Sanittanong, "The Role of Japanese Investment in Thailand," in *Readings in Thailand's Political Economy*, ed. Vichitvong Na Pombhejara (Bangkok: Bangkok Printing Enterprise, 1978), pp. 254–267.

6

Social Organization Within the Thai Nation-State

Social life among all the peoples of Thailand has been shaped by their religious worldviews. The vast majority of these peoples share fundamental assumptions about the world that stem from their belief in Theravada Buddhism.[1] Although Buddhists differ on how certain doctrines are to be interpreted, all would agree that one's position in life is fixed to some degree by the consequences of *kamma* inherited from a previous life. The law of *kamma* is not, however, as some have suggested, a fatalistic theory that leads people to accept their lot without question or complaint. One's previous *kamma* determines only in a general way the constraints of one's present life, leaving individuals a considerable degree of freedom to decide how they will act. A good Buddhist will choose to act in ways that are morally positive, thereby generating positive kammic consequences not only for his or her future life but perhaps also for the present one. Although one's ability to act is, therefore, constrained by a kammic heritage that situates an individual in a particular position within the social world, each individual is understood to be ultimately morally responsible for his or her actions— an orientation toward social life that may lie at the root of behavioral patterns that many observers have interpreted in terms of John F. Embree's characterization of Thai society as a "loosely structured social system" in which a "considerable variation of behavior" is tolerated.[2] Such interpretations have, however, often ignored many of the constraints on Thai social life, ones that Thai themselves may explain as the consequences of past *kamma*.

122

BASES OF SOCIAL LIFE AMONG THE BUDDHIST THAI

Thai Buddhists, like Theravada Buddhists elsewhere, conceive of the world as based on *kamma* and divided into three distinct domains: that of the gods above; that of animals, demons, and spirits below; and that of humans. Within the human realm, they believe that each person's location in the hierarchy reflects the consequences of *kamma* and that although one may in the course of one's lifetime change one's position in the hierarchy, one will still always have to acknowledge in speech and action people of higher and lower status. Caste, which in India is seen as an expression of a kammically determined hierarchy, was not adopted by the Thai except in limited form for distinguishing royalty. Royal status is the only hierarchical status that the Thai hold to have been absolutely fixed at birth, and even royal status is not transferred intact from parent to child. A child acquires, by what has been called a "declining-descent rule," a lower rank than that of his or her father.

The Thai believe that other social differences, in particular those associated with gender and kinship, have been determined at birth. Observable sexual differences are interpreted by the Thai with reference to ideas about gender differences shaped not only by Buddhist thought but also by notions inherited from pre-Buddhist traditions common to many peoples in Southeast Asia. All Tai-speaking people, like the neighboring Burmese and Khmer, believe there is an inherent link between women, earth, and rice. All three are seen as having nurturing qualities, such nurturance being not only biological but also spiritual. The nurturing qualities of earth and rice are conceived of as being embodied in goddesses. The *khwan*, the vital essence of the person, after having been transmitted along with the seed of the male to the mother's womb, is nourished by the mother's body before birth, then by mother's milk, and finally by rice, the essential food. Buddhist ideas have added another dimension to the image of woman as nurturing mother, making her the source of well-being not only for her own offspring but also for the monks who are the spiritual descendants of the Buddha. While men realize their religious potential by being ordained into the Buddhist order, women realize theirs by providing alms and food for the monks.

The Thai conceive of the essence of maleness as potency. This potency is manifest in the power men have to plant the seed of new life in women and the seed of rice in the earth. A man of extraordinary potency is also able to control the actions of others. The inherent quality of potency in maleness poses a religious problem for men; too great an accentuation of the quest for power can lead a man to commit immoral acts, ones that produce negative *kamma*. The only way a man can control the passion for power is to subject himself to the discipline of the monkhood. Although few Thai men become monks for life, many—more today in rural areas than in the cities—become monks for a period of at least three months, during which time they learn to temper their natural desires.

Although Thai conceptions of males and females appear to relegate women to domestic roles and men to public ones, the more basic idea that every individual—male or female—is responsible for his or her own destiny affords women as well as men the opportunity to choose a variety of ways of acting. In rural communities, aside from agricultural work in which men and women participate more or less equally, women tend to accentuate domestic activities—preparing food, caring for children, producing cloth, and managing the household economy—while men accentuate public roles—serving in village leadership positions, administering shrine and temple property and functions, and interacting with government officials. Yet even in villages, women do not always conform to normative expectations. Unlike Muslim women in communities in southern Thailand, Buddhist women from rural areas, and especially from the rural northeastern region, have migrated in large numbers to Bangkok and other centers of economic growth in search of nonagricultural work. Some migrant women become prostitutes, but many have found work in factories and commercial establishments, and some have established small businesses in the cities or back in their home villages. Other women from rural backgrounds have, through education, qualified to become clerks, nurses, or teachers; indeed, the primary school teacher in Thailand is increasingly likely to be a woman rather than a man.

In urban areas, many middle- and upper-class women have become professionals (especially in the educational and medical fields), and some have become the owners or managers of major commercial enterprises. On the other side of the coin, urban women who remain in domestic roles often find themselves more estranged from their husbands than do rural women. Not only is an urban housewife cut off from her husband's workplace, unlike in villages where men and women work in the fields together, but she rarely sees her husband in the latter's public roles, again unlike in the villages where women witness much of what the men do in their meetings or ritual activities. Moreover, the pattern of a man's seeking sexual pleasure from prostitutes is much more common among urban than among rural men. The marked tension in relations between the sexes in urban areas has been the subject of recent critical commentary by a growing number of women's groups and feminists.

Just as every Thai is born either male or female, so too is every Thai born as the child of particular parents who, in turn, are linked to other people through kinship ties. Unlike the Chinese, Thai (and today even many Sino-Thai) do not give particular recognition to their descent from the father's side of the family. Among many rural Thai—especially in northern and northeastern Thailand—the mother's side of the family is considered the more important. In the rural north and northeast, although men are entitled to inherit land from their parents, it is more typical that after marriage a son will move out and reside near his wife's family and inherit land from them while a daughter will remain with her parents and she and her husband will inherit land from her parents. Echoes of a matrilineal emphasis can also be found in rural districts in central Thailand and even among some people in urban areas.

Although in northern and northeastern Thailand households connected through matrilineal links often cooperate with each other in agricultural work and participate in some common ritual activities, they do not form corporate kin groups. The absence of such groups throughout Thailand makes kin ties less significant than they are, say, for Chinese or Indians, who see corporate kin groups as the basic units of society. Even the parent-child relationship, which is viewed by the Thai as basic to social life, is understood in light of the Buddhist idea that, ultimately, each individual is responsible for his or her own actions. Parents encourage their teenage children to leave the family to make their own way in life, through either homesteading in a different area of the country or, more commonly today, finding work in the city. At an even earlier age, parents may give a child to another relative or even to a patron to be raised because the future opportunity for the child is considered to be more important than the present attachment of parent to child. These facts do not mean that kinship is unimportant in Thai society. Many Thai, in urban as well as rural areas, retain very close ties with their families, and it is exceedingly rare that at least one child in a family will not assume responsibility for aged parents. Thai do not, however, invest kin ties with the marked significance that people in neighboring societies do.

The language of kinship is used by the Thai as an idiom to express how nonkin relationships are ordered hierarchically. Friends become "elder sibling–younger sibling" (*phinǫng*) to each other, and members of a community or an association are considered "siblings together" (*phinǫngkan*). The followers of a patron are typically referred to as "children and younger siblings" (*luk nǫng*), and the patron may be called a "nurturing father" (*phǫliang*). The idiom of kinship permits people who find a common interest with others in some aspect of social life to invest their relationships with a moral flavor. Kinship implies obligations that transcend the particular shared-interest situation.

ETHNIC AND RELIGIOUS MINORITIES

Many Thai use an extended kinship idiom to express their identification with a people (*chat*) who share a common heritage (*morodok*). Such ethnic identities have their roots in the premodern social order of Siam but have been given new significance in the context of the modern nation-state. During the reign of King Chulalongkorn, integrative reforms were linked with the promotion of a national identity—one called *"chat Thai,"* (Thai nation)—among all subjects living within the boundaries of the Siamese state. This promotion stimulated many people to reflect on their preexisting identities and to reformulate these identities to make them relevant to their lives in the modern world of the Thai nation-state.

For many peoples other than Tai-speaking Buddhists living in the core area of the premodern kingdom of Siam, state-defined Thai nationalism created a sense of tension with ethnic identities rooted in the premodern situation. Such a tension under certain circumstances in recent Thai history has impelled people to organize into social movements to assert their presumed right to retain valued aspects of their ethnic identities. The state's response to these movements has, in turn, led to a further reformulation of ethnic identities within modern Thailand.

Northeastern and Northern Thai

In northeastern Thailand at the end of the nineteenth and during the early twentieth century, the state first removed power from all local lords, crushed a millenarian revolt by the populace, and then imposed, in a rather heavy-handed way, the power of the central government as administered by central Thai officials. More recently, during the 1950s, a number of highly respected northeastern politicians who had come to the forefront of political life were murdered by the police. These actions, coupled with the facts that the northeast remains the poorest part of the country and that even in recent years the government has made only modest efforts to improve this situation, have led many Lao-speaking peoples in the northeast to see themselves as belonging to a disadvantaged regional minority. The region, and those living in it or coming from it, are referred to as Isan, meaning northeastern. For local inhabitants of the region, this term evokes a sense of their position in a Thai-dominated world, and politicians from the region have played on this sense to promote the ethnoregional interests of the peoples of the northeast.

Northern Thailand was similarly subordinated to the Siamese state. This process, together with a conflict in the 1930s between the Thai sangha and a highly charismatic monk from northern Thailand, Khruba Srivijaya, has contributed to the emergence of a northern Thai (Khon Muang) ethnoregionalism. Khon Muang identity has not, however, had quite the same salience as Isan identity has had, in part because northern Thai customs and language, unlike those of the northeastern Thai, have been viewed rather more positively in the national press and in movies. The fact that the king and queen built a palace overlooking Chiang Mai, the major city in northern Thailand, and often entertain foreign visitors there has added to the positive image of the north. Since at least the early 1950s, many temples in northern Thailand have become popular pilgrimage destinations for people from Bangkok and central Thailand. In recent years, the Thai government has also promoted the north as an attractive destination for tourists. There is potential, nonetheless, for Khon Muang ethnoregionalism to become more significant, and some people in the region today see the violent central Thai government reaction in the 1970s against the Farmers' Federation of Thailand, based as it was primarily in the Chiang Mai valley and first led by a northern Thai villager, as justification for a more aggressive Khon Muang movement.

Tribal Peoples

Northern Thailand is also home to most of the tribal peoples of Thailand. Although some of these peoples, such as the Karen, feel some kinship with the Khon Muang, most are not in a position to make such a claim even if they wanted to do so. Up until the 1950s, the Thai government effectively ignored the tribal peoples. Following Mao's successful revolution in China, the outbreak of tribal rebellions in Burma, and the growing conflict in Laos, tribal peoples from these neighboring areas began to migrate in increasing numbers into northern Thailand. Some of the migrants retained close relations with politically active tribal peoples in Burma, Laos, and China. The government of Sarit Thanarat, with its primary concern for national security, determined that there was a "tribal problem," that is, that the tribal peoples posed a threat to Thailand's internal security. In addition to the security question, the government also became increasingly concerned about the fact that most tribal peoples engage in swidden, or shifting, cultivation, a form of agriculture deemed damaging to the forests and the watershed and inimical to economic development.

The government soon came to believe that the Hmong (referred to by the Thai as the Meo) were the major cause of the "tribal problem." Most Hmong are recent migrants from Laos or southern China, have

Tribal peoples: Karen woman spinning while her daughter watches, northern Thailand. (Photo by author)

little loyalty to Thailand, and do have kin ties to the presumed "communist" Hmong of those countries. Their practice of slash-and-burn agriculture for both opium and other crops is viewed by the government as a major cause of environmental degradation in the hill areas of northern Thailand and, at the very least, as an embarrassment in light of the international condemnation of trade in opium and opium products. But although the largest number of new migrants into the hills of northern Thailand have been Hmong, they are, in fact, far outnumbered by the Karen, who are still the largest tribal population in Thailand, numbering over one-half of the estimated 400,000–500,000 tribal people now living in the country. Unfortunately, because of their focus on the Hmong rather than on the Karen or other tribal peoples, the Thai government has formulated policies toward tribal groups that have seriously hindered official relations with them. These policies presume that most tribal people are recent migrants, that they grow opium poppies, and that they have few ties to Thai peoples. These characterizations all apply to the Hmong but hardly to the Karen. Other tribal people such as the Mien (Yao), Akha, Lisu, and Lahu have also been treated according to the conception of "hill tribes" (chao khao) based on characterizations of the Hmong.

In the mid-1960s, the government decided that the tribal peoples were sympathetic to if not outright supporters of the communist movements in Thailand and Laos, and direct military action was taken against some tribal peoples in the northwestern part of the country. Napalm was used to destroy a number of Hmong and Mien villages, and members of many tribal groups were forced to resettle in new areas determined by the government. Contrary to what the government intended, these actions stimulated certain tribal groups, especially the Hmong, to support the communist-led insurrection. Thai military action against tribal groups suspected of being pro-communist continued well into the 1970s and ended only when the change of government in Laos in 1975 resulted in a large-scale outflow of Hmong and other tribal refugees into Thailand. Although the tribal refugees from Laos showed the Thai government that tribal peoples were not necessarily communists, the government still refused to permit these refugees to become permanent Thai residents lest they create yet another "tribal problem."

The concern that tribal people pose a threat to national security led not only to occasional armed conflict between Thai military forces and tribal peoples deemed to be supporters of a communist-led insurrection but also to programs designed to assimilate tribal peoples into Thai society. In the mid-1960s, the Border Patrol Police was charged with establishing schools in tribal villages. When these schools are considered to be functioning well, they are turned over to provincial educational authorities to be run as regular government schools. Some tribal village children have also been brought by various government agencies as well as by Christian missionaries to study in schools in northern Thai towns. As a consequence of these educational programs, an increasing number of tribal people have acquired literacy in Thai, and some have gone on to obtain secondary and even tertiary educations. For many tribal peoples, however, education has only made them increasingly aware that they belong to a disadvantaged minority.

A second program aimed at assimilating tribal people, also begun in the mid-1960s, entailed the sending of Buddhist missionaries into tribal communities. This missionary program was inspired by and competitive with long-standing Christian missionary work among tribal peoples. Unlike Christian missionaries, monks who have served in the Buddhist missionary program have rarely established persisting relations with tribal communities. Few missionary monks have ever learned a tribal language, although some tribal men have themselves been ordained as monks and have returned to work as missionaries. Some tribal people have converted to Buddhism, but the more significant consequence of the program has been to accentuate the distinction between Buddhist Thai and non-Buddhist tribal peoples.

The Thai government has also sought to encourage tribal peoples to abandon swidden cultivation and especially to give up the growing of opium poppies. Both efforts have had only modest success to date. Tribal peoples who have given up swidden cultivation have often found themselves in an even more marginal position in the Thai economy, and despite the efforts of a project sponsored by the king, economically viable substitutes for poppies have yet to be found. Although it would be possible for the Thai government to destroy opium poppy fields, as the U.S. government has encouraged it to do, the government has not done so out of concern that, deprived of the source of their livelihood, tribal opium-producers would become dependent on welfare or would turn to antigovernment activities.

Tourist interest in recent years has generated some new sources of income for some of these tribal peoples. Tribal handicrafts are marketed not only in northern Thailand but also in Bangkok and abroad, and some tribal communities regularly host trekkers into the hills of northern Thailand. Although tourism has benefited some tribal peoples, it has also served as a means of subordination of tribal peoples to the Thai. Thai middlemen present tribal dances, handicrafts, and even whole communities as being primitive in comparison to similar aspects of Thai culture and society. Even in its most benign effects, tourism serves to accentuate the distinctiveness of tribal peoples within Thai society.

Since the mid-1960s, members of the royal family have become patrons of tribal peoples. The princess mother, and the king and queen, have made well-publicized visits to tribal communities to open schools, sponsor rice banks, and assist those who have suffered some calamity. The king sponsors a project to improve agricultural production in tribal areas, and the queen and princess mother both sponsor the production and sale of tribal crafts. There is little question but that the patronage role played by the royal family has enhanced the image of tribal people in Thai society. At the same time it has also underscored the idea that tribal people are viewed as a "problem" within the Thai system.

Tribal people have not yet organized into any pantribal groupings comparable to the American Indian movement in the United States. By considering that the different peoples belong to a common category—"hill tribes"—and by implementing policies based on a presumption that tribal peoples are essentially the same, the government has, however, created a basis on which some pantribal organization might be meaningful, especially to those tribal peoples, whatever their actual background, who have had common experiences in dealing with the government.

Southern Thai, Thai Muslims, and Thai Malays

The majority Tai-speaking Buddhists of southern Thailand were historically within the kingdom of Siam and are culturally quite similar to the Central Thai. Such characteristics have not, however, precluded some southerners from espousing the cause of southern Thai ethnoregionalism. Like peoples in northern and northeastern Thailand, southerners have also experienced a sense of having little ability to influence the government whose policies directly affect them. Such alienation spurred some, especially in the mid-south, to join a communist-led insurrection in the late 1960s and 1970s. Thai-speaking Muslims in southern Thailand, as well as Thai Muslims elsewhere (mainly in Bangkok and in areas around Bangkok), recognize that their religion makes them different from other Thai, but to date they have tended to accentuate their "Thai-ness," as manifested in their language and their sense of shared tradition with other Thai, rather than their religion. Thai Muslims, although often feeling alienated from the central Thai government and resenting the heavy-handed actions of local Thai officials, have not joined Malay separatist movements. Some appear, however, to have joined the Thai communist movement.

Malay-speaking Muslims in southern Thailand do not have the bonds that link Thai Muslims to the Thai nation. Moreover, the types of government programs instituted in the area have often led these people to feel excluded from the national order. The government has recruited very few Thai Muslims but even fewer Thai Malays into government service, and those it has recruited have rarely been posted to areas with majority Muslim populations. Thus, Malay Muslims in southern Thailand have found themselves constrained to deal with officials who almost never speak their language and who not only do not understand Islam but may also be hostile to it. Schools in the far south where the Thai Malays live, like schools throughout the country, provide instruction in the Thai language and present a Thai view of both the past and the present. Not surprisingly, schools in the Malay areas of southern Thailand have among the lowest attendance rates of any in the country, and few Malay-speakers go beyond the compulsory primary grades. The government has also made use of coercive power in the far south to a more marked degree than almost anywhere else in the country, a policy that has been rationalized as necessary because of the "banditry" and "insurrection" in the area.

The alienation of Thai Malays in Thailand has been most strongly felt among those living in Pattani Province since Pattani was once a semi-autonomous Malayan sultanate. In the early 1970s, a separatist organization, the United Pattani Freedom movement, attracted considerable support from the local populace. The movement received aid from Libya and perhaps other countries as well. It has also proved to be something of an embarrassment to the Malaysian government, which while not supporting the movement dares not openly join with the Thai government in suppressing it for fear of alienating Malays living in the northern part of Malaysia who are sympathetic to the movement. By the mid-1980s, the movement appeared, however, to have lost much support and to have become largely ineffective.

Although the Thai government has yet to make major changes that would create a better situation for Malay-speaking Thai, the king has used his position to attempt to make Muslims and other non-Buddhists feel a part of the Thai nation. In recent years, the king has had many well-publicized meetings with Muslim leaders and has presented awards for study of the Koran to students from Muslim schools. Although these actions, like comparable ones directed toward the much smaller Christian community in Thailand, reflect efforts to recognize the special needs of Muslim and Christian communities, school curricula and the cycle of national holidays still reflect the primacy of Buddhism in Thai national ideology.

Christians in Thailand

Christians, although numerically a much smaller group than Muslims (no more than 200,000 Christians as compared with about 1.5 million Muslims), have had a very different relationship with the national society than Muslims have had. Although in the seventeenth century Catholic missionaries converted a few people in the kingdom of Ayutthaya, missionaries were not allowed into the country in any significant numbers until the early nineteenth century. Few constraints have ever been placed on missionary activity, but converts have in fact been few and limited primarily to peoples of Chinese or Vietnamese descent or to tribal peoples. Only in northern Thailand were missionaries successful in converting some people from Buddhist backgrounds. Despite such limited success, Christian influence has been considerably more significant than the number of converts would suggest, largely because many members of the Thai elite, today as in the past, send their children to Christian (and especially to Catholic) schools.

The schools and church organizations of both Catholics (who constitute about three-quarters of the Christian population) and Protestants (most of whom are affiliated with the Church of Christ in Thailand) have facilitated the integration of Christians into Thai society. A number of Christians have attained high-ranking positions in the military, held high bureaucratic positions, assumed significant positions in commerce and banking, and have been appointed to positions in the major academic institutions. Only for tribal Christians has Christianity sometimes been a divisive factor, for becoming Christian serves to set them even more apart from the dominant Buddhist Thai.

Chinese, Sino-Thai, and Other Immigrant Minorities

Between the mid-nineteenth century and the outbreak of World War II, hundreds of thousands of Chinese migrated to Thailand. As in other Southeast Asian countries, many of the Chinese migrants stayed on permanently in Thailand where they prospered and became middlemen, traders, and skilled craftsmen. But unlike in other countries in Southeast Asia, including Vietnam where a similar culture might have seemed likely to facilitate assimilation, the descendants of Chinese immigrants who settled in Thailand assimilated to their country of adoption to a remarkable extent.

Several factors contributed to this unique transformation. Of primary importance was the fact that in Thailand the Chinese had to learn Thai to speak to members of the elite whereas in the colonial domains they learned French, Dutch, or English. The school system also promoted linguistic assimilation. During the 1920s and 1930s, when a compulsory system of education was first being established, the government insisted that the primary language of instruction in all schools, including those run by Christians as well as by Chinese, be Thai. Although Chinese-run schools also offered classes in Chinese, most children of Chinese parents acquired their basic education through the Thai school system. Yet another factor conducing to assimilation was religion. Chinese could become Theravada Buddhists without having to abandon their own religious practices, including ancestor worship. This openness of Buddhism made it a more appealing religion to Chinese immigrants than Islam was in the countries that were to become Malaysia and Indonesia. Finally, since attaining independence from their erstwhile colonial overlords, other Southeast Asian countries have enacted legislation restricting the rights of Chinese while Thai governments since World War II have increasingly eliminated or rendered irrelevant prewar anti-Chinese legislation. Given these factors, it is not surprising that by the mid-1950s, G. William Skinner found that most third-generation descendants of Chinese migrants had "become Thai" in that they were Thai citizens with Thai names, spoke Thai as their primary language, and professed adherence to the Thai form of Buddhism.[3]

Skinner's findings notwithstanding, not all Chinese have assimilated to Thai culture. There remain today areas in Bangkok where Chinese languages are still spoken in the shops and on the streets and where Chinese dress and Chinese customs can be observed. Even assimilated

Chinese have, for the most part, become "Sino-Thai" rather than just plain "Thai." Sino-Thai continue to recognize their links with a Chinese past, often through some form of ancestor worship (which may be combined with Buddhist practices). They are also likely to accord greater importance than other Thai to kinship ties, especially patrilineal ones. Sino-Thai also tend to be set apart by their occupations. Most are in commerce, trade, banking, or the professions; very few are in agricultural occupations. Because an increasing number of ethnic Thai are moving into occupations that have long been filled primarily by Chinese or Sino-Thai, there is today something of a convergence between Sino-Thai and ethnic Thai in middle-class occupations and culture.

While the Chinese were migrating to Thailand, a much smaller number of Indians also made their way to the country. Most of these people also found jobs in trade, especially the textile trade. Indian communities are to be found today in Bangkok, Chiang Mai, and a number of other towns. Members of the Indian community do not constitute a single ethnic group; they are divided by religion, some being Hindu, others Sikh, and still others Muslim.

In the early part of the nineteenth century, a small number of Vietnamese Catholics fled persecution in Vietnam and settled in Thailand. In addition to this old community, the descendants of which have assimilated to Thai culture to a marked degree, although still remaining Catholic, other Vietnamese came as refugees after the 1954 partition of their country. Thai governments have granted very few of these refugees and their descendants the right to remain in Thailand or to obtain citizenship. In the 1960s and again between 1977 and 1979, Thai governments conducted negotiations with Vietnam in an attempt to arrange for the repatriation of these people. Some—perhaps a third— were returned to Vietnam. A few, primarily those born in Thailand, have quietly been allowed to become Thai citizens. Vietnamese refugees who have fled Vietnam since 1975 have, for the most part, first sought asylum in countries other than Thailand, but some have gone to Thailand. Thailand insists that these refugees be resettled in third countries or be allowed to remain only until arrangements can be made for their repatriation. In short, Thai policies have effectively prevented the formation of any significant Vietnamese community in Thai society.

Although it is Thai policy today to prevent significant numbers of non-Thai peoples from entering and settling permanently in the country, past migrations as well as the drawing of state boundaries have resulted in the presence of large sectors of the people having distinctive ethnic, ethnoregional, or ethnoreligious identities. For the most part, these people are not pushing for formal political recognition for their communities largely because the way in which *chat Thai* ("Thai nation") is defined makes it possible for people to have distinctive identities and still also see themselves and be seen by others as "Thai." For example, villagers in a community in the northern province of Chiang Rai might identify themselves locally as Lue, regionally as Khon Muang or Northern Thai, and nationally as Thai.[4] Even peoples such as the Mon in central Thailand and the Khmer and Khmer-related Kui in northeastern Thailand, although speaking distinctive domestic languages and following distinctive cultural traditions, have become sufficiently bilingual and bicultural to find no difficulty in also identifying as Thai.[5] This "Russian doll" relationship between local ethnic identities and national identity is easiest for those who adhere to Buddhism and speak Thai fluently as a first or second language. The national community does not, however, appear to provide for Malays or for many tribal peoples a place they find acceptable. There is always a danger that a future government might revert, as some rightists have strongly advocated, to a narrowly construed definition of Thai nationalism, one that would force some non-Buddhist or non-Tai groups to see themselves as marginal to the national community. At present, however, ethnic, ethnoregional, and ethnoreligious identities serve primarily as a means for peoples to organize themselves into distinctive groups within Thai society rather than into potential national groups opposed to the dominant Thai.

PATRON-CLIENT RELATIONS

In premodern Siam, the basic hierarchical cleavage in society was between the royalty and nobility on the one hand and the peasantry on the other. So-called slaves constituted yet a third category, one that included people who were either personal servants of the royalty and nobility or bondsmen attached to the relatively small holdings belonging to certain members of the elite or, in rare cases, to a temple. Slavery, which differed considerably from that found in the United States, was abolished by King Chulalongkorn in 1872–1873, although his decree was not fully implemented until the 1890s. The relationship between peasants and their "lords and masters" (caonai) was based, with only a few exceptions, not on the latters' owning the land on which the peasants lived and worked, but on the premise that adult male peasants owed personal service in the form of corvée labor or military service to their lords and masters. Peasants were subject to taxes, the most important of which was a head tax. In return for personal service and head taxes, the lords and masters were expected to ensure that the world in which the peasants (and the lords and masters) lived was an ordered one. That is, lords assumed responsibility for adjudicating conflicts among their subjects, controlling banditry, and assisting their overlord in defending the realm. The order that the lords maintained was also a religious one; they set an example as the leading supporters of the sangha and participated in rituals deemed by peasants and lords alike as essential for bringing their mundane existence into harmony with a cosmic system.

The traditional personal linkages between the people of different classes has persisted in the modern period in the form of patron-client relationships. Underlying the practice of patronage is the idea that each individual is situated, however temporarily, in a particular position in a hierarchy of relative power. Those higher up in the hierarchy seek validation of their power from among those below them, and in return those lower down expect tangible benefits from their superiors. Patron-client relations, as conceived of by the Thai, would seem to be inimical to a class system since individuals can, and do, change their positions in the hierarchy during their lifetime. Many patron-client ties are formed, for temporary periods, among people who belong to the same status group, especially in the bureaucracy and the military. In rural Thailand, however, other "entourages"—to use a term proposed by Lucien Hanks,[6] a major interpreter of Thai social life—tend to be formed among people who share a common and stable socioeconomic position while the patrons come from a different stratum of society.

Patronage roles typically are filled by officials who wield power by virtue of their positions in a state-created hierarchy. More recently, politicians and middlemen have also sought to establish patron-client relations with their constituents or producers and customers. Ties between patrons and their clients are often bolstered by ritual activities in which members of the sangha play key roles. The rite of *thǫt kathin*[7] is perhaps the rite of patronage par excellence in Thailand today. At the end of Buddhist lent, members of the laity are expected to offer in the *thǫt kathin* rite new robes to monks and novices who have resided for the prescribed period within a particular *wat*. Many would-be patrons in local *wat*s up-country emulate the king and queen who conspicuously give alms of robes and other gifts to various royal temples, primarily those located within the greater Bangkok metropolitan area. The members of the sangha, who are essential for the performance of Buddhist rituals in the *wat*s of the country, can be seen as the pivot on which the modern statewide version of the patron-client system turns. The patronage system has, however, begun to be undermined, especially through the national system of education and by new principles of stratification based on the distribution of power and wealth in the society. Although many people in Thailand, especially those in rural communities, continue to find salience in a patron-client ideology, an increasing number are beginning to view themselves as members of classes within a stratified social order.

THE SANGHA AS A STATEWIDE INSTITUTION

Social Organization of the Sangha

The sangha consists of those males who have been ordained either while under the age of twenty as novices (*samanen* or *nen;* from Pali, *samanera*) or after the age of twenty as monks (*phra* or *phikkhu;* from Pali, *bhikkhu*). Women cannot become members of the sangha; the white-robed "nuns" (*maechi*) are, technically speaking, only devout laywomen. Whereas laypeople "make merit" (*tham bun*) by offering food, clothing, medicine, and shelter to members of the sangha, they do not do so by offering the same types of alms to nuns. The distinguishing characteristic of members of the sangha is their submission to "the discipline" (*winai;* from Pali, *vinaya*), the rules of the order that, according to tradition, were first set forth by the Buddha. A monk will be "defeated," that is, forced to leave the order, if he has sexual intercourse, takes the life of a human, steals, or claims to have the powers of a saint. In addition, both monks and novices must lead ascetic lives by taking no more than two meals a day, the last one before noon; by consuming no alcohol or drugs; by handling no gold or silver (modern currency is not considered to be the equivalent of gold and silver by many monks); by dressing without adornment in clothing (that is, by wearing the robes of monks) that could be deemed to hold attraction for others; by avoiding entertainment, by living separately from laypeople in monastic communities; and by sleeping only on a simple mat or mattress, not on a comfortable bed. Monks meet together once a month to chant the rules of the order, to confess to each other any infractions of the rules they may have committed, and to determine penalties for those who have committed infractions. Serious cases may be referred to sangha courts for action.

Most monks and novices live in local *wat*s, temple-monasteries built and sustained by people living nearby. Some may live in forest *wat*s, that is, retreats designed to facilitate the practice of meditation. All monks and novices must adhere to the prescription of the Buddha that during the rainy season or "lent" (called *phansa*—from Pali, *vassa*—in religious language) they remain in a particular *wat*. Except during that period, monks may become wandering mendicants, living in the forest alone or traveling from shrine to shrine. Although most rural *wat*s have no wealth-generating property and are supported by donations from members of the local community, some urban *wat*s own very valuable property from which considerable revenues are generated. These

Ordination of a Buddhist monk in Mae Sariang, northern Thailand. (Photo by author)

revenues are managed by lay stewardship committees, and neither the property nor the revenues are considered, unlike in Sri Lanka, to belong to the abbot of the *wat* or to the other monks residing there.

Unlike in the Catholic church, the men who take holy orders in the Theravada Buddhist tradition of Thailand do not commit themselves to remaining apart from the world for life. Quite to the contrary, in Thailand a man acquires considerable esteem by becoming a member of the order even for only one lenten period. Because of the pattern of temporary membership in the sangha, the ranks of the order swell considerably during the lenten period. It has been estimated that in the 1960s and 1970s, in any one lenten period about 1 percent of all adult males in the country were in the monkhood and another 0.5 percent of boys were novices.[8] Because of the greater secularization of life in the cities, observance of the practice of temporary service in the sangha is much more common among rural than urban men, and because of local tradition, the pattern is strongest among rural peoples in the northeast and parts of central Thailand.

In premodern Siam, the major temples of the country were headed by monks who had come from elite families. During the twentieth century, it has become increasingly uncommon for members of elite families to become permanent monks as a consequence of both their greater exposure to nonreligious education and their markedly better opportunities to attain high status in secular occupations. Today, monks in most *wat*s throughout the country, urban as well as rural, and the majority of the monks in the sangha hierarchy are now men of nonelite, usually rural, backgrounds.

The sangha in Thailand today is divided between the large Mahanikai order and the much smaller Thammayut order. The Thammayut, as discussed earlier, emerged during the nineteenth century because of reforms first instituted by King Mongkut during his period in the monkhood. Royal patronage meant that Thammayut leaders were able to assume dominance of the unified national sangha created by an act promulgated by King Chulalongkorn in 1902. This dominance, especially during the time (1910–1921) when Prince Vajirañana was supreme patriarch, also made it possible for Thammayut monks to impose their ideas when reform of the entire sangha was undertaken during the first decades of the twentieth century. This reform became institutionalized primarily through the curriculum that was then established in religious schools throughout the country—schools that became separate and distinct from those providing general education for the populace at large.

Few members of the sangha spend much time studying the standardized curriculum of religious education since most are ordained for only a temporary period, during which time they devote themselves to performing the traditional rituals of their home communities. Completion of at least the basic grades of this education is essential, however, if a monk is to be appointed as a "preceptor," that is, to be authorized to perform ordinations—a position open only to monks who have been in the order for at least ten years—or to move on to offices higher than that of local abbot. Religious education has also proved to be a means of upward social mobility for a number of young men from rural backgrounds. Some village boys who start as novices in religious schools eventually make their way to one of the two religious universities in Bangkok—Mahamakut or Mahachulalongkorn. Many, perhaps most, of the people who obtain degrees from one of these two universities leave the monkhood. Although a few former monks who have graduated from the religious universities have entered the upper echelons of the elite, most have found middle-level jobs in secular educational institutions, in government service, or in business.

Sangha and State in Thailand

Since the promulgation of the 1902 act unifying the sangha into a national institution, the state has made use of the sangha to legitimate its authority. The sangha hierarchy created as a consequence of this act directly parallels the provincial administrative hierarchy, and monks of appropriate rank are invited to perform rituals at formal state functions or in conjunction with state holidays. In the early decades of the twentieth century, monks were co-opted by the government to teach in the new state schools. In the 1960s, when the government became concerned about security problems in the rural areas and among tribal peoples, the government supported the creation of moral rearmament and Buddhist missionary programs. Many of the monks recruited for the *Thammathut* (literally, "ambassadors of the *dhamma*") program, which sought to strengthen adherence to establishment Buddhism in the countryside, and for the *Thammacarik* (literally, "wandering *dhamma*") program, which aimed at converting tribal peoples to Buddhism, were from the religious universities in Bangkok.

The sangha has not been made over entirely into an instrument of the state, however. Since most monks, unlike bureaucrats, are recruited primarily from local communities and depend on the latter for their support, the sangha has remained much more responsive to local interests than the bureaucracy. Some high-ranking monks have also sought to promote programs not approved of by the government. One such monk, Phimonlatham, who was inconclusively prosecuted for alleged left-wing activities during the Sarit Thanarat regime, has reemerged in recent years as the leader of a village-based popular meditation movement. In the 1970s, a hundred or so educated young monks became actively involved in supporting student, farmer, and labor groups in their confrontations with the government. At the other end of the political spectrum, the very outspoken Kittivuddho Bhikkhu, the leader of a monks' movement that lay outside the official sangha structure, inflamed public opinion by claiming that it was meritorious to kill communists. Even though some right-wing military men supported Kittivuddho, he gained little backing from the religious and political establishments. Politicized monks have not become as common in Thailand as they are in Sri Lanka, or as they were in the past in Burma, but the pressures on highly educated monks to take an active interest in social problems makes it likely that at least some will continue to involve themselves in political or quasi-political activities.

The most highly respected monks are neither those who are active politically nor those who have been awarded the highest state-validated ranks. Rather, they are those who epitomize the religious ideal of world-rejection. A small number of monks, mainly of the Thammayut order and mostly followers of Acan Man Phurithat (1870–1949), a monk who is now acclaimed a saint, have founded forest monasteries where the practice of meditation is emphasized. In their teachings, the meditation masters offer a radical critique of all action predicated on the desire for power, wealth, or esteem. When the forest monks first began to achieve a degree of recognition in the 1950s and early 1960s, the government initially was suspicious, even suggesting that monks who placed themselves outside the sangha hierarchy might be communists. In the late 1960s and early 1970s, however, there was a shift in the official attitude, and forest monks came to be seen by many people as practicing a purer form of Buddhism than establishment monks.

Since the early 1970s, the royal family has been conspicuous in offering support to the leading meditation masters and in leading the funerary rites for several such monks. Even more significant, the forest retreats of these monks have become popular centers of retreat for a segment of the educated elite. Several hundred men who hold high positions in the civil bureaucracy or the military, and even some in business, have been ordained for a lenten period at one of these forest monasteries. Other members of the elite, both male and female, have also spent periods of time as laypersons in these retreats. In addition to forest monks, a number of other leading meditation masters—including some laymen and laywomen—have established centers in or near Bangkok where laypeople, mainly from the elite, come to learn how to act in the world without being driven by worldly passions. Although Buddhism, through the established sangha, has been used to legitimate a particular type of social order, it has also provided the means for some people to adopt a critical stance toward that order.

THE BUREAUCRACY AND THE MILITARY

The reforms instituted under King Chulalongkorn at the end of the nineteenth and beginning of the twentieth centuries replaced local political institutions in the semiautonomous polities of the traditional Siamese order with new institutions that were uniform throughout the state and centered on Bangkok. These reforms brought into existence a bureaucracy that became and still remains for most people the embodiment of the Thai state. The creation of a national army was closely linked with the establishment of a bureaucracy in extending uniform control throughout the state.

Although in English the Thai civil bureaucracy is often spoken of as a "civil service," the Thai call officials "servants of the crown" (*kharatchakan*). The difference in terminology leads the Thai to see bureaucrats, not as serving the people in whom sovereignty resides, but as representing the crown, or its government. The 1932 Revolution, if its rhetoric is taken at face value, should have changed this situation, for it brought into existence both a constitution specifying that sovereignty

Thai soldiers on parade. (Photo by author)

rested with the citizenry of the nation and a National Assembly whose elected members were to represent that citizenry. The governments that ruled Thailand between 1932 and 1944 and especially between 1944 and 1947 did attempt to make the system more democratic, but real power lay with members of the two status groups—the civil bureaucracy and the military—that had staged the 1932 Revolution. Although members of the civil bureaucracy continued to be referred to as "servants of the crown," with the monarchy in eclipse they became in effect instruments of civilian and military officials who constituted the "king's government."

Between 1947 and 1973, state power was wielded with even less regard for the elected representatives of the people than had been the case previously. Instead, it was employed primarily to advance the interests of the upper ranks of the civil service and the military. For this reason, Fred Riggs characterized the Thai system as a "bureaucratic polity."[9] Although such a system could be exploitative of the populace, the Thai civilian bureaucratic and military elites have seen it to be in their interest to provide some services for the populace. The "good of the people" has, however, been defined from above rather than through institutions representing the citizenry.

The reforms of King Chulalongkorn were designed to create a bureaucracy organized along functional lines and committed to actions guided by impersonal laws and regulations. This intent was frustrated by the fact that after 1932, the civilian bureaucracy and the military were effectively accountable to no one—neither the discredited monarchy nor the populace through their representatives in a weak parliament—for their performance. Within the bureaucracy and the military, personal relationships between patrons at higher levels and clients at lower levels rather than legislated principles or professional standards became the primary basis on which actions were evaluated. Under the new system, the most powerful local officials were the district officers (*nai amphoe*) and district and provincial chiefs of police. Such officials often assumed the right of premodern agents of the monarch to *kin myang*, or "eat the country," that is, to extract from the populace not only the taxes imposed by the state but also additional money or labor for their own personal benefit. As government programs multiplied during the post–World War II period, so did the potential for increased demands by officials on the populace.

Only a very small proportion of the bureaucrats hold positions of actual power; the vast majority are petty officials who perform routine administrative or clerical functions. Those who serve as petty officials are typically recruited locally while higher officials tend to have been educated in Bangkok and then posted to other than their natal provinces. Because of their lesser educational qualifications, petty officials are rarely promoted to more powerful administrative positions. Lower-echelon officials often feel torn between their responsibilities to their bureaucratic superiors and their personal ties with people in the communities from which they have come.

Until recently, members of the populace had almost no institutional means with which to challenge the authority of local officials. They attempted to minimize friction by seeking help from petty officials whom they knew personally and by showing proper deference to the more powerful officials whom they called "lords and masters" (*caonai*).[10] Beginning in the early 1970s, the press, together with student and other groups, began to investigate and make public instances of administrative abuses of power. Although such efforts came to an abrupt halt following the October 6 coup in 1976, by the late 1970s, they were again being undertaken by various self-designated public-interest groups. Members of parliament during the 1974–1976 period and, to a lesser extent, in the period since 1978 have also asked questions on behalf of their constituents regarding specific actions by certain local officials. Questions about actions of military officers have, however, invariably brought very strong negative reactions.

While outside groups were taking an increasingly critical stance toward the civil bureaucracy, the composition of the latter was undergoing change. During the 1960s, large numbers of highly trained people were recruited into the middle echelons of the bureaucracy. Although performance based on technical competence or professionalism has become a significant criterion for recruitment and advancement primarily only in ministries and agencies that have little direct involvement in the exercise of power, such as those concerned with the economy or with foreign affairs, that criterion has begun to be important for even some of the new recruits in the Ministry of Interior.

Pressures from outside groups and from internal tensions between technocrats and old-style officials have not yet led to a transformation of the bureaucratic polity, but the civil service elite can no longer manipulate the instruments of state power for their own ends with total impunity. The military elite, however, continues to remain almost immune from any criticism by outside parties. Even though professionalism in the military became more highly valued in the 1960s and 1970s than it had been previously, personal relationships continue to be of primary significance. This situation can be clearly seen in the case of the Young Turks who organized themselves on the basis of personal ties established while they were classmates at the military academy. Despite their vaunted professionalism, they still sought to exert influence through personal relationships, in their case through Generals Kriangsak and Prem. When these efforts failed, their frustration led them to attempt a coup in April 1981 and some to try again in September 1985.

Although the military elite draws its members primarily from middle- and upper-middle-class families in Bangkok, the rank and file in the military come mainly from rural backgrounds. In theory, the Military Service Act of 1954 made all males over the age of twenty-one subject to conscription for two years, but because only a few of those eligible are inducted, the majority never serve. Not only are rural males more likely to be conscripted because they form a much higher percentage of the draft-age populace, they are also less able to obtain waivers than are urban men. Because of the composition of the Thai military, many rural men who have served in the military return to civilian life with a strong sense of belonging to a national society, but one in which class lines are clearly drawn.

EDUCATION AND CLASS IN THAI SOCIETY

Compulsory Education and Educational Mobility

Class distinctions in Thai society as a whole are perhaps most clearly drawn through the system of national education. The present educational system was designed by state agencies to promote state-defined objectives; thus, it contrasts significantly with the traditional educational system, which was vested in the hands of the Buddhist sangha and organized to inculcate religious rather than secular knowledge. When a statewide system of education was first designed during the reign of King Chulalongkorn, many monks suddenly found themselves transformed into state school teachers, and until recently most schools continued to be located at local *wats*. By the early 1930s, this compromise system was beginning to be phased out, and secular teachers replaced monks. Even today some village schools are still located in *wat* buildings, but the vast majority are housed in separate structures built according to Ministry of Education standards. In contrast to Indonesia, where Islamic leaders have resisted state efforts to replace religious schools with secular ones, the Buddhist sangha in Thailand has not attempted to protect its traditional educational role.

In Thailand, all children must attend primary school. Initially, primary education was compulsory for four years, but in 1962, the number of years was increased to seven. Before the seven-year requirement could be generally implemented, however, the system was changed, and primary education was made into a six-year program. By the early 1980s, nearly all primary chools throughout the country provided six years of compulsory education.

The system of compulsory primary education has made Thailand's population one of the most literate in the world, even if a literacy rate of 90.2 percent in 1981 as reported in official statistics[11] cannot be taken at face value. Compulsory education has also facilitated the participation of rural as well as urban people in the market economy and has given them access to written materials relevant to their economic lives. The high degree of literacy among Thai women has contributed to the success of birth control programs. Through compulsory education, the vast majority of the Thai populace has acquired knowledge of the basic elements of national culture—the national language, national history, and the national symbols of monarchy, Buddhism, and nation. The populace throughout the country has also been prepared to act within a state-defined social world organized around the bureaucracy.

Although people throughout Thailand have complied to a significant degree with the compulsory education requirement, only a small percentage of the populace has gone beyond the required primary schooling to acquire further education. Those who do pursue secondary and tertiary education are mainly townspeople rather than villagers. Not only do few parents in rural communities see the relevance of secondary or tertiary education for agricultural occupations, but rural schools also provide poor preparation for those seeking higher education. Moreover, schools in up-country towns are not the equal of the best schools in Bangkok or Chiang Mai, some of which are privately operated by

TABLE 6.1
Educational Attainment of Population of Thailand 6 Years of Age and Older for
1960, 1970, and 1980
(In Percentages)

Educational Level	1960	1970	1980
None	37.7	25.9	15.8
Primary[a]	54.6	66.8	71.4
Secondary[b]	6.2	4.8	9.3
Tertiary[c]	0.4	0.7	2.2
Other[d]	1.0	0.5	0.2
Unknown[e]	---	1.5	1.1
TOTAL[f]	99.9	100.2	100.0

Sources:
> Thailand. Central Statistical Office, National Economic Development
> Board, Thailand Population Census 1960: Whole Kingdom (Bangkok, 1962);
> Thailand National Statistical Office, Office of the Prime Minister, 1970
> Population and Housing Census: Whole Kingdom (Bangkok, 1973); Thailand.
> National Statistical Office, Office of the Prime Minister, 1980
> Population and Housing Census: Whole Kingdom (Bangkok, 1983).

Notes:
> a. Primary education included grades prathom 1-4 in 1960 and grades
>   prathom 1-7 for 1970 and 1980.
> b. Secondary education included grades matthayom 1-6 and two grades of
>   pre-university schooling in 1960. In 1970 and 1980 it included
>   grades matthayom suksa 1-5, and secondary levels of vocational and
>   teacher training education.
> c. In the 1960 census tertiary education was equated with "college,
>   university or equivalent" while in the 1970 and 1980 censuses,
>   tertiary education was broken down by "general, vocational, and
>   teacher training."
> d. In the 1960 census, the "other" category was broken down into
>   "religious" and "all other." The "all other" category included the
>   "unknown." In the 1970 and 1980 censuses no separate figures are
>   given for "religious" education.
> e. In 1960 the "unknown" was subsumed with the "other."
> f. Totals do not always equal 100 percent owing to rounding.

Christian organizations or are connected to the major universities. The
differences among primary schools, as well as those among secondary
schools and institutions of higher education, both reflect and create class
differences within Thai society.

   As can be seen on Table 6.1, there was a significant decline between
1960 and 1980 in the number of people who had no education, but
there was also only a modest increase in the percentage of those who
went on from primary to secondary school. In 1981, the percentage of
school-age children enrolled in secondary (and equivalent) schools was
28.3 percent as compared with 97.7 percent of those eligible enrolled

in primary schools. The drop in secondary school graduates going on to higher education was also dramatic. In 1981, only 4.5 percent of those aged eighteen to twenty-three were enrolled in higher education institutions, although if figures for Ramkhamhaeng University, which has an open admissions policy and allows most of its students to pursue studies on a part-time basis, were added, the percentage rises to 12.6 percent.[12]

The people who do go on to tertiary education assume quite different class-linked statuses depending on what institution they attend. The surest way to gain admission to the ruling elite is to attend the Chulalongkorn Royal Military Academy. Admission to the academy, which was reorganized in 1948 and graduated its first class in the post–World War II period in 1953, is highly selective. Until the early 1970s, all those admitted had to be "native Thai," able to demonstrate that both grandfathers had been born in Thailand. While this anti-Chinese regulation was dropped after the revolution of October 1973, it still remains very difficult for those of Chinese descent to overcome a long-standing practice. Although not the equal of the military academy, the naval and air force academies also are considered to be desirable institutions for the upwardly mobile.

Until quite recently, most members of the civil bureaucratic elite were graduates of the two oldest universities—Chulalongkorn, which evolved from a school for civil servants founded by King Chulalongkorn, and Thammasat, founded by Pridi in 1934 primarily for the purpose of training officials who would show a democratic orientation, although this aim has been obscured over time. In the past few decades, there has been a marked expansion in the number of universities and colleges in Thailand, some of which have a rather specialized character. The National Institute of Development Administration, an institution offering only graduate education, is as clearly linked to training people for the upper echelons of the civilian bureaucracy as it was when only a program at Thammasat University. Some, like Mahidol University, an institution built around a medical school affiliated with Sirirat Hospital, or Sila-pakorn, the Fine Arts University, were founded as specialized institutions but have evolved into full-fledged universities with standards that are almost as selective as those of Chulalongkorn and Thammasat. Kasetsart University was originally founded to promote more knowledge of and expertise in scientific agriculture; even though it has added a number of nontechnical faculties, it remains organized primarily around an agricultural curriculum. Although many Kasetsart graduates initially take technical jobs, some have been able to use these as springboards into the upper echelons of the elite, especially in such agencies as the Royal Irrigation, Land, and Forestry Departments.

Although all the above institutions are located in or around Bangkok, a number of universities are also to be found in the provinces. In the 1960s, the government founded three provincial universities—Chiang Mai in the north, Khon Kaen in the northeast, and Songkhla in the south. Although located in provincial areas, most students at these universities continue to come from Bangkok. Chiang Mai and, to a lesser extent, Khon Kaen and Songkhla are considered the next most desirable universities after the major ones in Bangkok.

The open university of Ramkhamhaeng in Bangkok, which was founded in 1971 in response to an escalating demand for higher education; Sri Nakharinwirote University, a conglomerate linking former branches of Prasarnmitr, the education college; and all teacher and vocational colleges that offer tertiary education leading to degrees produce graduates who rarely are able to advance to the highest echelons of the bureaucracy. Rather, the graduates of these institutions typically take positions in primary and secondary education, acquire skilled-labor jobs, or work in commerce and business. Private colleges and universities have been allowed to exist since the early 1970s, but as yet none has acquired a clear class-linked identity. Payap College, an institution founded by the Church of Christ in Thailand and located in Chiang Mai, has considerable support among middle-class Christians and is beginning to find something of a niche in the educational order.

Parental influence does sometimes help students gain places in one of the elite institutions, but most places are allocated on the basis of entrance examination scores. The most competitive students who take such examinations typically graduate from the best private and public secondary schools, the majority of which are located in Bangkok or Chiang Mai. Most students at even the major provincial universities come from Bangkok. Students who have attended secondary schools in provincial towns, with the major exception of Chiang Mai, usually have to settle for a lesser institution if they wish to go on for more education.

As a national system of status markers, educational attainment serves as a clear indication of position within the national society. Not only does the school, academy, college, or university one has attended determine the opportunities open to a person, but so also does education acquired abroad.

Until the late 1950s, higher education abroad was limited almost exclusively to children of upper- or upper-middle-class families. In the 1960s and 1970s, an increasing number of families who had benefited from the rapid growth of the economy, especially in Bangkok, sought to send their children to colleges and universities. As the number of places at such institutions in Thailand was quite limited, they began to send their children abroad in increasing numbers. Most chose institutions in the United States, but some sent their children to other English-speaking countries such as Great Britain, Australia, and Canada or to English-speaking institutions in India and the Philippines. The U.S. government, through the Agency for International Development and the Fulbright Program, made a large number of scholarships and fellowships available to Thai students, thus enabling some with limited financial resources to gain higher education abroad as well. During the 1960s and 1970s, there was a rapid increase in the number of Thai obtaining college and university degrees abroad, but many graduates discovered that their degree was not the hoped-for passport to success as the Thai government began to discriminate among foreign-degree holders. Although any foreign degree ensured some upward mobility, especially for students from provincial backgrounds, only those who had attended colleges and universities in the United States and, to a lesser extent, Great Britain, Canada, and Australia for which there existed in Thailand alumni associations composed of members of the elite could be assured that their foreign education would be a passport to elite status.

Until the 1960s, the educational system tended to perpetuate a traditional division of the population between the modern *caonai*, the bureaucrats, and the subjects of the king, most of whom lived in rural areas. The economic boom of the 1960s and 1970s created, however, a large number of new jobs in commerce and industry, and increasingly the qualifications Thai acquire through the educational system also determine access to these jobs as well as to traditional positions of status. As will be seen in the next chapter, Thailand's integration into a world market economy has become almost as significant as its transformation into a modern state in shaping the organization of Thai society.

NOTES

1. Because of space considerations, it is not possible to discuss the worldviews of non-Buddhist peoples in Thailand, especially those of Muslim peoples who constitute the largest non-Buddhist population in the country.

2. John F. Embree, "Thailand—A Loosely Structured Social System," *American Anthropologist* 52 (1950), pp. 181–183. Embree's formulation has been the subject of considerable debate. Most of the issues are addressed in the papers contained in *Loosely Structured Social Systems: Thailand in Comparative Perspective*, ed. Hans-Dieter Evers, Southeast Asia Studies, Cultural Report Series, 17 (New Haven: Yale University, 1969).

3. G. William Skinner, *Chinese Society in Thailand: An Analytical History* (Ithaca, N.Y.: Cornell University Press, 1957). See also his "Change and Persistence in Chinese Culture Overseas: A Comparison of Thailand and Java," *Journal of the South Seas Society* 16 (1960), pp. 86–100, and Skinner, "The Thailand Chinese: Assimilation in a Changing Society," *Asia* 2 (1964), pp. 80–92.

4. See Michael Moerman, "Ethnic Identity in a Complex Civilization: Who Are the Lue?" *American Anthropologist* 67 (1965), pp. 1215–1230, and Moerman, "Being Lue: Uses and Abuses of Ethnic Identification," in *Essays on the Problem of Tribe*, ed. June Helm, Proceedings of the 1967 Annual Spring Meeting of the American Ethnological Society (Seattle: University of Washington Press, 1967), pp. 153–169.

5. Brian Foster found that Mon identity was salient as a local identity in central Thailand among those Mon who had distinctive economic roles; see Brian L. Foster, "Ethnicity and Commerce," *American Ethnologist* 1:3 (1974), pp. 437–448, and Foster, *Commerce and Ethnic Differences: The Case of the Mons in Thailand*, Papers in International Studies, Southeast Asia Series, 59 (Athens, Ohio: Ohio University Center for International Studies, Southeast Asia Program, 1982).

6. Lucien M. Hanks, "The Thai Social Order as Entourage and Circle," in *Change and Persistence in Thai Society: Essays in Honor of Lauriston Sharp*, ed. G. William Skinner and A. Thomas Kirsch (Ithaca, N.Y.: Cornell University Press, 1975), pp. 197–218.

7. *Thǫt kathin* literally means "laying down the *kathina*," the *kathina* in India being the frame on which monk's robes were woven. Thai use the term *kathin* to refer to the robes and other items as well as money that are given during the rite at the end of Buddhist lent. The ways in which the *thǫt kathin* rite serves to express and create patron-client relations in modern Thailand are examined at length by Christine Gray in "Thailand: The Soteriological State in the 1970s" (Ph.D. dissertation, University of Chicago, 1985).

8. Frederica M. Bunge, ed., *Thailand: A Country Study* (Washington, D.C.: Government Printing Office for the American University, Foreign Area Studies, 1981), p. 102.

9. See Fred W. Riggs, *Thailand: The Modernization of a Bureaucratic Polity* (Honolulu: East-West Center Press, 1966), esp. chap. 10.

10. See Herbert J. Rubin, "Will and Awe: Illustrations of Thai Villager Dependency upon Officials," *Journal of Asian Studies* 32:3 (1973), pp. 425–445.

11. Thailand, National Economic and Social Development Board, *Khrụangchi phawa sangkhom khǫng prathet Thai, Ph.S. 2524* [Social indicators: Thailand, 1981] (Bangkok, 1983), table 3.

12. Ibid.

7

The Thai Economy and Change in Rural and Urban Society

A religion that places its highest value on world-rejection might be expected to have constrained economic activities leading toward capitalist development, but Thailand's dominant religion, Theravada Buddhism, has not, in fact, generated such constraints. Because Buddhist doctrine makes each individual morally responsible for his or her own destiny, Thai Buddhism has been very tolerant of a variety of practical actions. What Winston Davis, a student of Japanese religion, has said about Japan can equally be said of Thailand: "One could argue that this kind of toleration was another way in which religion failed to get in the way of development. . . . Toleration (the religious face of pragmatism) and flexibility (the secular side of toleration) have undoubtedly enhanced the stability of Japan's [read Thailand's] rapidly developing society."[1] This tolerance has extended to the distinctive ethic of the Chinese and Sino-Thai, an ethic that, as the sociologist Frederic Deyo has shown,[2] has provided positive motivation for capitalist activity. Moreover, by serving for a temporary period in the monkhood or by practicing meditation under the guidance of forest monks or other meditation masters, many lay Buddhists have acquired the ability to dampen personal desire even while acting in the world. This religious ethic in the context of Thailand's expanding economy lends itself to the pursuit of capitalist types of endeavor.[3]

AN OPEN ECONOMY AND THE TRANSFORMATION OF THAI SOCIETY

The Roots of Thailand's Open Economy

If religion has not restricted economic development in Thailand, the same can not be said of the political system. Between the opening of Siam to the world economy with the signing of the Bowring Treaty in 1855 and the early 1950s, the Thai economy became increasingly commercialized, but it did not develop in the sense that there was "an increase in the use of capital and land relative to labor, and/or improvement in technique of production."[4] Until after World War II, governments in Thailand gave priority to guaranteeing the country's political independence, a commitment that led to the adoption, in part under the guidance of foreign (usually British) economic advisers, of very conservative fiscal policies. The remarkable expansion of rice production to meet external demand during the period was accomplished with only minimal investment in infrastructure by successive governments. Thai farmers created a rice surplus for export by expanding holding size, not by changing techniques of production.

Although agriculture, especially rice production, has been the mainstay of the Thai economy since the nineteenth century, the Phibun government predicated its development program on creating a manufacturing sector rather than on improving agricultural technology. It decided to use public revenues to establish a number of new firms, which in turn were to be placed under the control of various ministries. The decision to establish state industries was not based on a commitment to socialist ideals; rather, it reflected a deep suspicion of the Chinese, who dominated what private enterprise existed in the country. The effort to create a state system of industries that could lead the country to economic development proved, in any event, to be a failure. The inefficiency and corruption of these enterprises made them a net drain on government revenues.

Following Sarit's coup in 1957 and his assumption of power in 1958, a major shift in economic policy was instituted. Sarit's government abandoned Phibun's policy of state investment in new industries and, instead, adopted a policy of promoting private investment in the non-agricultural sector. In part, this shift of policy was stimulated by a World Bank report that strongly recommended that Thailand should encourage development by the private sector and limit intervention by the state.[5]

Of even greater significance was the change in the economic role of the Chinese. Chinese migration to Thailand effectively ended with World War II; as a result, the continuing (and soon rapidly growing) demand for wage labor in Bangkok (and to a lesser extent in other parts of the country) came to be met by people from rural Thailand rather than rural China. Thus, the labor force created by an expanding industrial sector was becoming Thai rather than Chinese. Moreover, the 1949 revolution in China led many Chinese in Thailand to decide to retain their savings for investment in Thailand rather than remit them to families in China. Although remittances did not end, they were markedly reduced. The commitment to retain surplus wealth in Thailand was also associated with a commitment on the part of many Chinese, and particularly descendants of Chinese, to "become Thai." To ensure the "Thai-ness" of the new enterprises that were created, many members of the bureaucratic and military elites joined these companies as board members while the Chinese provided the capital. Although such a system, as James Ingram observed, "is obviously subject to abuses . . . it may facilitate the process of assimilation and could lead, in time, to the emergence of a group of Thai entrepreneurs." In fact, as Ingram goes on to note, by 1970 "Thai managers [had] already emerged in many foreign and joint-venture firms."[6]

The Sarit government also sought capital from external sources to invest in economic development. In 1959, the Board of Investment was created to promote investment of foreign capital in the private sector by providing incentives such as tax credits. By the early 1960s, a significant number of foreign firms had begun to invest in the country. In addition, Sarit and his successors sought grants and loans from foreign sources—primarily the United States, the World Bank, and West Germany—for investment in the infrastructure, including hydroelectric and irrigation projects, road systems, improved port facilities, and other public works. During the period of military dictatorship (1957–1973), such foreign grants and loans added at least 50 percent to the money the government invested in such projects from its own revenues.

Economic Growth Since the 1950s

The investment-oriented economy that emerged in the late 1950s, and which continues to the present, has generated a remarkable degree of economic growth in Thailand. Whereas between 1951 and 1958 the GNP grew at an annual rate of 4.7 percent per year at constant prices, it grew at a remarkable 8.6 percent per year between 1959 and 1969. Although this growth rate was fueled in the late 1960s to some extent by the U.S. military presence, the boom was not an artificial one. In the 1970s, the rate of growth slowed, but it still averaged 6.9 percent per year between 1970 and 1979. For the first two years of the 1980s, it averaged 6.3 percent, and in 1984 it still grew at a rate of 6 percent—very respectable figures given the worldwide recession. The forecast for 1985, however, was for a growth of less than 5 percent.[7] During the first part of the growth period, from 1951 to 1969, inflation rose at only 1.9 percent per year, "which [was] probably one of the lowest rates in the world in this inflationary period."[8] In the wake of the oil crisis, however, the Thai economy became subject to significant inflation, reaching an average of 8.5 percent per year for the last three years of the 1970s and 16.2 percent per year for the first two years of the 1980s.[9]

This high inflation has not continued, however. In 1984, the rate was said to have dropped to 0.9 percent, "the lowest in more than a decade."[10]

The growth of the Thai economy has resulted in a marked imbalance in development. The growth sectors have been in industry and services while agriculture, which has continued to generate the vast bulk of export revenues, has been neglected. Between 1951 and 1984 there was a dramatic shift in the contribution various sectors made to economic growth in Thailand with the agricultural sector's contribution declining from 50.1 to 19.9 percent, the service sector growing from 31.6 to 43.6 percent, and the industrial sector growing from 18.0 to 36.3 percent.[11] These changes have occurred, however, without a commensurate shift of population from agriculture into nonagricultural occupations. In 1954, 88.0 percent of the labor force was in agriculture; in 1981, agriculture still accounted for 71.9 percent of the work force.[12] Although these figures are somewhat misleading, since many people whose primary occupation is agriculture also work part-time in nonagricultural jobs, they still indicate a markedly lower degree of growth in the sector employing the vast majority of the Thai population.

Even though all sectors of the economy, including agriculture, have grown significantly since the early 1950s, the primary growth has been in mining, electricity and fuels, construction, manufacturing, trade, banking, and services. Tin has long been mined in Thailand, and for most of the past century it ranked next only to rice and rubber among the country's major exports. It continues to be one of Thailand's major exports, accounting for more than 8 percent of total exports during the 1970s.[13] In recent years, tungsten, fluorite, and especially gems have been mined and sold to external buyers. The large number of gems sold in the 1970s, however, did not all come from internal sources; many came from Burma or Cambodia and were then sold in Thailand. Thailand has other natural resources—antimony, tungsten, manganese, and lignite, to mention just a few—that are also being exploited to a certain degree. Another natural resource, teak, which was long a major Thai export commodity, has not been exported in any sizable quantities since the late 1970s, when the government determined that teak forests had become so depleted that it was necessary to place severe limits on the amount of teak cut and sold.

The natural resource that has proved to be of particular significance to Thailand's economic development is water. Beginning with the construction of the Bhumibol Dam on the Ping River in northern Thailand, a project completed in 1964, the country has built a number of hydroelectric projects that provide more than enough electricity for most of the country. Lignite-fired electricity generating plants have also been constructed in southern Thailand. By the early 1980s, sufficient electricity was being generated not only to supply industries in the urban sector but also to provide electricity, through a major rural electrification program, to most households in the kingdom. But even though Thailand meets most of its own electrical needs, it still has to depend on imports for its petroleum needs. Oil explorations have not met with much success, although in recent years significant quantities of natural gas have been discovered in the Gulf of Thailand. With the growth of the economy, Thailand's needs for petroleum have grown substantially, and the need to import large quantities of oil has been a major contributing factor to a growing balance-of-payments problem.

During the 1960s and much of the 1970s, construction was the most rapidly growing sector of the economy as many infrastructure projects (roads, dams, public buildings, refineries, and so on) were undertaken by the government, and factories, warehouses, and buildings were put up by private enterprises. Construction has probably employed a much higher percentage of the labor force than statistics indicate; many villagers who are employed in farm work during the rainy season migrate to urban centers for construction work during the dry season. Statistics on labor in Thailand underestimate the significance of such seasonal employment.

The growth of manufacturing has been especially dramatic since about 1970 and reflects the investment of a large number of private firms. Between 1969 and 1983, the value of manufacturing in the gross domestic product rose from 19.2 billion baht to an estimated 172.5 billion baht.[14] Although many of the larger concerns have been financed in part by foreign capital, even these have more than 50 percent of their capitalization from Thai sources. Japan has been the major source of foreign capital for the new industries, a majority of which produce goods primarily for internal consumption. Whereas in the 1960s most manufactured goods offered for sale in shops in villages and small towns—canned foods, clothing, soap, medicines, cooking implements, and tools—were made abroad, today most have been manufactured in Thailand. Increasingly, electrical equipment, bicycles, motorcycles (although only assembled in Thailand), and a considerable range of small machines are also likely to have been locally manufactured. By the mid-1970s, Thailand was exporting clothing and canned goods in significant amounts; in 1975, manufactured goods accounted for about 9 percent of exports.[15] In the subsequent decade there was a boom in the production of manufactured goods for export so that in 1984, manufactured goods accounted for 43.4 percent of the total value of exports from the country.[16] Low costs of labor and electrical power and recent devaluations of the baht have made not only canned foods and textiles but also other goods such as electronic circuits manufactured in Thailand increasingly competitive with those from Taiwan, Korea, and other East and Southeast Asian countries.

The growth of trade has been closely linked to a growth in transportation facilities. Until well into the 1950s, most goods transported in Thailand were carried by the Royal State Railways, the rail system itself being a replacement of traditional transport by boats on rivers and canals. As the road system expanded, the government initially controlled internal transport by requiring that goods for many types of activities be carried by trucks belonging to the government's Express Transport Organization. The government also operated the interprovincial bus system. By the late 1970s, however, government control of transport was rapidly being overshadowed by new, privately owned trucking and busing firms. Government regulation, together with considerable corruption associated with the granting of licenses, still hinders the private development of transportation, making it very difficult for small operators to maintain their businesses.

Until the 1950s, little of the capital invested in what firms existed in Thailand passed through banks. Many Chinese families had their own system of moving capital from one place to another. Ordinary people who had surplus wealth tended to purchase gold and other jewelry as a form of savings. The 1960s, however, saw a remarkable change in the role of banks in Thailand. By 1969, there were 604 bank offices with at least one in each of the 71 provinces as compared with 84 in 24 provinces in 1952. At the same time, there was an extraordinary growth in privately held time deposits, a phenomenon that "reflects the increasing monetization of the economy, but more than that indicates . . . a growth in private saving and public confidence in both the baht and banking system."[17] Private savings have continued to remain very high, averaging 13.8 percent of the GDP for the period 1977–1981.[18] In recent years, the high tariffs placed on many types of imports, which depress consumer spending, coupled with the continuing growth of the economy have contributed to the high rate of savings. Although banks are now encouraged to extend more credit to farmers, they are structured in a way that makes it difficult for them to extend loans to even relatively well-off villagers. There has been increased investment, especially since the mid-1960s, but much of the new wealth generated in rural areas and funneled through banks has found its way into investments, not in the rural sector, but in urban-based firms in the greater Bangkok metropolitan area.

The growth in the economy has markedly spurred a concurrent rise in the demand for services. Even at the village level, many people today make a significant portion of their family income by providing such services as tailoring and sewing, hairdressing, or the repair of machinery, motorcycles, and even trucks and cars. Other aspects of the expansion of the service sector in Thailand have resulted directly from the country's involvement in the world economy. Tourism, which has been strongly promoted by the government as a means to generate more foreign exchange, has been a major stimulus to the growth of services. Recently, however, tourism has come under strong criticism because it has been closely linked with the growth of prostitution, a "service" much in demand by many middle-class Thai males as well as by foreign visitors. Although prostitution is illegal, the government has done little to enforce the law, and massage parlors, nightclubs, and other facilities that provide a thinly disguised cover for prostitution have proliferated.

Most prostitutes in Thailand come from rural rather than urban backgrounds.[19] Many rural women are drawn into prostitution because of the poverty of their families and because they have few qualifications for equivalently paid jobs in the urban sector of the economy. In other words, the high rate of prostitution in Thailand must be understood as a consequence at least in part of the growing disparity between the rural and urban economies.

Development and the Agrarian Economy

Prior to World War II, agriculture—especially rice agriculture in the central plains and the northeast and rubber cultivation in the south—generated most of the surplus wealth of the country. In 1950, rice still accounted for 50.8 percent of exports and rubber for 21.8 percent. Despite the importance of agriculture for the economy, government development policies, at least until quite recently, have discriminated against agriculture. Under the first three five-year plans (covering the period from 1962–1977), the government did invest some money in agricultural research and irrigation projects. This investment, together with government-supported road construction for "security" purposes, provided some stimulus to the agrarian sector. The slowness of Thai farmers in adopting high-yield varieties of rice in most parts of the country is indicative, however, of the limited attention given by the government to adapting such varieties for cultivation in Thailand and to the lack of adequate extension services to assist farmers in substituting the high-yield rice for traditional varieties. Although average rice yields in Thailand have improved in recent years, they still remain among the lowest in Asia.

Significant growth in the agricultural sector since the mid-1960s resulted less from government policies than from farmers' response to world demands for crops other than rice. Farmers have learned of this demand, as well as about appropriate seed varieties, fertilizer needs, and processes to prepare crops for the market, from middlemen in the private sector rather than from government agents. As farmers have responded to demands for other crops, the relative significance of rice as an export crop has declined markedly, accounting for only about 15 percent of exports in 1984 as compared with over 50 percent in 1950. In the 1960s and 1970s the most important new crops were maize and cassava, both produced for animal feed. In the early 1980s, demand for these commodities dropped owing to restrictions placed on them by the EEC and Japan, the two major destinations to which the commodities were sent. Sugar, a boom crop for Thailand in the latter half of the 1970s, became of minor importance in the early 1980s because the price of sugar on the world market made it uneconomical for Thai farmers to produce this commodity and because Thailand has a low quota for sugar exports. In short, while Thai farmers have become increasingly willing to produce crops to meet the international demand, in so doing they have made themselves increasingly vulnerable to fluctuations in world market prices. The government, in its turn, has done little to help farmers withstand sharp drops in the price of major export crops.

The vulnerability of the small farmer to changes in the international market is one factor that has contributed to the marked growth of tenancy in certain parts of rural Thailand. Other factors include population pressures, the closing of the land frontier, and the interest of some investors in acquiring land for agribusinesses. Tenancy, which prior to the boom of the 1960s and 1970s had been restricted to a very small portion of central Thailand, has become increasingly common. By 1976, some 21 percent of farmers throughout Thailand held some or all of the land they cultivated under tenancy arrangements.[20] Tenancy has become especially characteristic of the central plains and of the Ping River valley in northern Thailand. In a study made of four villages in the Ping River valley in 1980, it was found that 20 percent of the farmers rented all the land they cultivated and an additional 31 percent rented at least part of their land.[21] Even in areas where tenancy is not significant, farmers often do not have full title to their land. Only in recent years has a serious effort been made to extend a cadastral survey throughout the country and to speed up the process of granting titles.

The underdevelopment of the agricultural as compared with the nonagricultural sectors of the economy is most evident in the growing discrepancies between income in predominantly rural areas and that in Bangkok (see Table 7.1). Per capita income of all regions of the country save for the central plains declined significantly relative to the per capita income of Bangkok in the period between 1960 and 1983, with the worst decline being in the northeastern region where the largest proportion of Thailand's rural populace lives. The imbalances in economic development in Thailand were of major concern in a World Bank study

TABLE 7.1
Per Capita Income in Thailand by Region for Selected Years, 1960–1983
(Baht, in current prices)

Region	1960	1970	1980	1983
Whole Country	2,106	3,849	14,743	18,770
Bangkok Metropolitan Area[a]	5,630	11,234	41,300	51,441
Central Plains[b]	2,564	4,662	15,646	24,002
South	2,700	3,858	13,745	16,148
North	1,496	2,699	9,866	12,441
Northeast	1,082	1,822	6,012	7,146

Sources:

Saneh Chamarik, Problems of Development in Thai Political Setting (Bangkok: Thai Khadi Research Institute, Thammasat University, Paper No. 14, 1983), p. 15, table; Khryangchi sangkhom 2524/Social Indicators: Thailand, 1981 (Bangkok: Office of the National Economic and Social Development Board, 1983), p. 103, table; National Income of Thailand, 1983 (Bangkok: Office of the National Economic and Social Development Board).

Notes:
    a. Includes Bangkok and Thonburi.
    b. For 1980 and 1983 statistics excludes eastern and western subregions.

carried out in 1976.[22] Although the World Bank recommendations were given little attention by the Thanin government, they have been significant in the development policies formulated by the governments of both Kriangsak and Prem. Nonetheless, although there has been some shift in emphasis in government policies, under the fourth development plan (1977–1981), agricultural growth was only 3.0 percent per year as compared with an overall growth rate in the GDP of 7.3 percent and growth rates in industry of 9.0 percent and in mining of 11.2 percent. The fifth plan (1982–1986) projected a somewhat better growth rate for agriculture (4.5 percent) relative to the general growth rate (6.6 percent) as well as to the growth rate of industry (7.6 percent) but not of mining (16.4 percent).[23] Even if these targets are realized, the majority of the rural population in Thailand is still likely to be relatively worse off in comparison to the urban population at the end of the fifth development plan than they were before it began.

CHANGES IN THAI RURAL SOCIETY

Political-Economic Transformation of Rural Thai Society

More than 70 percent of the people in Thailand still live in rural communities. The traditional village, whether among the Siamese in central Thailand, the Lao in northeastern Thailand, the Khon Myang in northern Thailand, the Southern Thai, or the Mon and Khmer and Khmer-related peoples, was defined primarily as a ritual community organized around the local Buddhist *wat* and a shrine dedicated to the spirit of the village.[24] The religious practices that all members of a village participated in gave them a sense of belonging to a moral as well as a social community. Although there were differences in wealth, in knowledge (particularly of important religious and magical texts), and in participation in village leadership, no fundamental social cleavages, such as caste or class, separated some villagers from others. The close relations between members of villages were most marked in long-settled areas where kinship ties also bound villagers to each other. Only on the frontiers, where new settlements were often formed by families coming from different home communities and where most energy had to go into opening new land, were ritual activities less emphasized.

In the 1890s, the government of King Chulalongkorn organized the rural populace into administrative collectivities called *muban*, literally, a "cluster of houses." In the long-settled areas of northern, north central, northeastern, and southern Thailand, existing villages were simply accepted as the new administrative entities. In the lower central plains, however—an area that had only recently been settled and one in which households tended to be strung out along canals rather than clustered in nucleated settlements—somewhat arbitrary collectivities of households constituted a *muban*. As a consequence, local administrative units rarely corresponded with existing ritual communities. In more recent years, the government has subdivided many of these villages into two or more *muban*, yet further separating the administrative unit from the ritual community.

The government recognizes as head of a *muban* a village headman (*phuyaiban*). Although each village elects its own headman and often chooses someone who would have been a traditional elder, the role of headman is defined in accordance with state, not village, interests. Headmen sometimes accentuate their ties to their fellow villagers by not drawing officials in to help settle disputes or by foot-dragging in complying with orders to organize villagers to participate in some government-determined project. Other headmen, especially those who have become *kamnan*, or heads of the larger local units known as *tambon*—a collectivity of about ten to fifteen villages—may accentuate their position as a government agent and use the authority of this position, backed up by official patrons, for their own ends.

The state has intruded into rural society in another important way. During the late 1920s and especially during the 1930s, state schools were established throughout rural Thailand, and beginning in the 1950s and accelerating in the 1960s, the government provided funds to construct

Village headman, northeastern Thailand. (Photo by Jane Keyes)

Village children, northeastern Thailand. (Photo by Jane Keyes)

school buildings separate from the *wat*s. With separate facilities, school districts increasingly do not correspond to *wat* parishes. Although rural school teachers typically come from village backgrounds, they often choose to live in towns where they can maintain a middle-class standard of living and commute to their rural schools by bus, motorcycle, or even private car. Yet even when they live in towns, rural school teachers normally retain close ties to villagers. Being betwixt and between rural and urban society, village school teachers are able to comprehend urban-based politics and to translate this understanding into terms meaningful to villagers. As a consequence, village school teachers have increasingly been sought as organizers and recruiters by both legitimate and illegal political parties.

Rural society has also been transformed by the increasing involvement of villagers in production for the market. This transformation has led to an expansion in the significance and numbers of people who play another role that connects rural with urban society, namely, that of the "middleman." Middlemen in Thailand are often thought to be ethnically distinct and usually Chinese, but while this is often still the case, an increasing number come from local, often rural, backgrounds and are Thai in origin. Indigenous middlemen in traditional rural society were known by such terms as *nai họi* ("mister trader"), *cao phọ* ("lord-father"), or *phọliang* ("father-nurturer"), although today even Thai middlemen may be called *tawkay*, a term of Chinese origin. Most middlemen who control traffic in large or expensive goods are male, while those

Open-air market in Mae Hong Son, northern Thailand. (Photo by Jane Keyes)

who deal in local produce in daily markets are usually women, who are referred to as *maeliang* ("mother-nurturer").

Emergence of a New Agrarian Order in Central and Northern Thailand

The economic transformation of rural Thai society has been the greatest in the lower central plains, the area that has long produced and still produces the major share of Thailand's rice for export. Rice agriculture in the central plains has become increasingly mechanized, with tractors replacing water buffalo as the major source of power for pulling plows, harrows, and other farm equipment and mechanical pumps being used to shift water from field to field rather than having to be shoveled by hand as in the past. The lower central plains have benefited more than any other area of the country from the government's investment in irrigation works. By 1979, dam projects on tributaries of the Cao Phraya River together with a diversion dam on the Cao Phraya made it possible to control the water supply to 1.3 million hectares (3.2 million acres) during the rainy season and about 450,000 hectares (1.1 million acres) during the dry season.[25] Farmers in the central plains have also widely adopted the high-yield varieties of rice and are more likely to employ sufficient amounts of fertilizers and insecticides with these varieties than are their counterparts elsewhere in the country. Although rice is the major commercial product of the lower central plains, a considerable amount of land in areas close to Bangkok has been converted into market gardens and poultry farms to meet the rapidly escalating demands for higher quality food by the Bangkok middle and upper classes.

The second area of greatest agricultural transformation has been in northern Thailand, especially in the Ping River valley and to a somewhat lesser extent in the area around Lampang. These areas have also benefited from improved irrigation, which has made double cropping a very common practice. Although some rice is produced for sale in the area, tobacco, peanuts, garlic, and fruit (especially longans, or what are called *lamyai* in Thai) as well as market garden crops and poultry are of major significance.

The growing demands for rice and other products from the central plains and parts of northern Thailand, together with the significant changes in technology that have made double cropping and higher yields possible, have made land an attractive investment. As a consequence, land is increasingly passing out of the hands of local farmers and into the hands of commercial farmers or agribusinesses. Tenancy is highest in the country in these two areas, involving as many as 75–85 percent of the farmers in the areas immediately around Bangkok and between

25 and 50 percent in other areas that have a high concentration of commercial activity. In addition, an increasing number of people in these areas have become landless. In the late 1970s, it was estimated that the landless numbered between 500,000 and 700,000; most such people came from the central plains or the north.[26] Although many of the landless in the lower central plains have the option of seeking work in the Bangkok metropolitan area, this is not an option for most of the landless in the north. There, the increasing number of landless farmers has contributed to a new and growing problem, namely, that of illegal (from the point of view of the government, although not necessarily from that of the villagers involved) squatting on forest reserve lands.

During the period of civilian rule in 1975, the government passed a Land Reform Act designed to alleviate some of the problems associated with the growing number of tenant or landless farmers. Although interest in enforcing this law waned after the coup of October 6, 1976, recent governments have undertaken to use the act to grant titles to people who are considered to be illegal settlers in forest reserves. Little has been done, however, to improve the situation for tenants or for landless farmers who have not settled on forest reserve lands. There has been strong opposition from landlords, many of them from the middle and upper classes, to implementing those provisions of the Land Reform Act that would permit the government to acquire and redistribute land in areas of high tenancy.

The land poor and the landless provided much of the support for the Farmers' Federation of Thailand and the farmer protest movements of the mid-1970s. With the assassination of the leaders of the FFT and its disappearance after the coup of October 6, 1976, these people have found it difficult to make their concerns known to the government. They also are finding that the village as a moral community no longer has meaning for them, for they rarely receive help from fellow villagers who have become large landowners or even from small landowners who are increasingly oriented toward the market. Anomie, tensions, and even open conflict between villagers have become increasingly common in villages in these areas.

Underdevelopment and Ethnic Separateness in Rural Northeastern and Southern Thailand

In northeastern Thailand, where over a third of the rural population of the country lives, the transformation of rural society brought about by inclusion in the market economy has been, for the most part, less profound than in other parts of the country. In the northeast in the mid-1970s, less than 10 percent of households rented any land, and no more than 3 percent rented all the land they cultivated.[27] Moreover land-holdings were large, in 1974 averaging 25 *rai* (a little less than 10 acres) per holding for the region as a whole.[28] There has been little alienation of land since that date, and landlessness is still negligible. The rapidly growing population in the northeast has been able not only to maintain a sizable land base but actually expanded it in the 1960s and 1970s. Northeasterners have accomplished this feat by converting to their own uses large tracts of land previously classified as "forest" areas. In 1956, 61.5 percent of the total land area in the northeast was classified as forest land; by 1977, the percentage had dropped to 15.8 percent.[29] This dramatic expansion into forested areas has led the government to regard many northeasterners as illegal cultivators. Because little of the land in the northeast that is classified as "forest" but is being cultivated is considered valuable for other commercial purposes or essential for the protection of watersheds, it is likely, however, that most "illegal" holdings will be reconstrued by the government as legal ones.

Despite the fact that the vast majority of the small landholders in the northeast own farms whose size would seem to make their owners the envy of most of the rural peoples of Asia, northeasterners are, in fact, by far the poorest of all rural peoples of Thailand save for the relatively much smaller number of tribal peoples. Table 7.1 shows that the average per capita income in the northeast has been consistently the lowest in the country and that taken as a percentage of per capita income in Bangkok, the average per capita income in the northeast has declined from 19.2 percent in 1960 to 13.9 percent in 1983. Although there were some absolute improvements in income levels in the 1960s and early 1970s, World Bank data still show that in 1975-1976, 44 percent of the population of northeastern Thailand lived below the poverty line. This compares with 33 percent in the north, 31 percent in the south, 14 percent in the center, and 12 percent in Bangkok.[30] Conditions of poverty prevail throughout much of the northeast because the natural ecology of the region, particularly its rainfall patterns and soil characteristics, does not lend itself well to the production of commodities for sale and because there has been only limited technological change that would enable farmers to overcome these natural constraints. Most northeastern farmers still produce rice primarily for home consumption and generate cash income only through the sale of surplus rice and a few other commodities such as cassava, kenaf, and maize. With the mechanization of agriculture in the central plains, the demand for water buffalo, long exported to the central plains from the northeast, has declined, and the demand for cattle, which might have developed from Japan, has not grown because of uncontrolled hoof-and-mouth disease. Probably the major export from the northeast is labor. There is a well-developed pattern throughout the region of villagers, both men and women, going to Bangkok and other industrial centers to find work temporarily or even permanently. In the early 1980s, northeastern men (although few women) were also migrating in significant numbers to the Middle East to take up temporary employment there.

Changes in social differentiation in rural northeastern society since the 1950s have not been as great as those found in much of central Thailand or in parts of the north. Northeastern villagers still tend to see themselves as united both as villagers (*chao ban*) and as Lao with reference to the central Thai government and its locally appointed officials, whom they feel have done little to alleviate the poverty of the region. Although wary of officials, some northeastern villagers have developed firm contacts with middlemen and others in the business sector, in part because economic development, insofar as it has occurred in the region, has come about primarily as a result of communication through the marketing system rather than as a consequence of government assistance. Not only have some northeastern villagers built up relationships with locally based merchants and middlemen, but many have gone to Bangkok and found employment there in firms that have been willing to give them on-the-job training. To a considerable extent, northeastern villagers have replaced the poor peasants of southeastern China who first went to Bangkok seventy-five to a hundred years ago in search of new opportunities. Today, some of the descendants of that earlier wave of migrants are now the owners and managers of many of the firms in which northeasterners are seeking their opportunities.

The economic development of the rural south has roughly paralleled that of central Thailand, although the southern economy is more diversified, with rubber as its major agricultural commodity and fish and fish by-products as the major commodities produced by the inhabitants of coastal villages. In addition, tin mining has provided some local wage labor in the south. In agricultural villages, rubber land has become, like paddy land in central Thailand, a valuable commodity, and its value has increased since the early 1960s when new methods of cultivation resulting in higher rubber yields were introduced. Tenancy in the south, while not yet of the proportions found in the lower central plains or in parts of the north, is still significant in rubber-planting areas. Internal differentiation of rural society has also been increasing in fishing villages, where many have become employees on boats owned by fellow villagers or by people living in nearby towns.

Village solidarity does not appear to have been undermined in the south to the extent it has been in the north. Both Thai-speaking and Malay-speaking villagers, however, frequently feel alienated from government officials, particularly as the latter are usually ethnically Central

Thai rather than Southern Thai or Malay. Although southerners, like northeasterners, have a more positive attitude toward the market than toward the government, they still see themselves as barred by ethnic distinctions from entering into business. As Ruth McVey, a political scientist who has worked in southern Thailand, has written, "[southern] peasants cannot hope to enter the world of business, as, except for a peripheral and struggling sector, trade is dominated by the Chinese who depend on kin ties for financing and enforcing deals and do not readily admit outsiders."[31] More than anywhere else in Thailand today, with the exception of tribal areas of the north, social relations in the south, especially the far south, continue to be organized around ethnic differences: Chinese, Malay, and Southern Thai are differentiated from each other and at the same time all see themselves as distinguished from the dominant Central Thai.

The south has been marked by "banditry" as well as by its Malay Muslim separatist rebellion and two communist (Malaysian as well as Thai) insurrections. Such unrest bespeaks a social world in which assumptions about the basis of the social order and ways in which conflicts within that order can be mediated are not shared by at least some of its groups. The Thai government has made considerable efforts to alter this situation by strengthening state institutions—most notably the school system—and by co-opting the sangha as a state-legitimating institution. These efforts appear to have met with some success. The relatively limited unrest in the south and the failure of the Communist party of Thailand to win wide adherence for its revolutionary program suggest that much of the populace has been willing, whatever social and ethnic distinctions may exist, to act with reference to premises that define a Thai national order.

Although local and ethnic loyalties remain strong among rural peoples in Thailand, many have become increasingly conscious of social differences based on class. In areas where there are high tenancy and landless rates, class differences are becoming significant even within rural communities themselves. Most rural peoples see themselves, however, as sharing a common situation in contrast to that of the urban dwellers who control power and wealth in the larger social order. Meanwhile Urban Thai society, which means primarily Bangkok society, has itself become increasingly differentiated in the wake of the changes that have occurred, especially since the 1950s.

BANGKOK AND URBAN SOCIETY IN THAILAND

Social Stratification in Bangkok

In the transformed social order of Thailand, Bangkok has assumed an overwhelmingly dominant place. Although Bangkok, like certain other cities of the world—such as Rangoon or Cairo—is a "primate city," the degree of Bangkok's primacy is exceptional. Following the Bowring Treaty, Bangkok became an entrepôt, the center to which all commodities produced in the country were transported for shipment abroad and the port of entry for all incoming imports. Although in recent years there have been some efforts to develop alternative ports on the east coast, Bangkok's role remains unchallenged. When Chulalongkorn's reforms were put into effect at the end of the nineteenth century, Bangkok also became the sole administrative center of the country. Again, while there has been talk in recent years about a devolution of authority to local government, little has been done to effect such a change, and Bangkok remains the locus of all significant power.

Because of its primacy, Bangkok has a more complex social strucure than is found elsewhere in the country. It retains remnants of the old hereditary royalty and nobility, some members of which are extremely wealthy as a result of their ownership of large tracts of real estate in the greater Bangkok metropolitan area. Today, however, two elites—the bureaucratic-military elite that controls the government and the capitalist elite that controls the major industries, trading firms, and financial institutions—run the country. Although probably the vast majority of the capitalist elite members are of Chinese descent, because of assimilation and personal identification as Thai they no longer possess the ethnic distinctiveness of their forebears. Similarly, while most in the bureaucratic-military elite are descendants of Thai, an increasing number (perhaps as many as a quarter to a third) today are Sino-Thai. These people also no longer define their interests in the same ethnic terms as did their predecessors in the pre–World War II period. But even with the decline of ethnic tension and considerable intermarriage between members of the bureaucratic-military and capitalist elites, and although many members of the former sit on boards of corporations owned or managed by members of the latter, these two elites still have distinctive interests that lead to periodic conflicts between them. Debates over the devaluation of the baht in the 1980s provide one such example. Although the business leaders supported devaluation because they thought it would stimulate exports and encourage the purchase of domestic products over imported goods, many in the bureaucracy and especially the military opposed it because it would increase the cost of imported luxury goods that have become part of their style of life and would make the cost of imported arms, considered crucial to maintaining power, almost prohibitive.

Differences between these two elites are also reflected in the way they treat their immediate subordinates. In the bureaucracy, and even more so in the military, subordinates tend to be advanced because they have secured the patronage of powerful senior individuals. Although personal, and especially kinship, ties are important also for the capitalist elite, subordinates in this latter stratum are often rewarded for impersonal abilities, such as efficiency, that contribute to the maximization of institutional profits.

Before 1950, Thailand could be said to have had only an embryonic middle class. The basic social distinctions were those dividing officials from nonofficials and upper- from lower-echelon officials. The ranks of business and commercial occupations were filled mainly by Chinese, who had an uncertain future in Thai society. The rapid economic development of Thailand since the mid-1950s has brought about a marked expansion of occupations in trade, banking, and manufacturing. Recruitment into these new occupations is no longer limited to Chinese or even to Sino-Thai; many ethnic Thai have also taken up jobs in the business sector. At the same time, while the bureaucracy expanded, albeit at a more modest rate than it had done in the 1930s, the ruling elite did not; thus many in the bureaucracy, especially those with technical skills, found themselves at relatively young ages without much prospect of further upward mobility.

The economic boom also generated an increasing demand for medical, dental, legal, educational, and other professionals. Many of these professionals, technically trained officials, and middle-echelon businessmen had attended good, but often not the top, primary and secondary schools in Bangkok and had gone to one of the new colleges or universities. Others had studied abroad, especially in the United States. Many also acquired a sense of belonging to a middle class through reading the same periodicals, such as *Chao Krung* [People of the City], and newspapers. The coalescence of middle-class identity has been strongest among the people who have settled in the new housing developments that began to spring up around Bangkok. New clubs and associations, such as those promoting sports for men and charitable activities for women, have further solidified such an identity.

Although the new middle class in Thailand is based predominantly in Bangkok, it has extensions and counterparts in many up-country cities and towns. Sino-Thai business people, professionals, and teachers in secondary schools and colleges and universities (where these latter exist) often form the core of up-country middle-class communities. Bangkok officials posted up-country often have, however, only a marginal relationship to such communities. Because their families prefer to remain in Bangkok, officials often take up their posts up-country without their families.

Some up-country towns and cities are, nonetheless, beginning to emerge as relatively self-contained social worlds. This is most evident in Chiang Mai, Thailand's second-largest city, located in northern Thailand. Because of its more equable climate, the beauty of its physical location, its proximity to the winter palace, and its considerably smaller size, Chiang Mai is becoming a preferred place to live even among some members of the Bangkok elite. Officials posted to Chiang Mai are more likely than officials elsewhere to take their families with them. Chiang Mai also has sizable business and professional sectors from which a local elite with distinctive local interests has emerged. There also exists in Chiang Mai a cultural elite, found primarily in Chiang Mai University, the teachers' college, and among the sangha, which self-consciously promotes Chiang Mai and Northern Thai identity. Patterns similar to those found in Chiang Mai also exist in a number of cities and towns in northeastern Thailand, especially Khon Kaen, Khorat (Nakhon Ratchasima), and Ubon Ratchathani, and in southern Thailand, most notably in Nakhon Si Thammarat and Songkhla. Saraburi in the central plains, Chonburi on the eastern seaboard, and Hatyai in the far south represent a different type of urban society—one in which Chinese and Sino-Thai businessmen are dominant and local cultural elites are conspicuous by their almost total absence.

Although Bangkok is increasingly assuming a middle-class character, the city depends on a large population of skilled and unskilled workers and service employees for its work force. This populace does not constitute a working class in any formal organized sense; save for a small percentage of mainly skilled workers, few belong to unions or organizations that bring workers together. In mid-1979, fewer than 100,000 workers belonged to unions, and the number of unions was small—185, of which 100 (mostly the larger ones) were located in Bangkok. Even in 1985 the total of registered unions in Thailand totaled only 282. But while the movement has been weak, it has succeeded in pressuring the government to raise the minimum wage from 12 baht (about $.60) a day in 1972 to 45 baht (about $2.25) a day in 1980 (the rate is lower up-country).[32] Members of labor unions also joined with student groups to protest government proposals to raise bus fares in Bangkok—protests that the government has heeded. Labor unions have also been active in protesting periodic government decisions since the early 1970s to raise the price of rice. Such protests clearly set the labor movement, and other urban workers, against the farmers, who would benefit from increases in the price of rice.

Workers and service people in Bangkok can be distinguished in part by the areas of the city or by the quarters in which they live. As the Bangkok metropolis has grown, it has absorbed nearby villages. Some of these formerly rural communities kept their distinctiveness until increases in land values forced members of these neighborhoods to search for cheaper housing in peripheral areas of the city. Contrary to what many people think, most of the slums—the densely settled sections of the city with poor housing and poor facilities—are not inhabited by recent migrants to the city.[33] Instead, most of the slums are long established and have grown in density because of natural population growth and concentration following encroachment on land bordering the slums by commercial institutions. Some slums, like the well-known one at Klong Toey near the Port of Bangkok, grew up in conjunction with nearby commercial activity. Although some of the transient workers in Bangkok—i.e., those who come to the city seasonally or for temporary periods—sometimes live in slum areas, many are housed in dormitories provided by their employers or else find shelter in *wats* (this latter option being especially true of migrants from northeastern Thailand). The women who become bar girls, masseuses, and prostitutes by other name also tend to live at their work sites.

Although one sees some beggars on the streets of Bangkok, they do not constitute a significant element in the city's population. Unlike many other cities in Asia, Bangkok has not attracted a large number of unemployed. Although official unemployment statistics for Bangkok—averaging less than 3 percent for the five-year period from 1977 to 1981[34]—are difficult to accept at face value, they are indicative of the fact that only a very small number of people in Bangkok are reduced to begging from others in order to survive.

One of the most dramatic differences between the Bangkok of today and the pre–World War II city lies in its present "Thai" flavor. In the prewar period, except in the area around the Grand Palace and government offices, the city had a strongly Chinese character. Today, the Chinese predominate in only a small part of the city, namely Yaowaraj, sometimes referred to as Bangkok's "Chinatown."

Also more muted today is the religious character of the city. When Thonburi and Bangkok became the centers of secular power, they also became the sacred centers of the kingdom, and successive monarchs built important shrines in different parts of the old city. In addition, many members of the aristocracy and nobility endowed other *wats* throughout the area of the old city. Today, while the most important shrines such as the Temple of the Emerald Buddha, Wat Pho (the Temple of the Reclining Buddha), and Wat Maha That—all of which are near the Grand Palace—and Wat Bencamabophit (the Marble Temple) near parliament, and some others still dominate the areas in which they are located, many of the other old *wats* have been eclipsed by the commercial worlds that have surrounded them. Indeed, in many cases *wats* have allowed much of their land to be used for very worldly purposes.[35] Such conversion of temple lands from sacred to secular uses indicates the growing dependence of many urban *wats* on revenues other than

Bangkok as a religious and cultural center. (Photo by author)

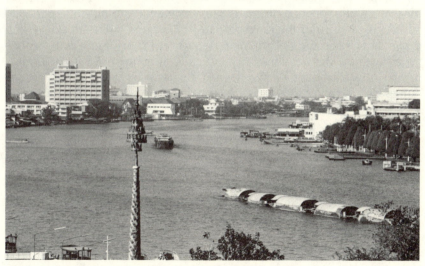

View of Cao Phraya River and Bangkok. (Photo by author)

those provided by members of local communities. Indeed, many *wats* today no longer have their erstwhile "parish" character, and their resident monks are likely to be of rural origin rather than coming from Bangkok itself.

Between Rural and Urban Worlds

Bangkok has increasingly become socioeconomically as well as culturally a world that is radically different from that in which villagers live. To an increasing extent, up-country towns—especially the larger ones like Chiang Mai, Khon Kaen, Khorat, and Hatyai—have similar characteristics to Bangkok and, thus, are also alien worlds to villagers. Significant numbers of villagers move every year between these worlds, and some remain permanently in Bangkok and other cities. Although aggregate data on temporary and permanent migration of villagers into Bangkok and other Thai cities are not adequate, a function of the way in which such data have been collected, a number of microlevel studies suggest that migration rates from at least northeastern and central Thailand (which account for nearly two-thirds of the rural populace of the country) have been high since the 1950s.[36] Moreover, they have been increasing. In a study made in six villages in Roi-et Province in northeastern Thailand in 1979, it was found that during the three-year period from 1976 to 1979, over three-quarters of all the households in the sample had at least one member away in Bangkok and that a quarter of the sample population had been migrants during this period.[37] Although some rural migrants to Bangkok acquire sufficient on-the-job experience to become skilled laborers, such as factory workers or drivers or mechanics, the vast majority never qualify for any but the most menial or demeaning work. Women migrants typically take jobs as domestics or as prostitutes, and many male migrants are hired in positions such as gas pump operators in which they also perform services for the richer inhabitants of the city. As most villagers are only temporary sojourners in the city, they eventually return to their villages with a strong sense of the class and cultural differences that separate them from permanent city inhabitants.

The larger world of Thai society, which encompasses both villagers and townspeople, albeit in very different guises, has become increasingly differentiated as a consequence of Thailand's "openness" to the world economy. This transformation has its roots in the period between the Bowring Treaty in 1855 and World War II, but it has been most dramatic since the Thai economy began to grow rapidly in the 1960s and 1970s. This transformation has undermined cultural assumptions, ones derived primarily from the traditions associated with Buddhist temple-monasteries that once were shared by townspeople and villagers.

NOTES

1. Winston Davis, "Religion and the Development of the Far East" (Paper presented at an MIT-Harvard Joint Seminar on Political Development, March 21, 1984), p. 31.

2. Frederic Deyo, "Ethnicity and Work Culture in Thailand: A Comparison of Thai and Thai-Chinese White-Collar Workers," *Journal of Asian Studies* 34:4 (1975), pp. 955–1015.

3. See, in this connection, Charles F. Keyes, "Economic Action and Buddhist Morality in a Thai Village," *Journal of Asian Studies* 12:4 (1983), pp. 851–868, and Keyes, "Buddhist Practical Morality in a Changing Agrarian World: A Case from Northeastern Thailand," in *Attitudes Toward Wealth and Poverty in Theravada Buddhism*, ed. Donald K. Swearer and Russell Sizemore, forthcoming.

4. James C. Ingram, *Economic Change in Thailand, 1850–1970* (Stanford: Stanford University Press, 1971), p. 209.

5. World Bank, *A Public Development Program for Thailand* (Baltimore: Johns Hopkins Press, 1959).

6. Ingram, *Economic Change in Thailand*, p. 231.

7. Different sources give somewhat different figures for the rates of growth of the Thai economy. I have taken the figures for the 1951–1958 and 1959–1969 periods from ibid., p. 223; also see p. 222, table. I have calculated the figure for the period 1970–1979 by taking the figure in Frederica M. Bunge, ed., *Thailand: A Country Study* (Washington, D.C.: Government Printing Office for the American University, Foreign Area Studies, 1981), p. 122 for 1970–1978 (7.1 percent per year) and factoring in the figure for 1979 (5.0 percent) as given in Thailand, National Economic and Social Development Board, *Khryangchi phawa sangkhom 2524* [Social indicators, 1981] (Bangkok, 1983), p. 106. I have also calculated the figure for 1980–1981 on the basis of information given in the same work, p. 106. Whereas the growth rate for 1977–1981 can be calculated as averaging 6.7 percent per year, an article in the *Far Eastern Economic Review* (October 22, 1982, p. 85) reports that in the government's new five-year plan, the rate for this same period was given as 7.3 percent. The 6 percent figure for 1984 is from the *Far Eastern Economic Review*, January 24, 1985, p. 69. In the *Far Eastern Economic Review*, August 15, 1985, p. 60, it is reported that "the annual average gross domestic growth of just above 5% during 1980–84 is a far cry from the average of more than 7% in the previous three decades. . . . The central bank has projected a 5% GDP expansion this year [1985]—against a 4.5% forecast by the Bangkok bank."

8. Ingram, *Economic Change in Thailand*, p. 221.

9. Thailand, *Khryangchi phawa sangkhom*, p. 100, table.

10. *Far Eastern Economic Review*, January 24, 1985, p. 69.

11. These statistics have been calculated from data in Ingram, *Economic Change in Thailand*, p. 235, and from information provided by the National Economic and Social Development Board, Office of the Prime Minister, Thailand.

12. Ingram, *Economic Change in Thailand*, p. 235, and Thailand, *Khryangchi phawa sangkhom*, p. 119, table.

13. Bunge, *Thailand: A Country Study*, p. 286, table.

14. The 1969 figure is from Ingram, *Economic Change in Thailand*, p. 235, table; the 1983 estimate is from data provided by the National Economic and Social Development Board, Office of the Prime Minister.

15. Ingram, *Economic Change in Thailand*, p. 147.

16. Bank of Thailand, *Raingan setthakit raidyan* [Monthly economic report] 25:3 (June 1985), p. 52.

17. Ingram, *Economic Change in Thailand*, p. 307.

18. Thailand, *Khryangchi phawa sangkhom*, p. 102, table.

19. See Pasuk Phongpaichit, *Rural Women in Thailand: From Peasant Girls to Bangkok Masseuses* (Geneva: International Labour Office, World Employment Programme Research Working Papers, 1980).

20. Chayan Vaddhanaphuti, "Cultural and Ideological Reproduction in Rural Northern Thai Society" (Ph.D. dissertation, Stanford University, 1984), p. 143, table.

21. Ibid., p. 169, table.

22. World Bank, *Thailand: Toward a Development Strategy of Full Participation—A Basic Economic Report*, Report no. 2059-TH (Washington, D.C., 1978).

23. *Far Eastern Economic Review*, October 22, 1982, p. 85, table.

24. See, in this regard, Michael Moerman, "Ban Ping's Temple: The Center of a 'Loosely Structured' Society," in *Anthropological Studies of Theravada Buddhism*, by Manning Nash et al., Cultural Report Series, 13 (New Haven: Yale University Southeast Asia Studies, 1966), pp. 137–174.

25. Bunge, *Thailand: A Country Study*, p. 114. Also see Leslie Eugene Small, "Water Control and Development in the Central Plain of Thailand," *Southeast Asia* 3:2 (1974), pp. 679–697, and Small, *Returns to Public Investments in Water Control in Southeast Asia: A Case Study of the Greater Chao Phraya Project of Thailand*, Cook College Bulletin, 342 (New Brunswick: New Jersey Agricultural Experiment Station, 1975).

26. See Chayan, "Cultural and Ideological Reproduction in Rural Northern Thai Society," p. 143, and Bunge, *Thailand: A Country Study*, p. 133. Also see Ansil Ramsay, "Tenancy and Landlessness in Thailand: How Severe a Problem?" *Asian Survey* 22:11 (1982), pp. 1074–1092.

27. Charles F. Keyes, *Socioeconomic Change in Rainfed Agricultural Villages in Northeastern Thailand* (Seattle: University of Washington, Department of Anthropology, Thailand Project, 1982), p. 66, table. Also see Bunge, *Thailand: A Country Study*, p. 133.

28. See World Bank, *Thailand: Toward a Development Strategy*, p. 39.

29. Keyes, *Socioeconomic Change*, p. 49.

30. Oey Astra Meesook, *Income, Consumption, and Poverty in Thailand, 1962/63 to 1975/76*, World Bank Staff Working Paper, 364 (Washington, D.C.: World Bank, 1979), p. 52.

31. Ruth T. McVey, "Change and Consciousness in a Southern Countryside," in *Strategies and Structures in Thai Society*, ed. Han ten Brummelhuis and Jeremy H. Kemp (Amsterdam: Universiteit van Amsterdam, Antropologisch-Sociologisch Centrum, 1984), p. 119.

32. Bunge, *Thailand: A Country Study*, pp. 167–168; also see Bevars D. Mabry, *The Development of Labor Institutions in Thailand*, Data Paper, 112 (Ithaca, N.Y.: Cornell University Southeast Asia Program, 1979); Arnold Wehmhorner, "Trade Unionism in Thailand," *Journal of Contemporary Asia* 13:4 (1983), pp. 485–491; and *Far Eastern Economic Review* (August 29, 1985), p. 24.

33. See Akin Rabibhadana, "Rise and Fall of a Bangkok Slum," in *The Studies of Social Science* (Bangkok: Social Science Association of Thailand, 1978), pp. 40–91, and Susan Morell and David Morell, *Six Slums in Bangkok: Problems of Life and Options for Action*, 2 vols. (Bangkok: United Nations Children Fund, 1972).

34. Thailand, *Khryangchi phawa sangkhom*, p. 117, table.

35. See Richard Allan O'Connor, "Urbanism and Religion: Community, Hierarchy, and Sanctity in Urban Thai Buddhist Temples" (Ph.D. thesis, Cornell University, 1978).

36. Theodore D. Fuller, Peerasit Kamnuansilpa, Paul Lightfoot, and Sawaeng Rathanamongkolmas, *Migration and Development in Modern Thailand* (Bangkok: Social Science Association of Thailand, 1983).

37. Paul Lightfoot and Theodore Fuller, "Circular Migration in Northeastern Thailand," in *Strategies and Structures in Thai Society*, ed. Han ten Brummelhuis and Jeremy H. Kemp, p. 86.

8
Cultural Ferment in a Changing World

The cultural life of the vast majority of the peoples of Thailand traditionally centered on the *wat*, the Buddhist temple-monastery. Whether they were villagers or townspeople, commoners or nobles or princes, the Buddhist *dhamma* transmitted by the monks provided the vast majority of the inhabitants of premodern Siam with the ultimate basis for making sense of the world. The centrality of the sangha—whose members could come from commoner or elite ranks—as arbiters of culture precluded the emergence of a significant gulf between popular culture and elite culture, such as existed in traditional China and Vietnam. Despite differences between popular and elite cultures, both members of the elite and ordinary villagers shared a common epistemology rooted in the tradition of Theravada Buddhism.

TRADITIONAL BUDDHIST CULTURE

Before being converted to Buddhism through contact with the Buddhist Mon, the Tai-speaking people who were the ancestors of most of the modern peoples of Thailand had been animists. Like the tribal peoples who live on the peripheries of Thailand today, these early Tai had propitiated a variety of spirits, known as *phi* by Tai-speaking peoples. They also believed that each person was animated by a vital essence (*khwan*). Ritual specialists, known as *mǫ* (and sometimes by other names), ensured that rites propitiating the spirits and securing the vital essence were properly performed. When the Tai became Buddhists, they did not abandon their beliefs in spirits or in the vital essence; rather, such beliefs were subsumed within a Buddhist cosmological scheme. In Buddhist terms, spirits, like humans and deities, are regarded as subject to the inexorable law of *kamma*. The *khwan* was reinterpreted as an essence transformed at death into the *winyan* (from the Pali

178

viññana, or "consciousness"), which in Buddhist thought links one life with another. Although most of the Tai-speaking peoples, like the Mon, Khmer, and Khmer-related peoples also living in the country, came to accept the reinterpretation of animistic beliefs within a Buddhist cosmological framework, many, particularly those living in villages, continued to accord considerable ritual attention to the *phi* and *khwan.*

Animistic beliefs were less significant among the elite, especially at the Siamese court, than they were among villagers. The Siamese elite gave greater attention, however, to practices associated with the cult of Hindu deities (especially Brahma, Siva, and Visnu), cults borrowed from the Hinduized Khmer court of Angkor. At the court, a small coterie of Brahmins receiving royal patronage performed rites for which the texts were in Sanskrit (even if the Sanskrit was imperfectly understood). "Folk Brahmanism," as A. Thomas Kirsch, a student of Thai religion, has termed it,[1] was not unknown among villagers, but the distinctive cult activity found in the courts was absent at this level. The observance of Brahmanical rituals at the court did not indicate, however, that the elite followed a religious tradition different from that of villagers. Like villagers, the elite also accepted the fundamental Buddhist dogma of *kamma.*

Neither elite nor villagers obtained their understanding of *kamma* through direct study of the *Tripitaka* or "three baskets" of the *dhamma,* the Buddhist scriptures. The *Tripitaka* has never filled for Buddhists the same role the Koran does for Muslims or the Bible (at least since the Reformation) has for Christians. Most Thai Buddhists today, as in the past, have gained their understanding of the *dhamma* less from scriptural texts than from ritual presentations, dramatizations, or, more rarely, reading vernacular texts based on Buddhist commentaries and mythical literature.

Three texts—or, more properly, several versions of three texts—define for most Thai Buddhists today, as in traditional Siam, the basic parameters of a Theravadin view of the world. The *Trai Phum Phra Ruang* [The Three Worlds according to Phra Ruang], a treatise in which a systematic cosmology is set forth, is believed to have been composed in Thai in the mid-fourteenth century by a man who would later become king of Sukhothai.[2] Versions of this cosmology are standard items in almost every monastic library throughout the area. Monks still draw on this text for many of the sermons they deliver to their congregations. Stories from the *Trai Phum* have also been the source for many of the mural paintings found in Thai temples.

The *Trai Phum* discusses how inherent differences among humans in beauty, health, and status and differences between humans, spirits, demons, and deities are the consequences of particular morally significant actions, that is, consequences of *kamma*. A long section of the text concentrates specifically on the role of kings. It provides both a justification for rule by monarchs, who are seen as embodying an extraordinary amount of merit with which a very few are born into this world, and a guide as to how kings should conduct a morally tempered rule. For most people in traditional Siam, the *Trai Phum* was the source of their understanding of a world organized as a moral hierarchy based on the law of *kamma*.

The second major text from which the Siamese draw their Buddhist understanding of the world relates the story of a monk known to the Thai as Phra Malai.[3] *Phra Malai* appears to have first been composed in northern Thailand in the fifteenth century and is based on Sinhalese and perhaps ultimately Indian sources. In vernacular translations it became a popular sermon not only among Tai-speaking peoples but also among most Buddhists in mainland Southeast Asia. Like the *Trai Phum*, *Phra Malai* has also been a source for temple mural painting as well as a source for sermons.

The monk, Malai, visits both hell and heaven and relates his observations to the people still on earth. His description of hell portrays in graphic detail how particular punishments are meted out to those who have committed specific immoral actions (adultery, theft, murder, and so on). To escape these punishments, Malai admonishes those still living in the world to avoid acts that involve such consequences. On his visit to heaven, Malai sees people enjoying the consequences of positive *kamma*. Although both the *Trai Phum* and *Phra Malai* are concerned primarily with making the doctrine of *kamma* understandable to ordinary people, the former underscores the consequences in this world of past actions while the latter emphasizes the importance of acting in morally appropriate ways in this life in order to ensure a good rebirth in the next one. *Phra Malai* adds another dimension to Buddhist belief. In heaven, Malai meets with Ariya Maitreya (called Phra Si An in Thai), the future Buddha. Malai admonishes those people who seek to be reborn at the time of the coming of Maitreya, and thus to ensure that they will achieve *nibbana*, to listen to the sermon of the "Great Life." This sermon is unquestionably the most important of the three traditional texts.

The "Great Life"—*Maha Chat*—story is a version of the last of the "birth stories" (*jataka*) of the Buddha.[4] *Jataka* stories are thought by many scholars originally to have been folk tales that the Buddha or his disciples adapted to make doctrinal points easier to grasp. Subsequently, they came to be identified as stories of earlier incarnations of the Buddha. According to ancient tradition, 547 *jataka* constitute the stories of his previous lives as told by the Buddha. Although only brief allusions to most of these tales exist in the canon, the full tales have long been accorded a quasi-canonical status.

The last ten *jataka*, the *dasa-jataka*, of the 547 have a special place in popular Buddhist thought. Each of these is said to show how the Buddha-to-be acquired one of the ten transcendent virtues that were essential preconditions of his becoming the Buddha. And of the *dasa-jataka*, the last, the *Vessantara-jataka*, the story of how the Buddha-to-be as Prince Vessantara (Thai, Wetsandǫn) acquired the virtue of "generosity," has attained by far the greatest popularity among all Theravada Buddhists, including those in Thailand.

Although the story of Prince Vessantara, *Maha Chat*, is alluded to in Thai records from the fourteenth century, the earliest recension in Thai known of the work is the *Maha Chat Kham Luang* (literally, "the royal poem of the Great Life"), which was written in the fifteenth century.[5] The "Great Life" is known widely throughout Thailand to this day. It is frequently presented to the populace in the form of a sermon, typically in conjunction with a major festival; the story is also dramatized in folk opera and in theater; and scenes from it appear in art. In recent years, the *Vessantara-jataka* has been used as the source of themes in modern fiction and has even been presented in a film version. There is probably no Buddhist in Thailand beyond the age of ten or so who could not give at least a synopsis of the story, and many people especially in villages, can quote passages in the same way English speakers can quote parts of the Bible or selections from Shakespeare.

For Thai, the Wetsandǫn/Vessantara story provides moral models for the most important social relationships: those of father and child, husband and wife, mother and child, ruler and subject, world-renouncers and people who remain in the world. Above all, it validates the supreme religious significance of the sacrifice of possessions through acts of generosity. Ordinary people emulate Prince Wetsandǫn, not by giving their goods to anyone who asks for them, but by offering alms to those most worthy of receiving them, the members of the sangha.

The *Vessantara-jataka* or "Great Life" story, the *Phra Malai*, and the *Trai Phum* constituted what might be termed the "key" texts of both popular and elite traditions of traditional Siam. The large number of other sermons, ritual texts, legends, and folkloric texts familiar to villagers and the poetry and histories of the courts and certain monasteries can be said to have been understood in light of the Buddhist world view projected in these key texts.

THE ROOTS OF CULTURAL CHANGE

In the nineteenth century, the Buddhist worldview shared by most of the people of premodern Siam began to be challenged by new interpretations of the world when some members of the Siamese court and some intellectuals were exposed for the first time to Western thought.[6] The process of secularization was not solely a function of Western influences, for it also had roots in the cultural revival initiated in the first reigns of the Chakri dynasty. Anticipation of a new, less religious worldview is evident, for example, in the poetry of Sunthon Phu (1786–1855), the gifted and prolific commoner author who gained the patronage of King Rama II. In some of his most famous works, Sunthon Phu explored an emotional world that is anchored more in actual experience than in Buddhist assumptions about experience.

Such innovations notwithstanding, neither Sunthon Phu nor other early-nineteenth-century Siamese writers and thinkers undertook any serious critical reflection on the religious tradition. Such reflection was first initiated from the 1830s on by Mongkut, especially during his period in the monkhood before he ascended the throne, and by a number of Mongkut's close associates both within and outside the sangha. Mongkut came to be directly influenced by Western thought, especially by those aspects of Western thought transmitted by missionaries who were then going to work in Siam in increasing numbers. Although Mongkut never showed any inclination toward converting to Christianity, he did adopt certain aspects of the Protestant stance toward religion, in particular coming to hold that religious belief should be a matter of conviction rather than simply of received tradition. He was disdainful of the mixture of folk culture and religion in traditional Thai Buddhism and, as king, issued an acerbic denunciation of the linking of the preaching of the *Maha Chat* sermon with secular festivals.[7] Mongkut encouraged monks to look beyond the texts from which most Thai acquired their understanding of the *dhamma* to the sources of the *dhamma*. In particular, he stressed the study of the scriptures and of the major commentaries. The reform Buddhism initiated by Mongkut and later institutionalized in the Thammayut order with Mongkut's son, Prince Vajirañana, at its head continued to regard the doctrine of *kamma* as central but, in contrast to traditional Thai Buddhism, emphasized the significance of self-conscious moral action as opposed to customary collective merit-making activities.

Mongkut not only encouraged a critical stance toward traditional religion but also evinced a strong interest in Western science. Although his own knowledge of science remained that of an informed layman, his interest led other Thai to begin to think about the world in naturalistic as well as cosmological terms. The new interest in science was associated with a gradual secularization of society from the middle of the nineteenth century on.[8] This process was stimulated yet further during the later part of the century as Bangkok began to undergo rapid social and economic change. Traditional ideas no longer made sense in what had become a pluralistic society linked to an international economy.

The development of both reform Buddhist and secular thought in late-nineteenth-century Siam was spurred by the introduction of printing for the communication of ideas. Written works in traditional Siam had been produced by the laborious process of inscribing texts with a stylus on specially prepared palm leaves or by writing them by hand on folded manuscripts made of paper, which itself had taken much labor to produce. When missionaries first began to work in Siam in the early part of the nineteenth century, they determined to make the Christian message available through print. The first missionary press using Thai characters was apparently made in Burma around 1810, and from 1836 on, works printed in Thai were produced within Siam. Initially, very few works were printed; they consisted mainly of Christian tracts and a few government documents. By the beginning of the reign of King Chulalongkorn in 1868, however, the potential of the printed word had begun to be realized, and a number of presses had been established. Although the government had its own press, most of these new presses were privately owned. "Print capitalism," to use Benedict Anderson's term,[9] was to have far-reaching consequences for Thai culture.

Prior to the 1870s, English was the primary language of print, but the pattern had been reversed by the end of the nineteenth century when the majority of printed works were in Thai. The fact that Siam was never colonized meant that, unlike neighboring countries in Southeast Asia, no Western language ever became the official language of the country. The publication of materials in Thai contributed markedly to the establishment of Thai as the national language of the country. Thai was not the only language, however, in which works were printed in Bangkok.

As large numbers of Chinese immigrants poured into Thailand in the latter part of the nineteenth century, a number of presses also began to turn out works—initially mainly periodicals but later novels and political tracts—in Chinese. Although Chinese and English works continue to be published in Bangkok to this day, the literary culture of most of the reading populace of Thailand since the late nineteenth century has been shaped by works printed in Thai. Even Western and Chinese works read by the people of the country have, for the most part, been read in Thai translation.

The new medium of print was used and continues to be used for traditional as well as modern works. Today, when monks read a traditional sermon or a village dramatic troupe performs a traditional play or folk opera, printed versions of traditional texts are more likely to be used than are handwritten texts. Indeed, printed works have replaced handwritten texts to such an extent that scholars today are trying to catalog, preserve, and reproduce the old works found in monastic libraries before such works disappear entirely.[10]

Although print has been used for traditional materials, its primary significance has been in the production of modern works. The literary culture that began to emerge at the end of the nineteenth century had two distinct strands. One was associated with the reform Buddhism initiated by Mongkut. The other was overtly secular and was closely associated with the transformation of urban elite society that took place in the wake of the political and economic changes that followed the signing of the Bowring Treaty in 1855. These two strands continue to exist in tension with each other as well as with persisting themes of the traditional culture.

MASS EDUCATION AND THE EMERGENCE OF A NEW LITERATI

Premodern Siam had a high degree of literacy promoted in monastic schools designed to give students access to texts considered to contain the teachings of the Buddha.[11] Although most monastic schools emphasized the importance of the same key Buddhist texts, they were not controlled by any centralized authority. Moreover, the knowledge acquired by the students who passed through such schools was used almost exclusively within local communities. Local monks preached and recited from texts found in local monastic libraries, while some laymen who had passed through monastic schools became local specialists in herbal treatments, spirit exorcism, soul-calling, and magic (especially love magic) or gained local reputations for their knowledge of legends and folklore. In other words, the traditional monastic schools provided popular as well as religious education.

State schools, which from the 1930s on were separated from monastic schools and staffed by lay teachers, have offered a very different type of education to that of the *wats* as the primary purpose of the former has been to inculcate a sense of citizenship.[12] Students throughout the country are instructed in the same version of the national language, or in what can be termed "standard Thai," no matter what dialect or language they speak at home. They learn the same version of Thai history, one that emphasizes the centrality of the Siamese monarchy and plays down the relatively recent incorporation of outlying areas of the country into the Siamese state. Throughout the country, children learn to sing the same songs and to play the same games and sports. The role of the school as a national institution is accentuated by the morning ritual of raising the national flag and singing the national anthem and by the periodic rituals associated with national holidays at which connection is made between the monarch (represented by a picture of the king), the nation (represented by the flag), and the religion (represented by a statue of the Buddha).

Literacy acquired during primary schooling is designed to provide students, not with access to the *dhamma*, but with the ability to read official documents, written materials such as agricultural manuals, and more general secular literature. The rudiments of scientific knowledge that students in primary schools are exposed to is supposed to enable them to acquire some understanding of the principles and laws underlying natural processes, especially those connected with agriculture.

Teachers (*khru*) serve as examples to students of educated people whose claim to knowledge is based on secular rather than religious education.[13] Their role is thus very different from that of the monk in the traditional educational system. The state teachers' knowledge is validated, not by their clear demonstration of the study of religious texts, but by credentials conferred by the state. Teachers, for village students, are more than just dispensers of knowledge; they are also state officials and, as such, represent other officials that the students will have contact with when they leave school. The fact that an increasing number of primary teachers are women also makes their role a new and different one in Thai society—one that again contrasts with that of the monk and, at the same time, offers a new possibility for emulation by Thai village girls.

With the rapid expansion of government programs and the changes in the economy since the mid-1950s, an increasing proportion of the populace has come to see the value of school education. Although few village children continue their formal education beyond the compulsory course of study, even the minimal compulsory education requirements have produced significant changes in the cultural orientation of people throughout Thailand.

In most Thai rural communities, the traditional culture associated with *wat*s continues to coexist with state-sponsored secular education and continues to be communicated through rituals, sermons, folk opera, and theater. In Bangkok and other cities, however, the traditional culture has been almost totally overshadowed by the pervasive secular culture, which is associated with a much higher average level of formal education than in the villages; a much higher rate of reading newspapers, periodicals, books, and other printed matter; a much greater degree of film and television viewing; a more intense involvement in a consumer economy; and a marked decline of participation in *wat*-centered activities. Thus, while schools have contributed to the overall secularization of Thai

society, rural society continues to be influenced by traditional culture
to a much greater extent than does urban society.

DEVELOPMENT OF A MODERN THAI LITERARY CULTURE

The Origins of Modern Thai Literature

Although the reading public in Siam at the end of the nineteenth
century was quite small and limited mainly to Bangkok, its character
and the nature of what it read were beginning to undergo significant
changes. Monks still composed the majority of the literate public, and
many of the first works printed were religious texts. Such texts differed,
however, from those handwritten works that were so significant in
traditional culture. In 1893, as part of an effort to make the scriptures,
rather than derivative works, the source of *dhamma*, King Chulalongkorn
had printed at government expense the whole of the *Tripitaka* in Pali
as transcribed in Thai orthography. Prince Vajirañana, perhaps the most
prolific of the early modern writers in Thai, produced a very large
number of exegetical works in which he sought to rid Buddhist practice
of superstitious accretions and to return it to its scriptural basis. A
number of the Prince's writings became the texts for a new religious
curriculum taught in monastic schools.

If monks still composed the most significant sector of the urban
reading public in the latter part of the nineteenth century, by the 1920s,
the literary culture of Siam had become decidedly secular. King Vajiravudh, who succeeded to the throne in 1910, was a major influence
in introducing new types of literature into the country. While a student
in England, he had been very taken by English literature, especially
plays and mystery stories. He translated not only a number of Shakespeare's plays into Thai but also several Sherlock Holmes stories. He
also wrote and produced a number of plays of his own. While Vajiravudh
and other members of the royal family and nobility who had studied
abroad introduced Western forms into Siamese literature, a number of
commoners of Chinese descent—many of whom were journalists—
introduced Chinese forms through their translations of Chinese stories
and novels. Both Western and Chinese influences were often linked to
traditional Thai forms—especially tales associated with *jataka* stories,
narrative poetry, and chronicles—to create a new Thai literature.

Thai fiction began in the form of short stories, and the first novels
in Thai appeared in the late 1920s. The first novel to achieve popular
acclaim, *Lakhǫn haeng Chiwit*, appeared in 1929. Its author, Prince Akat
Damkoeng called it "The Circus of Life" when speaking of it in English.

Prince Akat's promise was not to be realized, however, as he died at the early age of twenty-seven.

After Prince Akat's death, two other novelists and a third writer of short stories were to dominate Thai literary life during the 1930s and 1940s. Si Burapha, the pseudonym of Kulap Saipradit,[14] published a novel the year before "The Circus of Life" appeared, but *Luk Phuchai* [Son], did not have the impact of "The Circus of Life" and is not considered today to be one of Si Burapha's best works. His *Songkhram Chiwit* [War of life], published in 1932, is usually taken to be the best of his seven pre–World War II novels. Unlike Prince Akat, Si Burapha came from a commoner family whose rise in society had been made possible by the growth of the bureaucracy and the expansion of educational opportunities. It is not surprising, therefore, that his first story has as its main character a person who is highly upwardly mobile. Its optimistic tone gives way in his subsequent work to a more critical view of Thai society.

Dokmai Sot, the pseudonym of Buppha (Kunchara) Nimmanhemin, was without question the preeminent novelist of the pre-World War II period. Between 1929 when her first novel, *Sattru khọng Cao Lọn*, called *Her Enemy* in English, appeared and 1940, she wrote eleven novels as well as numerous short stories. Like Prince Akat, she was concerned with the moral choices facing people living in a world in which Western and traditional Thai values were in conflict. The ethical character of her work was noted by another woman writer, Nilawan Pintong, who commented on Dokmai Sot's novel *Phu Di* [The Good person] published in 1937: "'Dokmai Sot' is none but our preacher outside a pulpit. . . . All Dokmai Sot's novels often contain religious discourses in disguise. . . . The people in these (modern) Jataka are . . . our contemporaries."[15] Her fundamental concern was with changing relationships between the sexes. Dokmai Sot also provides her readers with cautionary tales on what can happen if Thai adopt Western patterns simply because they are Western without reflecting on their implications. In the short story "Fai" [Fire], she tells of three students, just about to take their entrance examinations for university, who are tempted by the hedonism of a Western-style dance hall where men drink whiskey and watch performances by scantily dressed women. One of the three succumbs to the temptations of the pleasure palace, but the other two are led by an older relative to see this imitation of the worst of Western culture as "an obstacle to the progress of our culture."[16]

The moral tone of Dokmai Sot contrasts with the stance taken by Malai Chuphinit, the most prolific story writer in Thailand both before and after World War II. Many of the characters in Malai's short stories find a place in the world, not by reaffirming their commitment to traditional values, but by their "modern" toughness. Malai's short stories were the vanguard of a new popular fiction in which the characters, while facing situations of conflict, do not view these situations as moral dilemmas.

Popular Fiction in the Post–World War II Period

Popular romantic and "tough guy" fiction has flourished since the 1950s. During the late 1950s and early 1960s, when the government cracked down on "leftist" writers and intellectuals, such fiction dominated the literary life of Thailand. Many of the romances written during this period turn on the same plot line in which a virtuous woman eventually triumphs over an immoral one to win the love of a strong man. The love triangle is also the most common theme in Thai films. For both romantic novels and romantic films, the main audience consists of middle-class women. Although such stories play on tried and true themes, they reflect an image of women that contrasts with the dominant one found in traditional Thai culture. In traditional literature, such as in the *Vessantara-jataka*, a woman's place in the world is defined primarily by her relations with her children. In modern popular romantic fiction and films, children (at least small children) rarely are significant characters, and a woman's relationship with a lover or a husband is stressed more strongly. Men are frequently portrayed in macho roles in which they swagger, dominate others, and surround themselves with modern material possessions. This image also contrasts sharply with the dominant ideal of a man as one who acts in accordance with Buddhist values by tempering his passions.

Some recent popular novelists have been able to transcend the usual formulas in creating more complex fictional worlds. One of the most successful of these is Kukrit Pramoj, a well-known journalist and politician who served as prime minister of Thailand in 1975 and 1976. Kukrit's *Si Phaen Din* [Four reigns], which first appeared in 1953, has been reprinted many times, and has also been translated into English,[17] is the history of a noble family during a period (1890s–1946) of marked social change. The story of Ploi, from her girlhood at the court of King Chulalongkorn, through marriage and her relations with her children, to her old age at the end of World War II, can be seen in some ways as a Thai *Forsyte Saga*. Most of Kukrit's other novels do not approach the quality of *Four Reigns*. Only *Phai Daeng* [Red bamboo], a novel first serialized in Kukrit's newspaper *Siam Rath* in 1954 and subsequently translated into English,[18] has been as well received by the reading public. *Red Bamboo*, a novel modeled on Giovanni Guareschi's *Don Camillo*, tells of the confrontation between the Buddhist tradition of rural society and communist ideology as personified by two friends, one a Buddhist abbot and the other an ordinary villager. The clear anticommunist message of the novel reflects the growing concern in Thailand in the mid-1950s about the perceived communist threat. Because of this theme, the United States Information Service sponsored the novel's translation into English and seventeen other languages as well.[19] Despite its political message, *Red Bamboo* represents one of the first significant efforts, albeit only a partially successful one, to construct a fictional world based on rural Thai society.

The fictional chronicle of a family in a changing world in Thailand, such as Kukrit provided in *Four Reigns,* has a counterpart in *Cotmai cak Myang Thai* [Letters from Thailand] by Botan (pseud. for Supha Lysiri). Instead of depicting the life of an upper-class Thai, Botan follows that of a Chinese migrant, Suang U, from his arrival in Thailand at the age of nineteen in 1945 to 1967. During this period, Suang U marries, prospers as a merchant, has a family, sees his children enter a very different world from the one he had come from, experiences the death of his wife, and as the novel ends, is on the verge of marrying his very up-to-date sister-in-law. The novel has continued to enjoy popularity since it was published in 1969, not because it was awarded the SEATO Prize for International Literature, but because it provides a detailed description of life in the Chinese quarter of Bangkok, presumably based on the actual experience of the author, and offers a Chinese perspective on Thai society. The novel was translated into English in 1977.[20]

The New Literature of Social Consciousness

Although *Letters from Thailand* is mildly critical of a political system in which a Chinese merchant must bribe officials if he is to prosper, it adopts a fundamentally positive attitude toward a nation in which a Chinese from a peasant background could rise to be a wealthy merchant. Other authors in the 1950s and 1960s were far more outspoken about the faults of the new social order that had emerged in Thailand.

Si Burapha, who had already become somewhat critical of society as early as the late 1930s, began to produce stories from 1949 on in which he "condemned the capitalist bourgeoisie and the aristocracy for taking advantage of the poor."[21] A later generation of radical writers was to claim Si Burapha as the forerunner of socialist realism in Thai fiction. To a certain extent this claim is true, but his concern with social injustice is rooted as much in Buddhist ethical ideas as in secular socialism.

Several other fiction writers in the early 1950s also adopted a critical stance toward the increasing social differentiation in Thai society. In *Pisat* [Evil spirit] published in 1953, Seni Saowaphong (pseud. for Sakchai Bamrungphong) makes his main character, a villager who rises in society, the evil spirit who threatens the established order. Many of the short stories of Itsara Amantakun "have as characters politicians and businessmen who exploit others with their wealth and authority, are arrogant, conceited, selfish and indulge in women and alcohol."[22] Although not a novelist, Jit Poumisak's critique of literature, *Sinlapa phya chiwit sinlapa phya prachachon* [Art for life, art for the people] later became the ideal a new generation of socially conscious writers sought to uphold.

After Sarit's coup in 1957, Jit, Itsara, and Si Burapha, along with other writers, were arrested and jailed for a number of years. Si Burapha, the first of the three released, left the country in 1958 and remained in exile in China until his death in 1974. After his release in 1964, Jit joined the communist insurrection and was killed under somewhat mysterious circumstances in 1966. Itsara spent five years in jail before he was released. The imprisonment of these and other writers strongly discouraged others from emulating their literary themes for a number of years. Not until the mid-1960s, after the death of Sarit, did socially conscious literature reemerge.

By the mid-1960s, the growing urban populace was becoming increasingly aware of its lack of access to political power, of the growing class differentiation in Thai society, of the increasing disparity between rural and urban worlds, and of the radically distorting effects U.S. influence was having on Thai life. The journal *Sangkhomsat Parithat* [Social science review], which first appeared in 1962, provided a vehicle for students, teachers, and others to express their concerns about changes in Thai society. A number of its contributers later became significant writers. In the late 1960s, several socially conscious writers developed a literary movement, called "new wave" (*khlyn luk mai*),[23] which anticipated the student uprising of the early 1970s. After the 1973 Revolution, members of the somewhat more radicalized element of the new wave took their inspiration from Jit Poumisak and designated themselves the "literature for life's sake" (*wannakam phya chiwit*) movement. They strongly criticized the romantic literature of the 1950s and 1960s and referred to much of it as "polluted literature" (*wannakam namnao*). Following the October 1976 coup, many writers who had emerged in the 1960s and 1970s either fled into the jungle to join the Communist party, were jailed, or fell silent. Wimon Ciamcaroen, whose work was attacked as exemplifying the qualities of "polluted literature," became the head of a censorship committee formed by the Thanin government.[24] By the early 1980s, the situation had once again been reversed, and most of the writers of the "new wave" and many of those associated with the "literature for life's sake" movement were again writing and publishing, although the tone of their writings had for the most part become less strident.

A number of the authors writing since the late 1960s have seen Thai society as being transformed into precisely what Dokmai Sot had warned against. In contemporary fiction, people who frequent nightclubs, massage parlors, and sex shows constitute a pervasive demimonde and have little hope of ever escaping from this world.

Contemporary Thai fiction also contains much explicit criticism of the misuse of power and the effects of the increasing capitalist domination of the economy. Characters in novels are often merely embodiments of particular social qualities rather than actors with complex personalities. In the popular novel *Khru Ban Nok*, which was later made into a film and translated into English under the title of *The Teachers of Mad Dog Swamp*, Khammaan Khonkhai successfully captures the flavor of the lives of rural school teachers, but in the end, even his characters become stereotyped exploiters, victims, and helpless onlookers.[25]

The short stories of the woman who writes under the pseudonym of Sri Daorueng (real name, Wanna Thappananoen) are much more subtle and more powerful in their literary effect. Sri Daorueng, as Anderson has said, is "as a writer peculiarly alone"[26] both because of her limited education (four years of primary schooling) and because of her firsthand experience both of village life and of urban factory work.

The work of Sri Daorueng approaches that of Khamsing Srinawk (pseudonym, Lao Khamhawm) whom many regard as Thailand's preeminent contemporary writer of short stories.[27] Khamsing, who was born in 1930, began writing in the 1950s, and his collection of short stories *Fa bo kan* [Heaven has no barriers] was first published in 1958. The collection was not looked on favorably by the Sarit government, and Khamsing fell silent until the late 1960s and 1970s. His second collection of stories, under the title of *Khamphaeng* [The Wall], appeared in 1975. After the October 6, 1976, coup Khamsing fled the country and eventually took up exile in Sweden for four years before returning to Thailand.

Khamsing writes mainly from the perspective of the rural villager, and his early stories paved the way for other writers "to bring the reality of peasant life to the attention of the urban society."[28] In his stories, villagers try to make a go of life in a world in which the environment is harsh and political and economic constraints are imposed from the outside. Even when Khamsing makes explicit his view of how social injustice has created difficulties and suffering for rural people, he never manipulates his characters simply to make a point.

A number of other writers also seek, like Khamsing, to create a fully rounded rural world for a basically urban reading public. One popular work is *Luk Isan* [Child of the Northeast] by Khamphun Bunthawi.

Like Khamsing, Khamphun is a native of the northeastern region. *Luk Isan*, which was first published in 1976 and won a prize as the best novel of that year, is actually less a novel than an autobiographical account of a rural childhood in the late 1920s. What comes through most strongly is the good humor and cooperativeness with which villagers confront a life of poverty in which the land may not yield enough to eat. In a stylistic innovation, Khamphun has most of his characters speak in Lao, the language of the people of northeastern Thailand. In the film version, the exclusive use of Lao with Thai subtitles in a Thai film caused a furor in official circles. Despite the criticism, the popularity of the film and the novel is indicative of some acceptance of the use of regional languages, despite the state's long-standing effort to make standard Thai the sole medium of national culture.

Although the works of Khamphun, Khamsing, and others are about rural society, they are written for urban dwellers who often have little direct experience of life in rural Thailand where the vast majority of the country's people still live. These writers seek to break down "the wall," to use Khamsing's metaphor, between the urban and rural worlds. Although their writings may help to do so for a literate public, rural people gain access to the world of the city through the popular culture communicated by the radio, television, films, and the press.

MASS MEDIA AND POPULAR CULTURE[29]

The influence of mass media was limited almost exclusively to Bangkok until after World War II. Even with the expansion since the early 1950s of the number of newspaper readers, radio listeners, moviegoers, and television viewers living up-country in small towns or villages, the presumed audience for the mass media continues to be an urban, essentially Bangkok-based one. The state directly controls radio and television broadcasting while film-making and newspaper and periodical publishing are in the hands of private owners. These differences in ownership are reflected in the ways that the film industry and especially the press on the one hand and radio and television broadcasters on the other attend to popular taste.

The Press in Thailand

The press is the oldest of the mass media in Thailand. Newspapers and periodicals first began to be published there in the mid-nineteenth century. Although few publications prior to World War II lasted for any period of time, the number of publications and the size of readership grew steadily, if rather slowly. Since World War II, press readership has grown dramatically. By 1972, there were 12 daily newspapers in Thai,

11 in Chinese, and 4 in English (all published in Bangkok); 58 weekly magazines; 20 fortnightlies; 140 monthlies; 37 quarterlies; 8 biannuals and 55 other publications in Thai, 13 in Chinese, and 11 in English.[30] By 1984, the number of daily newspapers appearing in Thai had jumped to 22, but the number of Chinese ones had dropped to 8, and there were only 3 in English.[31]

It is difficult to get any sense of how widely newspapers are read in Thailand today. In 1984, the most widely read paper, *Thai Rath*, was said to have had a circulation of 600,000–700,000, but its readership was estimated to be as much as ten times as great. Most newspaper subscribers pass their copies on to others, and there are multiple readers in coffee shops, restaurants, barbershops, hairdressing salons, and other such popular establishments. The government has recently promoted newspaper reading in the villages by creating reading centers in rural communities that make available a number of publications, usually selected by teachers. Although newspaper reading has increased among rural peoples, probably fewer than 10 percent of adults in rural communities read a daily paper, as against at least 80 percent in Bangkok. Nevertheless, major news stories published in papers are spread by word of mouth (sometimes with elaborations) in rural areas.

Newspapers and other periodicals in Thailand today enjoy a freedom that is unequaled in the rest of Southeast Asia, though the private press in Thailand has been subject to censorship from time to time. It was especially strict during World War II, during the period of Sarit's rule, and in the immediate aftermath of the October 6, 1976, coup. Even during these periods, however, the press was allowed to publish many nonpolitical stories that would have not been allowed in the newspapers of other countries. But even during periods of lax censorship, Thai newspapers have been very careful to present the royal family in a positive way and to allow almost no criticism of the monarchy. Only a very few periodicals, with a limited readership, have ever tested the limits of Thailand's lèse majesté laws. Although the monarchy has been relatively immune from criticism, other people in public life have, however, sometimes been depicted in the press in highly unfavorable ways. Moreover, there are no strong libel laws to protect the interests of those who feel they have been unfairly dealt with.

The most popular Thai newspapers print sensational stories of murders, robberies, sex crimes, accidents, and purported supernatural intervention in the success of a lottery winner, as well as reports of the national lottery and accounts of sporting events, especially Thai boxing. Intermingled with this yellow journalism are relatively brief reports of newsworthy events in Thailand, summaries of foreign news, film reviews, and columns by a few writers. Some papers also carry

serialized stories. Beginning in the early 1970s, articles based on in-
vestigative reporting also began to appear in some papers, including a
few even in *Thai Rath* and its imitators. Reporters who have inquired
deeply into cases of official corruption; collusion between businessmen
and government officials, as in the granting of licenses for timber cutting,
mining, trucking, and so on; or the flaunting of the law by industries,
as in the use of child labor, have, however, often exposed themselves
to personal danger. In the five-year period between 1979 and 1984,
forty-seven journalists were killed—most apparently as a direct consequence of the stories they had published or were planning to publish.
Very few perpetrators of these murders have been brought to justice,
and in not a few cases, the police have been directly implicated in the
murders.[32] In such an intimidating environment, official censorship is
not necessary to discourage papers from publishing stories sharply
critical of injustices within the society.

Newspapers and periodicals with a restricted urban readership
provide a more critical reflection on Thai society. The success of the
newspaper *Matichon* [Public opinion] suggests that more responsible and
critical journalism can be financially viable in contemporary Thailand.
In 1984, the circulation of *Matichon* stood at about 55,000 and included
not only people from Bangkok but also a growing number of teachers
and civil servants living up-country as well.[33] Although *Matichon* carries
significantly more foreign news than do the most popular Thai newspapers, the well-educated sector of Thai society is likely to turn to one
of the English-language newspapers published in Thailand, and especially
to the *Bangkok Post* or its chief competitor, the *Nation Review*, for such
news as well as for other versions of local news. It is estimated that
about three-quarters of the people who read English-language newspapers
in Thailand are native speakers of Thai.[34]

Although the readership of English-language newspapers has grown,
indicating a growth in the number of Thai who read English with ease,
the readership of Chinese-language newspapers has markedly declined
in recent years. The eight Chinese papers, with a combined readership
in 1984 of about 70,000,[35] concern themselves primarily with news about
the local Chinese community and events in China, Taiwan, Hong Kong,
and Singapore. The Chinese papers, by ignoring stories about Thai
society, tacitly recognize that most Chinese who are interested in such
stories will read them in Thai language papers.

Radio, Television, and Film

Although the press in Thailand is relatively free to present news
without reference to governmental dictates, radio and television stations
broadcast only news programs that have been cleared by government

representatives. The same news programs are broadcast in Thai at exactly the same time on all 269 radio stations throughout the country. Television channels provide somewhat different versions of the news, but there is little use of on-the-spot reporting or interviews, and commentaries are not provided. Government control of radio and television broadcasting makes it difficult for listeners to gain a nongovernmental view of political events in the country. During the height of the 1973 crisis, for example, those living up-country had to depend mainly on word-of-mouth reports (often based on rumors) about what was happening in Bangkok. Most were little prepared when the king came on the air to announce the resignation and departure from the country of the three leading members of the government. During the 1976 crisis, military-run radio and television stations kept up a steady barrage of patriotic music, inflammatory rhetoric directed against the student movement, and ad hominem attacks on particular individuals, such as Dr. Puey Ungphakorn, then the rector of Thammasat University. These stations urged right-wing groups to attack those who were deemed threats to "the monarchy, religion, and nation."

Aside from news, radio programming is rather more oriented toward local audiences than television is. During the 1950s, people throughout the country began to acquire radios, and by the 1980s, even the most remote village had at least one or two receivers while in many villages almost every household had a set of its own. Although local radio stations are owned by the government and often operated by units of the military, they are encouraged to broadcast some programs in local languages. In areas where little Thai is spoken, as in the Malay-speaking south or in the tribal areas of the north, summaries of the news (as determined by government agencies) may be presented in other languages. For the most part, however, local-language broadcasting has been primarily associated with programs of traditional music or of modern versions of such music. In northern Thailand one can hear *kham sǫ*, a traditional Northern Thai form of courting songs, on the radio; in northeastern Thailand one will hear performances of *mǫlam mu*, the traditional folk opera based on *jataka* tales or traditional legends; and even in Bangkok, where there is now a large Lao-speaking community of migrants from the northeast, there are stations that broadcast a considerable amount of *khaen* music, that is, music performed on the traditional Lao polyphonic reed mouth organ, together with musical commentary and jokes in Lao. A very popular musical form heard today on stations throughout the country is *phlaeng luk thung*, "songs of the children of the rice paddies." Typically, these are love songs, based on the traditional *mǫlam* form of northeastern Thailand, but they often express the concerns of modern day poverty-stricken peasants as well.

Although the most politically pointed of such songs are not broadcast on radio (although they may enjoy a wide audience through the circulation of cassette recordings), some of the songs that are broadcast convey some muted criticism of the growing discrepancy between rural and urban life.

By comparison with radio, television, which is acquiring a very large viewership as electricity is extended throughout the country, offers very limited and uninspired programming. John McBeth, a reporter for the *Far Eastern Economic Review*, has characterized television programming in Thailand as being almost without redeeming virtue:

> Government regulations effectively rule out independent political comment or meaningful current affairs programmes, but leaving that aside there is a woeful lack of made-in Thailand documentaries and other imaginative educational fare to balance a diet of soap operas, hours-long variety and game shows, Chinese martial-arts series and end-of-the evening Western shows. There appear to be no obstacles to documentaries on the countryside itself, where ordinary people rather than officials and the civilian elite are given a share of the limelight; it is a fact that many of Bangkok's more privileged residents have an appalling lack of knowledge of their own country, something TV could help correct as it also could create a greater awareness of the problems of the rural population.[36]

At the same time, television does little to give rural people any insight into the life of the vast majority of the people who live in Bangkok. Aside from depictions of the lives of the wealthy and the powerful, television projects a fantasy world for both rural and urban viewers that deflects attention away from the realities of the world in which most Thai live. Standing as a partial exception to this generalization are the advertisements presented on television. Most commercials have been made with middle-class urban viewers in mind, and the scenarios used to promote sales of soap powders, milk-based drinks, medicines, electrical appliances, and motorcycles provide brief glimpses of an idealized urban middle-class life.

Most films made in Thailand, like those appearing on television, also show a world that few Thai inhabit.[37] In recent years, there has been some break with standard romantic formulas as the films of a number of new wave directors, such as Cherd Songsri and Vichit Kunawut, show dramatic conflicts between believable characters or even view the world from the perspective of poor villagers, as Vichit Kunawut did in *Luk Isan*.

The productions of the Thai film industry, whether standard romantic or new wave fare, increasingly have been threatened by the growing number of video cassette players. Although such players are typically privately owned in Bangkok, up-country they are often owned by a shopkeeper or another entrepreneur who sets up a mini-theater. Thai firms have not yet responded to the demand for video cassettes and pirated editions of foreign films, but the potential is there for a more specialized film industry that can cater to different popular tastes, including those of up-country audiences.

Popular Culture and Folk Culture

Popular culture in Bangkok, and to a somewhat lesser extent in other towns, has become almost entirely severed from the traditional media of folk culture. Classical Indian-derived masked dances, or *khon*, can occasionally be seen on television and may also be witnessed at the shrines of the *lak myang*, or "pillar of the city," located near the Grand Palace and at the shrine of the god Brahma in the courtyard of the Erawan Hotel in Bangkok. At both shrines, it is deemed pleasing to the deities who are propitiated there to see performances of *khon*. There are also occasional performances at the National Theater or the Fine Arts School. Few Thai gather to see performances of *khon* at these shrines or watch performances on television or in other contexts, and it is highly likely that the largest audiences for traditional classical dance in Bangkok today consist of tourists. Like *khon* productions, other traditional forms of the dramatic arts—*like* (folk drama), *nang thalung* (puppet theater linked to the *wayang* of Java), or *lakhọn* (classical theater)— can occasionally be seen in Bangkok either on television or in special live productions, but again like *khon*, the numbers of people who see these other forms of traditional drama are almost insignificant compared to those who see films or watch soap operas and Chinese, Japanese, and Western popular dramas on television.

Even in the countryside, traditional dramatic, musical, and dance performances are being challenged by the cinema and increasingly by television. Nonetheless, the folk arts remain very vital in at least some parts of the country, perhaps nowhere more so than in northeastern Thailand, where it is still common for villages to have their own troupes of *mọlam mu* performers. The communities or individual who can afford it will still hire well-known professional or semiprofessional troupes to perform on the occasion of an ordination or a temple fair. A number of northeastern *mọlam* singers have become well-known popular singers throughout the country. Candidates for political office in the northeastern region, even if not Lao themselves, typically will have performers of *mọlam* or at least *khaen* players accompany them as they campaign. Traditional Lao music and musical drama of the northeastern region have given rise to an indigenous popular tradition, much as the popular spirituals of the U.S. South engendered jazz and country-western musical forms. This traditional music serves as a counterpoint to the imported and imitation Western forms that are so conspicuous in urban Thailand.

NOTES

1. A. Thomas Kirsch, "Complexity in the Thai Religious System: An Interpretation," *Journal of Asian Studies* 36:2 (1977), pp. 241–266.

2. This work has been translated into English; see Frank E. Reynolds and Mani B. Reynolds, trans., *Three Worlds According to King Ruang: A Thai Buddhist Cosmology*, Berkeley Buddhist Series, 4 (Berkeley: University of California, Group in Buddhist Studies, Center for South and Southeast Asian Studies, and Institute of Buddhist Studies, 1982). For an overview of the traditional literary culture of Siam, with some discussion of modern literature, see P. Schweisguth, *Etude sur la littérature siamoise* (Paris: Imprimerie Nationale, 1951).

3. See Eugène Denis, "L'Origine Cingalaise du P'rah Malay," in *Felicitation Volumes of Southeast Asian Studies Presented to His Highness Prince Dhaninivat* (Bangkok: Siam Society, 1965), pp. 329–338.

4. By far the best source in English on *Maha Chat*, or the story of Prince Vessantara as it is known in Thailand, is in G. E. Gerini, *A Retrospective View and Account of the Origin of the Thet Maha Ch'at Ceremony (Maha Jati Desana) or Exposition of the Tale of the Great Birth as Performed in Siam* (Bangkok: Bangkok Times Press, 1892). The work has recently been reprinted under the title *The Thet Maha Chat Ceremony* (Bangkok: Satirakoses-Naga-pradipa Foundation, 1976).

5. See Sombat Chantornvong, "Religious Literature in Thai Political Perspective: The Case of the Maha Chat Kamluang," in *Essays on Literature and Society in Southeast Asia*, ed. Tham Seong Chee (Singapore: Singapore University Press, 1981), pp. 187–205.

6. See, in this regard, Craig J. Reynolds, "Buddhist Cosmography in Thai History, with Special Reference to Nineteenth-Century Culture Change," *Journal of Asian Studies* 35:2 (1976), pp. 203–220.

7. See Mongkut's diatribe against the traditional ritual practices associated with the delivering of the *Maha Chat* sermon as translated and published in Gerini, *Thai Maha Chat Ceremony*, pp. 57–58.

8. See Craig J. Reynolds, "The Buddhist Monkhood in Nineteenth-Century Thailand" (Ph.D. dissertation, Cornell University, 1973), and A. Thomas Kirsch, "Modernizing Implications of Nineteenth-Century Reforms in the Thai Sangha," in *Religion and the Legitimation of Power in Thailand, Laos, and Burma*, ed. Bardwell L. Smith (Chambersburg, Penn.: Anima Books, 1978), pp. 52–65.

9. Benedict Anderson, *Imagined Communities: Reflections on the Origin and Spread of Capitalism* (London: Verso, 1983), esp. chap. 5.

10. During World War II, Phibun had many handwritten manuscripts destroyed because they were considered obsolete.

11. See Stanley J. Tambiah, "Literacy in a Buddhist Village in North-East Thailand," in *Literacy in Traditional Societies*, ed. Jack Goody (Cambridge: Cambridge University Press, 1968), pp. 85–131.

12. The following discussion of the role of the school is drawn primarily from Charles F. Keyes, "The Proposed World of the School: Thai Villagers' Entry into a Bureaucratic State," to appear in *Reshaping Local Worlds: Rural Education and Culture Change in Southeast Asia*, ed. Charles F. Keyes, forthcoming. Also see Chayan Vaddhanaphuti, "Cultural and Ideological Reproduction in Rural Northern Thai Society" (Ph.D. dissertation, Stanford University, 1984), esp. chap. 6.

13. See Robert Gurevich, "Khru: A Study of Teachers in a Thai Village" (Ph.D. dissertation, University of Pittsburgh, 1972), and Gurevich, "Teachers, Rural Development, and the Civil Service in Thailand," *Asian Survey* 15 (1975), pp. 870–881.

14. Thai authors commonly use pseudonyms, often to indicate that the work is fiction rather than to mask their identity. Some fictional writers do not use pseudonyms, however, and a few authors of other types of writing do use them. It is possible to find in the National Library the real name of almost any author who uses a pseudonym.

15. Wibha Senanan, *The Genesis of the Novel in Thailand* (Bangkok: Thai Watana Panich, 1975), p. 97.

16. Manas Chitakasem, "The Development of Political and Social Consciousness in Thai Short Stories," in *The Short Story in South East Asia: Aspects of a Genre*, ed. Jeremy H.C.S. Davidson and Helen Cordell (London: School of Oriental and African Studies, University of London, 1982), p. 69.

17. Kukrit Pramoj, *Si Phaendin* (*Four Reigns*), trans. Tulachandra, 2 vols. (Vol. 1, Bangkok: Duang Kamol, 1981; Vol. 2, Bangkok: Duang Kamol, n.d.).

18. Kukrit Pramoj, *Red Bamboo* (Bangkok: Progress Bookstore, 1961).

19. Sulak Sivaraksa, *Siam in Crisis* (Bangkok: Komol Keemthong Foundation, 1980), p. 321.

20. Botan, *Letters from Thailand*, trans. Susan Fulop Morell (Bangkok: D. K. Book House, 1977).

21. Manas, "Development of Political and Social Consciousness," p. 91, n. 17.

22. Ibid., p. 72.

23. Ibid., p. 85.

24. Ibid., p. 91, n. 19.

25. Khammaan Khonkhai, *The Teachers of Mad Dog Swamp*, trans. Gehan Wijeyewardene (St. Lucia: University of Queensland Press, 1982).

26. Benedict R. O'G. Anderson, "Introduction," in *In the Mirror: Literature and Politics in Siam in the American Era*, ed. and trans. Benedict R. O'G Anderson and Ruchira Mendiones (Bangkok: Duang Kamol, 1985), p. 61.

27. A number of Khamsing's short stories, mostly from an early collection, have been translated into English by D. Garden and published in *The Politician and Other Stories* (Kuala Lumpur: Oxford University Press, Oxford in Asia Modern Authors, 1973).

28. Manas, "The Development of Political and Social Consciousness," p. 78.

29. I use the term "popular culture" to mean that culture which is communicated through mass media as contrasted with "folk culture," which is transmitted through oral traditions.

30. Wibha, *Genesis of the Novel*, pp. 113 and 114n.

31. Paisal Sricharatchanya, "A Change for the Better," *Far Eastern Economic Review*, July 19, 1984, pp. 34–36. The statistics in the following discussion are also drawn from this article.

32. John McBeth, "Going to the Stake," *Far Eastern Economic Review*, July 19, 1984, p. 40.

33. Paisal, "A Change for the Better," p. 34.

34. Ibid., p. 35.

35. Ibid.

36. See John McBeth, "A Switched-off Service," *Far Eastern Economic Review*, July 19, 1984, p. 40.

37. On the Thai film industry, see Ian Buruma, "Thailand's Film-Makers Sing in a Morass of Money vs. Artistry," *Far Eastern Economic Review*, October 27, 1983, pp. 53–54, and Sanachit Bangsapan, "A Bleak Future for Good Films," *Far Eastern Economic Review*, May 3, 1984, pp. 63–64.

Epilogue

Ever since the reign of King Chulalongkorn, the state has construed the cultural traditions of the diverse pasts of the peoples living within the state as a single tradition common to a unified nation. This process has aimed, as Andrew Turton observes, at producing "what comes to be regarded, and has to be accepted, as *the* national tradition, *the* significant past."[1] Through the exercise of control over the Buddhist clergy, the institution of a statewide system of mass education, manipulation of the mass media, and the creation of public holidays that celebrate the nation, the state has attempted to impose a dominant national ideology on the populace. This process has, however, generated countertendencies, and although there is a widespread consensus today that Thai national culture is predicated on "nation, religion, and king" (*chat, sat, phra maha kasat*), there are significant differences, even among the elite, on how these elements of Thai tradition are to be understood.

NATIONAL IDEOLOGY AND THE LEGITIMACY OF POWER IN THAILAND

The process of creating a national ideology was initiated by King Chulalongkorn and those of his brothers who were his close advisers. King Chulalongkorn sought to redefine the relationship of the monarch to society by transforming many of the traditional rituals performed within the court into public events. Rather than being a remote, godlike figure living within a replica of a Hindu-Buddhist heaven, the king was to be seen publicly performing his ritual functions on behalf of his subjects throughout the country. At the same time, attitudes toward his subjects were being redefined. Prince Damrong, as minister of interior, ordered provincial authorities to cease using pejorative terms for the Lao of the northeastern region and the Yuan (also sometimes called Lao by the Siamese) of the northern region. Instead, all peoples who

201

spoke a Tai language were to be called "Thai" and were to be distinguished by regional rather than ethnic labels. Prince Vajirañana, as the head of the Thammayut order and later as supreme patriarch of the entire sangha, instituted an interpretation of the Buddhist tradition based on the reforms of Mongkut and his own reading of the scriptures and authoritative commentaries as the basis of religious education for all monks throughout the country. King Vajiravudh carried the process to the next stage by making explicit through his writings a national ideology predicated on the Thai nation, united in its adherence to the Buddhist religion and loyal to the monarch who sat on the throne of the Chakri dynasty.

The 1932 Revolution brought this formula into question when it became necessary to incorporate the notion of popular sovereignty, as symbolized by the constitution (*ratchathammanun*), into the national ideology. Phibun Songkhram, as prime minister from 1938 to 1944, attempted a further change by making the "leader" (*phunam*), who during that period was none other than Phibun himself, the embodiment of popular sovereignty and, implicitly at least, an alternative to the king. These attempted changes were not wholly successful, and under Sarit there was a return to the older formulation of King Vajiravudh. King Bhumibol was encouraged by Sarit, and by Thanom who succeeded Sarit, to take an active role in promoting this ideology. The activities King Bhumibol engaged in during the 1960s, as illustrated by the description given in the Prologue of the royal couple's visit to Mae Hong Son in 1968, show that he has taken a significant role in the process. At the same time, Sarit and his successors sought to promote the idea that the military had a special role in leading the nation as protectors of the religion and the monarchy.

This role came under attack during the student movement of the early 1970s, a movement that sought to restore the "constitution" as a central element of national ideology. The 1973 Revolution at first appeared to be successful, but it resulted only in an increasingly strident debate about the character of Thai nationalism.

When the 1973 Revolution demonstrated that many people did not accept as legitimate the dominance of a ruling military elite, some in that elite turned to coercive violence as a way to retain their hold on power.[2] During 1974–1976, many leaders of farm movements, leftist politicians, and others deemed to be "communists" or a threat to the nation were murdered; others were threatened by toughs known to be supported by influential members of the military and police. Organized into quasi-organizations such as Nawaphon and the Red Gaurs, these toughs were recruited primarily from the unemployed urban lower-middle class. Nawaphon and the Red Gaurs spearheaded the attacks on students during the October 1976 crisis, leading to the bloody climax of the October 6 coup. Other hoodlums, without benefit of organizational identity, were employed by corrupt businessmen to "neutralize" reporters and certain politicians who threatened to expose their activities. Human rights groups also reported numerous abuses of power by members of the Village Defense Corps, a paramilitary organization supported by the Border Patrol Police.

Although intimidation of certain sectors of the Thai populace still continues, it has never assumed a major role in Thai life. There are still some members of the elite who continue to sanction the use of coercive violence, but the majority seek legitimacy through a national ideology.

The quest for legitimacy continues to be predicated on the assumption that most Thai see themselves as belonging to a Thai nation whose roots are based in the dominant Buddhist tradition and as united in their loyalty to the institution of the monarchy. This assumption serves, however, only to define the parameters of a debate among several elements of the elite, as well as between elite and nonelite, about how each of the premises of national ideology are to be understood.

The Thai Nation and Regional, Ethnic, and Religious Identities

A consensus exists among the vast majority of people in Thailand today that the language used in contexts that are understood to have a national character is to be standard Thai rather than some other language. There is no "national language problem" in Thailand as there is in neighboring Malaysia, the Philippines, or Sri Lanka. Even the people who seek to champion regional or ethnic identities address themselves in Thai to Thai-reading or Thai-speaking audiences.

Until quite recently, there was little allowance for a positive expression of distinctive regional or ethnic identities in national culture. In popular films and fiction, the Lao dialects spoken by the people of northeastern Thailand are still often stigmatized as uncouth. Although a northern Thai accent in a young woman has sometimes been more positively treated in film, it is still presented in a patronizing way. In school curricula, regional history is almost totally ignored.

Since the early 1970s, there has begun to be some change in such attitudes, in part because of a government interest in promoting tourism.[3] Regional festivals, costumes, and other customs have suddenly been found worthy of positive official recognition. Peoples holding distinct ethnoregional identities are not necessarily eager, however, to see themselves presented as objects of tourist attention. Also indicative of change is a growing interest, spearheaded primarily by the faculties of provincial universities and teacher-training colleges, in including the study of regional cultures at college, secondary, and even primary school levels. This movement has been encouraged by certain national organizations, most particularly the Social Science Association of Thailand.

Prior to World War II, the most stigmatized ethnic identity in Thailand was that of the Chinese. King Vajiravudh wrote disdainfully of them, calling them on at least one occasion "the Jews of the East." Anti-Chinese feelings were exacerbated during the 1930s by anti-Chinese policies instituted by the government and by the chauvinist writings of of Luang Wichit Wadthakarn, the ideologist of the Phibun period. After World War II, the ending of Chinese migration and the increasing assimilation of Chinese into Thai society tended to soften anti-Chinese sentiments. It remained common, nonetheless, to find evildoers in popular fiction or films, or, more recently, television programs, characterized as being Chinese. Given the prevailing images, the popular acclaim given in 1969 to Botan's novel, *Letters from Thailand*, with its sympathetic portrayal of a Chinese migrant and his family and unflattering observations about the behavior of urban Thai, represents a shift in attitude. This shift can be traced to the rapid growth of a Sino-Thai middle class in the 1960s and to the rise into the elite of a significant number of people who have a stake in promoting the idea that a Thai national identity can be held by people of Chinese descent.

The king and other members of the royal family have also contributed to the view that Thailand is a country of peoples of diverse ethnic backgrounds who all are in a fundamental way "Thai." In the 1960s, the king and queen and the princess mother assumed the roles of patrons for the tribal peoples of the north. Although those involved in such royal projects have sometimes acted in patronizing ways, royal patronage has undoubtedly contributed to a growing acceptance of tribal peoples as members of the Thai nation. Similarly, by offering awards for study of the Koran to Thai Muslims, the king has also contributed to better acceptance of Muslim peoples into the nation. Few Malayspeaking or Thai-speaking Muslims or tribal people, however, have been able to achieve positive national recognition beyond that accorded by the king and royal family.

One of the underlying factors behind the virtual exclusion of tribal peoples and Muslims from national politics is the equation of Buddhism with the national religion. The only non-Buddhist religious groups that have been able to make themselves heard at the national level are the relatively small Protestant and Catholic communities. A number of well-respected intellectuals and writers are Christian, and Christians are active in the Coordinating Group for Religion and Society, perhaps the most significant human rights organization to emerge in the 1970s. Such inclusion of Christians in national affairs, in contrast to Muslims, bespeaks the long-standing relations that have existed between Buddhist and Christian communities that go back to the positive interactions between Mongkut and Western Christian missionaries. Christians appear to have accepted the fact that Thai national culture is rooted in Buddhism but have also gained acceptance for the proposition that Christians can still be Thai. A Muslim-Buddhist dialogue has, however, yet to begin.

Establishment and Other Buddhisms

The interactions between Buddhists and Christians during the second half of the nineteenth century stimulated a consciousness among the Siamese elite of that time of what being Buddhist involved. No longer were the premises of traditional Buddhist culture simply taken as given. This self-consciousness, in turn, spurred Prince Vajirañana, with the encouragement of King Chulalongkorn, to institute reforms that eventually made Buddhism a national religion. What can be termed "establishment Buddhism" was created by instituting a unified hierarchy that integrated the two sangha orders, by controlling entrance into the sangha through appointment by sangha authorities of those monks empowered to perform ordinations, and by inculcating a modern interpretation of doctrine based on a return to the scriptures and embodied in a common curriculum for religious education and used throughout the country.

Establishment Buddhism would seem to be susceptible to being used by the ruling elite to ensure compliance with a national ideology, but this possibility was not seized on prior to Sarit's coming to power in 1957. For most of the period between the promulgation of the 1902 law creating a national sangha and World War II, sangha efforts were directed primarily toward ensuring the incorporation into the national system of local monks who remained responsive primarily to local traditions. Although a modernized national sangha was in existence by World War II, Phibun Songkhram, who returned to power in 1948, did not seek to make it a national body and instead emphasized the more traditional uses of Buddhism. He was conspicuous in making offerings to the sangha, in building temples, and especially in his sponsorship of the 2500th anniversary celebrations of the Buddha's death in 1956 and 1957. Because Phibun permitted local monks to develop their own followings, Sarit, after he came to power, viewed the sangha as a potential threat.

Sarit challenged the sangha by instituting legal proceedings against one of its most senior members, Phra Phimonlatham, the abbot of Wat Maha That in Bangkok, whom many regarded as the most likely candidate to be the next supreme patriarch. Although Sarit was unable to have Phra Phimonlatham disrobed, he imprisoned him and stripped him of his rank. Sarit then instituted a new sangha law, bringing the sangha under much closer state control.

Since Sarit's time, governments have used the sangha directly to promote anticommunism, compliance with government development programs, and assimilation of non-Buddhist tribal peoples into the national society. Such government use of the sangha notwithstanding, the sangha has not become a tool for the spread of a national ideology by the ruling elite. Many highly respected voices in the sangha have continued to articulate views that are not in accord with a narrow Buddhist nationalism.

The Buddhist reforms set under way by Mongkut have served, ironically, to undermine the traditional belief in a hierarchical ordering of society whereby those who rule do so by virtue of their previous "merit." Reform Buddhism, as can be seen from the writings of Mongkut and especially Prince Vajirañana, emphasizes the doctrine of *kamma* but shifts the emphasis from *kamma* as destiny to *kamma* as responsibility.[4] What was once taken as being fixed in the world as a consequence of previous *kamma* is now stressed less than the responsibility of each individual to act in ways that reduce the likelihood of future suffering. This shift of emphasis in reform Buddhism was initially adopted by only a small number of the elite; the majority of the people continued to adhere to the older cosmological formulations of traditional Buddhism. As Vajirañana's new religious curriculum took hold, however, increasingly influential monks up-country as well as in Bangkok began to promote the new interpretation.

In line with this new interpretation, the monks who receive the highest respect in Thailand today are those who most clearly exemplify the ideals of detachment from the world and diligent cultivation of the "virtues" that conduce toward ultimate salvation. Such monks are most usually forest monks who live in meditation retreats located apart from towns and villages.

Although few Thai aspire to emulate the radical world-rejection of the forest monks, the forest monasteries offer opportunities for laypersons to engage in a period of retreat during which they practice meditation and lead ascetic lives. Laypeople who undergo such experiences hope to return to the world able to act in accordance with Buddhist moral precepts instead of being impelled by worldly passions. This ideal of being able to act morally yet dispassionately is central to the moral philosophies of two of contemporary Thailand's outstanding Buddhist theologians, namely Buddhadasa Bhikkhu and Caokhun Rajavaramuni (Prayut Payutto). Since the early 1950s, Buddhadasa, a monk from Chaiya in Suratthani Province in southern Thailand, has gained increasing recognition, particularly among the urban laity but also among villagers. His numerous sermons and writings as well as his "spiritual theaters" in Chaiya and Chiang Mai offer people the view that *"nibbana is in samsara,"* that is, that ultimate salvation (*nibbana*) is not to be attained through escape from the realm of sentient existence (*samsara*) but through cultivation of moral behavior and self-awareness while remaining within that realm.[5] In a more philosophical mode, Caokhun Rajavaramuni, especially in his monumental *Buddha-dhamma* (*Phutthatham*) published in 1982[6] but also in many of his shorter essays and lectures, has sought in the scriptures and commentaries the basis for Buddhist notions of individual ethical responsibility and social justice.

Buddhadasa and even Caokhun Rajavaramuni, despite his clerical rank, like the forest monks, stand apart from the established sangha. The sangha, even with the backing of the state, has no real power to enforce orthodoxy. Moreover, while it assumes responsibility for enforcing orthopraxy, or correct practice, its standards are those of the ancient disciplinary code of the sangha. Only in matters determining which monks have the right to serve as preceptors in ordinations and in enforcing the requirements that those who enter the monkhood not be subject to criminal prosecution (by the Thai state), be free of obligation to serve the (Thai) government, and have completed the required number of years of state education does the sangha hierarchy impose any significant constraints on its monks. Beyond these constraints, there is, as a direct consequence of the reform of Thai Buddhism, tolerance for Buddhist practices that lie beyond the control of the established sangha and the state associated with that sangha.

Such tolerance extends to an unwillingness on the part of the state to enforce some particular version of Buddhist morality through law. Contemporary Thai law is strikingly free of reference to religious authority, especially when compared to the legal codes of many states with dominant Muslim populations. This characteristic of Thai law also reflects the much greater secularization of Thai society as compared to most Islamic societies.

A Buddhist-based secular tolerance of what are considered to be matters of individual moral choice has contributed to the development of plural value-systems among the Thai. At one end of the spectrum, there is a subculture made up of those who have not internalized any of Buddhism's emphasis on temperate behavior and who pursue the hedonistic pleasures of drink, drugs, and sex. At the opposite end of the spectrum is the subculture of those ascetic monks who have turned their backs on all worldly temptations. Of particular interest are those subcultures—found especially among the Sino-Thai, the Lao of northeastern Thailand, and perhaps among other groups as well—that emphasize tempering desires for immediate gratification in order to accumulate capital to be invested for a future goal. This ethic, with its different sources in the Buddhist tradition of the Lao and the mixed Buddhist and ancestor-focused tradition of the Sino-Thai, has contributed in a significant way to the economic growth of Thailand since the 1950s.[7] Some groups, drawn primarily from the urban intelligentsia, have found in Buddhist thought the premises for criticism of the marked inequalities in wealth and power in Thai society. Although emphasis on individual moral responsibility has tended to preclude development of a rigid class structure, some people, especially in rural areas, have found in their shared ideas of morality derived from Buddhism the basis for common cause in protesting specific injustices.

Changing Images of the Thai Monarchy

The monarchy as an element of Thai nationalism has also been variously interpreted since the advent of the modern nation-state at the end of the nineteenth century. The success of the early kings of the Chakri dynasty in subordinating all potential alternative rulers to their overlordship meant that whatever role a royal family was to have in the modern nation-state, it would be assumed by members of the Chakri family. No descendant of the Ayutthayan royal house, nor of King Taksin of Thonburi, much less any descendant of the Chiang Mai or any other princely family of formerly autonomous polities has made, or could ever make, any viable claim to the throne of Thailand. The Chakri dynasty became fused in nationalist ideology with the concept of the Thai nation. At no time was this fact more evident than in the 1982 bicentennial celebrations of the founding of the Ratanakosin era, the era inaugurated by Chakri when he ascended the throne in 1782.

The 1932 Revolution could have ended the monarchy fifty years before these celebrations were held, but the Promoters of the revolution backed away from attempting to institute a Thai social order that lacked the monarchy. Although the monarchy was retained, King Prajadhipok was unable to redefine its role in postrevolutionary terms and soon abdicated. For twenty years thereafter, the monarchy was reduced to a symbol that could be manipulated according to the purposes of the government in power.

King Bhumibol has, for all practical purposes, been the only active monarch of the post-1932 period. His actions, as well as those of the queen and other members of the royal family, have projected a new image of the monarchy in Thai society. One of the king's first acts on his return to Thailand after many years of education abroad was to be ordained temporarily as a monk. Pictures of him as monk are still to be found in many homes throughout the country and today are often paired with pictures of the crown prince as monk. The king's ordination has been taken to symbolize his status as one who "has merit and virtue" (*mi bun mi barami*), that is, a great store of positive *kamma*. His subsequent highly publicized visits to various *wat*s to offer alms to the sangha and especially his presentation of Buddha images to all of the provinces of the kingdom have reinforced this perception. Since the 1960s, the king and queen and other members of the royal family have been conspicuous in showing their concern for the victims of drought and other natural calamities, for the poor in rural villages and tribal communities, and for soldiers and policemen injured while protecting the country. Their concern has been seen by many to indicate the deep compassion that only people with "merit and virtue" can display.[8]

Many people viewed the king's intercession in the political crisis of October 1973, when he personally came forward to ask the ruling triumvirate—Thanom, Praphat, and Narong—to leave the country in order to prevent serious civil strife, as yet further proof of his compassion. So unassailable was the king's reputation during the 1960s and early 1970s that the Communist party of Thailand, which certainly had long since determined to eliminate the monarchy if it ever came to power, never criticized him, at least publicly. Nevertheless, the king's direct involvement in politics in October 1973 led him and other members of the royal family into further political involvements, many of which were far more controversial and were to stimulate a new debate about the relationship of the monarchy to Thai nationalism.

In the mid-1970s, the king and queen became publicly linked with rightist elements and most notably with the *luk sya chao ban*, the Village Scouts, of which they became patrons. Thanin Kraivichien, the very conservative former judge who became prime minister after the October 1976 coup, was known to have been approved, if not actually chosen, by the king and queen. Their backing of him was clear when Thanin was appointed to the Privy Council following his removal from office by the coup of 1977. Of perhaps even greater concern to a wide segment of the population has been the moral character of Prince Vajiralongkorn. Because of his reputation for chasing women and especially for his apparent lack of interest in the welfare of the people, many people began to fear that he lacked the "merit and virtue" of his father. At the same time, the role assumed by Crown Princess Sirindhorn brought her great popularity. From the late 1970s on her active involvement in social welfare and educational projects as well as in ceremonial functions at which she represented her father led many people to speak of her as possessing great merit and virtue. In this connection, it is noteworthy that she chose to write her master's thesis on *barami*, the virtue that comes from adherence to the teachings of the Buddha and that has long been seen as especially associated with those deemed to be righteous rulers.

After the 1977 coup, the king withdrew from the active political role he had been playing since October 1973, and the royal family did not again enter the political scene until 1981 when they publicly sided with General Prem against the Young Turks who were attempting to overthrow him and thereby ensured Prem's survival. In 1982, the succession question became an immediate issue when the king fell seriously ill. Although he recovered and has since reassumed his public activities, on a restricted scale, the question has not dissipated. Since then, the crown prince has assumed a much more active role in carrying out not only many of the ceremonial functions previously performed by his father but also some of the patronage roles of both of his parents. Such actions have made perhaps a majority of the populace more accepting of the prospect of his succession.

During a period when many monarchies around the world were being eliminated as unwanted relics of a premodern era, King Bhumibol succeeded in restoring the Thai monarchy as a central pillar of the modern nation-state. The national consensus that emerged around the king in the 1960s and early 1970s contrasts strongly with conflicts that were threatening the unity of other nearby Buddhist states such as Burma, Laos, Cambodia, and Sri Lanka. Although this consensus was seriously threatened in 1976, in part because of the king's partisan role in the crisis leading up to the October 6 coup, a tenuous consensus has been restored since 1977. This consensus presumes tolerance for different value systems within a Buddhist kingdom as against an ideology based on a narrowly militant Buddhist or Buddhist-monarchical nationalism. If King Bhumibol or his successor were to support the promotion of the latter type of ideology, the consensus would undoubtedly collapse. So, too, would it collapse if the king or his successor were to give unqualified support to efforts by any military faction to extend its power through violent and coercive means.

The constraints on how the throne can be used to invest any particular political order with legitimacy derive from a Thai national culture that is not a mere reflection of a national ideology imposed by a dominant elite on the populace. Most Thai evince a significant degree of tolerance for pluralistic life-styles within their society. Given this tolerance, which has its roots in a reform Buddhism that accentuates individual responsibility and in the subsequent and consequent secularization of Thai society, insistence on unquestioning loyalty to the throne, or for militant defense of the religion, or for a violent "purging" of alien ethnic elements from the nation are unlikely to evoke the positive and wide response of comparable appeals in some neighboring societies, including ones with a Buddhist heritage. Although the Thai nation, Buddhism, and the Chakri monarchy are generally accepted as the "pillars" of Thai nationalism, most Thai would like to see these pillars support a large, open structure with room for a diversity of peoples rather than a small one with reinforced walls as barriers to alien influences.

NOTES

1. Andrew Turton, "Limits of Ideological Domination and the Formation of Social Consciousness," in *History and Peasant Consciousness in South East Asia,* ed. Andrew Turton and Shigeharu Tanabe, Senri Ethnological Studies, 13 (Osaka: National Museum of Ethnology, 1984), p. 119.

2. Turton, ibid., discusses at some length the use of coercive violence as a means of domination in Thailand.

3. See, in this regard, James Elliott, "Politics, Power, and Tourism in Thailand," *Annals of Tourism Research* 10 (1983), pp. 377–393.

4. For a fuller discussion of the two sides of the doctrine of *kamma,* see Charles F. Keyes, "The Study of Popular Ideas of Karma," and Keyes, "Merit-Transference in the Karmic Theory of Theravada Buddhism," both in *Karma: An Anthropological Inquiry,* ed. Charles F. Keyes and E. Valentine Daniel (Berkeley and Los Angeles: University of California Press, 1983), pp. 1–24 and 261–286.

5. Many of Buddhadasa's writings have been translated into English; see, for example, *Toward the Truth,* ed. Donald K. Swearer (Philadelphia: Westminster Press, 1971). Swearer, in *Buddhism in Transition* (Philadelphia: Westminster Press, 1970) and "Bhikkhu Buddhadasa on Ethics and Society," *Journal of Religious Ethics* 7:1 (1979), pp. 54–65, provides good introductions to Buddhadasa's thought. Also see Louis Gabaude, *Introduction à l'herméneutique de Buddhadasa Bhikkhu,* Thesis presented for the doctorate to the University of Sorbonne-Nouvelle (Paris, 1979).

6. See S. Sivaraksa, Review of *Phutthatham* (Buddhadhamma) by the Venerable Phra Rajavaramuni (Payutto), *Journal of the Siam Society* 70:1–2 (1982), pp. 164–170.

7. See, on this ethic, Frederic Deyo, "Ethnicity and Work Culture in Thailand: A Comparison of Thai and Thai-Chinese White-Collar Workers," *Journal of Asian Studies* 34:4 (1975), pp. 955–1015; Charles F. Keyes, "Economic Action and Buddhist Morality in a Thai Village," *Journal of Asian Studies* 12:4 (1983), pp. 851–868; and Keyes, "Buddhist Practical Morality in a Changing Agrarian World: A Case from Northeastern Thailand," in *Attitudes Toward Wealth and Poverty in Theravada Buddhism,* ed. Donald K. Swearer and Russell Sizemore, forthcoming. For a different view, see Eliezer B. Ayal, "Value Systems and Economic Development in Japan and Thailand," *Journal of Social Issues* 19:1 (January 1963), pp. 35–51.

8. The royal family has, however, displayed little public sympathy for the families of political and peasant leaders or students killed or injured in the conflicts of 1973–1976.

Appendix A

A Note on Names and the Spelling of Thai Words

In this work I use two different forms, "Tai" and "Thai," to distinguish between, on the one hand, any people speaking a language belonging to the Tai language family and, on the other, the Tai-speaking peoples (and in some cases non-Tai-speaking peoples) who are citizens of modern Thailand. Tai-speaking peoples are found throughout mainland Southeast Asia and southern China and include the Shan of Burma and southern China, the Tai Lue of northern Laos and southern China, the Lao of Laos, and various other Tai groups (such as the Tai Dam or Black Tai, Tho, Nung, and Chuang) of northern Vietnam, northern Laos, and southern China. The main Tai-speaking groups found today in Thailand are the Siamese or Central Thai, the Lao or Isan (or Northeastern Thai), the Yuan or Khon Mµang (or Northern Thai), and the Southern Thai. In addition, other peoples of different ethnic origin who are citizens of Thailand are also Thai in nationality. For some purposes, I refer to these peoples under labels suggesting a hyphenated identity: for example, Sino-Thai, Thai-Malay, and so on.

The name "Thailand" was adopted as the official, international name for the country only on the eve of World War II and was associated with the emergence of an extreme form of Thai nationalism under Phibun Songkhram, then prime minister. Prior to that time, foreigners had known the country as "Siam," a name that had been used since at least the early sixteenth century as the Western appellation for the kingdom of Ayutthaya and then from the late eighteenth century on as the name of the kingdom whose capital was at Bangkok. Although the name Thailand is a reasonably accurate translation into English of the Thai name for the country, *prathet* Thai or, more colloquially, *mµang Thai,* its adoption during the rule of a chauvinist right-wing government has led a number of leading intellectuals in the country to prefer the

213

name "Siam." A Bangkok group lobbying for a return to the old name of Siam wrote to the *Bangkok Post* in early 1985 (as reported in the *New York Times*, February 3, 1985), stating that the name "Thailand" has a negative connotation and is as "as out of date as the military dictatorships that thought it up when absolute monarchy was abolished half a century ago." Other people, particularly those who are not of Siamese or Central Thai origin, have reacted against the move for a name change, arguing that "Siam" implies Siamese domination of a state in which they are but one of a number of significant Tai-speaking peoples.

The fact remains that the official name of the country and the name by which it is generally known is "Thailand." For this reason, I employ the name "Thailand" both in the title of the book and in discussing events since World War II. I retain the designation "Siam" in those sections of the book that relate to the period prior to the official name change.

In rendering Thai words into romanized forms I have followed, with some modifications, what is known as the "General System of Phonetic Transcription of Thai Characters into Roman" devised by the Royal Institute of Thailand in 1939 and first published in the *Journal of the Thailand Research Society* in March 1941. The pronunciation of consonants is as in English with the following exceptions. Initial *k*, *p*, and *t* are unaspirated stops, and *kh*, *ph*, and *th* are aspirated. Note that *ph* is pronounced like the English *p* in "pony" and not as *f* as in "phone" and *th* is pronounced like the English *t* in "tail" and not as *th* as in "thing." *C*, which I have substituted for the Royal Institute's *čh*, is pronounced like the *cz* in "Czech," and *ch* is pronounced as in the English "which." In Thai, *ng* can occur at the beginning of a word as well as medially as in English "singer." Vowel sounds are as in Italian with the following exceptions: *Ae* is like the *a* in English "sang"; *ǫ* is something like the *o* in English "morn" or the *aw* in "dawn"; *oe* is approximated by the English *er* in "her," but without the *r*, or like the French *eu* in *peuple*. *Ų*, which I have substituted for the Royal Institute's *u'*, has no equivalent in English; it is something like the German *ü* but is more open.

In Thai, vowels can be long or short; in transcription, long vowels are indicated with a line over the vowel. For example, *khai* (with a rising tone) means "to unlock," and *khāi* (also with a rising tone) means "to sell." In the body of the text, I have not indicated vowel length, but I have done so in the Glossary. Thai is a tonal language with five tones: middle, low, falling, high, and rising. Because of typographical complications, tones are not indicated in transcribing Thai words into romanized forms in this book.

The rendering of Thai names in romanized form is more complicated than transcribing ordinary words. Thai surnames and many Thai first names have been derived from Indian sources, and the original Sanskrit or Pali spelling is preserved in the Thai orthographic renditions. The pronunciation of Thai names, however, often differs considerably from how those names are spelled. In the English press as well as in the Western literature on Thailand, some names follow the Indian forms, others follow the spoken forms, and few follow any standard system of transliteration. For example, the name of the present king of Thailand has appeared in English works as Bhumibol Adulyadej, now the official spelling, but also as Phumiphon Aduladej and Phumiphon Adunyadet. In this book I have used the most common form of a name if it is well known but have transcribed names for which there are no common romanized forms according to the modified Royal Institute system. In Appendix B, I list the most important figures mentioned in the book with both common and standard romanized forms of their names.

In referring to Thai people, their first, not their last, name is used. Thus, in talking about, for example, Kukrit Pramot—a well-known writer, politician, and former prime minister of Thailand—the name Kukrit rather than Pramot is used.

Appendix B

Major Thai Figures

Akat Damkoeng (Akāt Damkoeng Raphīphat), **Prince.** Writer (1905–1932) whose work "The Circus of Life" (*Lakhǫn hāēng Chīwit*) is considered to be the first novel in Thai.

Ananda Mahidol (Ānantha Mahidon). King of Siam/Thailand (1935–1946). Also known as Rama VIII.

Arthit Kamlangek (Āthit Kamlang-ēk), **General.** Commander in chief of the army, 1982–1985.

Bhumibol Adulyadej (Phūmiphon Adunlayadēt). King of Thailand (1946 to present). Also referred to as Rama IX.

Bowring, Sir John. British politician, colonial official, and diplomat who negotiated a treaty in 1855 with the Siamese court that opened the country to free trade.

Buddhadasa Bikkhu (Buddhadāsa Bhikkhu; Phutthathāt Phikkhu). Highly respected Buddhist monk and theologian. Born in 1906 and founder of a meditation center in his home province of Suratthani in southern Thailand.

Chakri (Cakkrī), **Cao Phrayā.** Former general who founded the present ruling dynasty of Thailand and became the first king (1782–1809) of the Bangkok period. As king he is known by the reign title of Yǫtfā and in English as Rama I.

Chulalongkorn (Culālongkǫn). King of Siam (1868–1910). Known in Thai by the reign title of Culacǫmklao and in English as Rama V.

Damrong Rajanubhab (Damrong Rātchanuphāp), **Prince.** Brother of King Chulalongkorn. As minister of interior (1892–1915) devised and implemented major administrative reform of the country. Also well known as historian and considered founder of modern Thai historiography.

Dokmai Sot (Dōkmai Sot), **pseud.** Real name, Mǫm Luang [M.L.] Bupphā Kunchara Nimmānhēmin. Writer (1905–1963) considered to be one of the pioneers of modern Thai fiction.

Jit Poumisak (Cit Phūmisak). Radical scholar and poet (1930–1966) whose works, especially his "The Face of Thai Feudalism Today" (*Chomnā khǭng Sakdinā Thai nai Pacuban*), have significantly influenced contemporary Thai thought.

Khuang Aphaiwong (Khūāng Aphaiwong). One of the Promoters of the 1932 Revolution. Prime minister, 1944–1945, 1946, 1947–1948.

Kittivuddho Bikkhu (Kittivuḍḍho Bhikkhu; Kittiwutthō Phikkhu). Influential Buddhist monk who provided Buddhist justification for extreme right-wing militancy in the mid- and late 1970s.

Kriangsak Chomanan (Krīāngsak Chomanan), **General.** Prime minister, 1977–1980 and commander in chief of the army, 1978. Subsequently elected to parliament and founded National Democratic party. Arrested as one of the leaders of the abortive coup of September 1985.

Krit Sivara (Krit Siwarā), **General.** Commander in chief of the army, 1973–1975. Supported the ouster of the military dictators, Thanom and Praphat, in 1973.

Kukrit Pramoj (Khǔkkrit Prāmōt). Lesser member of royalty (holds title of Mǫm Ratchawong [M.R.]), novelist, essayist, former editor of *Siam Rath* newspaper, founder of the Social Action party, prime minister, 1975–1976.

Man Phurithat (Man Phūrithat; Bhūridatto Thera), **Ācān.** Monk (1870–1949) who became the founder of the tradition of forest monks, acclaimed by many as a Buddhist saint.

Mano Pakorn (Manōpakǭn Nitithādā), **Phrayā.** First prime minister following the 1932 Revolution (1932–1933).

Mongkut (Mongkut). King of Siam (1851–1868). Known in Thai by reign name of Cǫmklao and in English as Rama IV.

Phahon Phonphayuhasena (Phahon Phonphayusēnā), **General Phrayā.** One of the Promoters of the 1932 Revolution. Prime minister, 1933–1938.

Phao Sriyanonda (Phao Sīyānon), **General.** Leader of one of the dominant political factions during the postwar Phibun government (1947–1957). Director general of police, 1956–1957. Died in exile in 1964.

Phibun Songkhram (Phibūn Songkhrām), **Field Marshal Luang.** One of the major leaders of the 1932 Revolution and a dominant political figure from 1932 until 1957. Prime minister, 1938–1944 and 1948–1957. Also known by given name of Plǣk Khittasangkha. Died in exile in Japan in 1964.

Phimonlatham (Bimaladhama, Āt Ātsapha Thēra), **Phra.** High-ranking monk against whom Sarit brought charges in the late 1950s for purported left-wing political activities. Remained a monk and continues to have considerable influence in the sangha.

Pote Sarasin (Phot Sārasin). Prime minister, 1957–1958.

Prajadhipok (Prachāthipok). King of Siam (1925–1935). Known in Thai by reign name of Pokklao and in English as Rama VII. Abdicated in 1935 in the wake of the 1932 Revolution. Died in England in 1941.

Praphat or Praphas Charusathien (Praphāt Cārusathīān), **Field Marshal.** Although never prime minister, shared power during the government of Thanom Kittikachorn (1963–1973). Served as deputy prime minister, minister of interior, and director general of the police. Founder and former leader of a political faction that still remains important in Thai politics.

Prem Tinsulanonda (Prēm Tinsūlānon), **General.** Former commander-in-chief of the army who became prime minister in 1980 and was reappointed several times, most recently following the election of July 1986.

Pridi Banomyong (Prīdī Phanomyong). One of the major leaders of the 1932 Revolution. Served in several prewar governments and became regent during the war. Headed the Free Thai movement in the country. Prime minister in 1946. Forced to leave the country in 1947 and after a failed coup attempt in 1949, spent the remainder of his life in exile, first in China and then in France. Died in France in 1983.

Puey Ungphakorn (Pūai Ụngphākōn), **Dr.** Economist, former governor of the Bank of Thailand and rector of Thammasat University at the time of the October 6, 1976, coup. For his championing of human rights was forced by the right wing to flee the country.

Rajavaramuni (Rājavaramuni; Rātchawaramunī; Prayut Payutto), **Phra** or **Caokhun.** Born in 1939. Leading Buddhist theologian.

Ramathibodi (Rāmāthibodī). Founder and first king of Ayutthaya. Reigned from 1350 to 1369.

Ramkhamhaeng (Rāmkhamhāēng). Third and most famous king of Sukhothai. Reigned from circa 1279 to 1299. Credited with having created the Thai system of writing.

Sanya Thammasak (Sanyā Thammasak), **Judge.** Appointed prime minister by the king following the revolution of October 14, 1973. Prime minister, 1973–1974.

Sarit Thanarat (Sarit Thanarat), **Field Marshal.** Military strongman who rose to become commander in chief of the army in 1957 under Phibun and then led successful coup against him. Prime minister, 1958–1963.

Seni Pramoj (Sēnī Prāmōt). Lesser member of royalty (holds title of Mǫm Ratchawong [M.R.]), political leader who first emerged as a leader of the Free Thai Movement outside of Thailand during World War II. Founded Democrat party after the war. Prime Minister, 1945–1946, 1975, and 1976.

Si Burapha (Sī Buraphā), **pseud.** Real name, Kulāp Sāipradit. Writer (1905–1974) who, together with Dokmai Sot, is considered to be a pioneer of modern Thai fiction. His postwar writing increasingly focused on subjects of social injustice. He was jailed after the Sarit coup and subsequently went into exile in China where he died in 1974.

Sirikit. Queen and wife of King Bhumibol Adulyadej whom she married in 1950.

Sirindhorn (Sirinthǫn). Princess and daughter of King Bhumibol and Queen Sirikit. Made eligible for succession to the throne and raised to rank of Mahā Chakri Princess in 1977.

Srisuriyawong (Sīsuriyawong, Chūām Bunnak), **Cao Phrayā.** Regent of Siam during the early part of the reign of King Chulalongkorn.

Srivijaya (Sīwichai, Sirivijayo Thera), **Khrūbā.** Renowned northern Thai monk (1878–1939) who led resistance to integration of northern Thai sangha into the national order of monks. Acclaimed by many in northern Thailand as a Buddhist saint.

Sunthon Phu (Sunthǫn Phū). Poet (1786–1855) whose works are considered to be classics of Thai literature.

Thamrong Navasawat (Thamrong Nāwāsawat), **Rear Admiral Luang.** One of the Promoters of the 1932 Revolution, close associate of Pridi in the Free Thai movement, and prime minister (on behalf of Pridi) in 1946 and 1947.

Thanin Kraivichien (Thānin Kraiwichīan). Appointed prime minister following the coup of October 6, 1976, and served until the coup of October 1977.

Thanom Kittikachorn (Thanōm Kittikhacǫn), **Field Marshal.** Close associate of Sarit; served briefly as prime minister in 1958 while Sarit was abroad. Became prime minister again in 1963 after Sarit's death and together with Field Marshal Praphat perpetuated the type of military rule instituted by Sarit until the revolution of October 14, 1973.

Thawi Bunyaket (Thawī Bunyakēt). One of the Promoters of the 1932 Revolution. Prime minister, 1944.

Vajiralongkorn (Watchiralongkǫn), **Prince.** Son of King Bhumibol and Queen Sirikit. Designated crown prince in 1972.

Vajirañana (Vajirañāṇa or Vajirañāṇavarorasa; Wachirayān[warorot]),
Prince. Brother of King Chulalongkorn, head of the Thammayut
order (reformed order) of monks from 1893 and supreme patriarch
(Sangharāja) of entire sangha from 1910 until his death in 1921.
Vajiravudh (Wāchirawut). King of Siam (1910–1925). Known in Thai
by reign name of Mongkutklao and in English as Rama VI.

Glossary

Terms covered in the glossary are Thai, except for a few words of Pali or, more rarely, Sanskrit (Skt.) origin. Pali and Sanskrit terms are used primarily for certain basic Buddhist concepts.

baht (*bāt*): basic unit of currency in Thailand. For most of the period from the late 1950s through 1980, the exchange rate between baht and dollars remained relatively stable at between 20 and 21 baht to the dollar. In the 1980s, the baht was devalued and allowed to float on the currency markets. In 1985, the baht fluctuated between about 26 and 27 to the dollar.

ban (*bān*): house; village.

bhikkhu (**Pali; Thai,** *phikkhu*): Buddhist monk.

caonai (*caonāi*): literally, "lord and master." Traditionally the term was used to designate royalty. In contemporary usage it refers primarily to officials, such as district officers, who wield power invested in them by the state.

cedi (**Thai,** *cēdī;* **Pali,** *cetiya*): also stupa, a shrine that contains a relic of the Buddha or is a "reminder" (the basic meaning of *cetiya*) of a shrine containing such a relic.

chat (*chāt*): nation, nationality, ethnic group.

chat, sat, phramahakasat **or** *chat, satsana, phramahakasat* (*chāt, sāt[sanā], phra mahā kasāt*): nationalist formula meaning (Thai) nation, (Buddhist) religion, and (Chakri) monarchy.

dhamma (**Pali; Thai,** *tham;* **Skt.,** *dharma*): the teachings of the Buddha; the way to salvation taught by the Buddha.

Hmong: the second largest tribal population in Thailand; referred to as Meo by the Thai. Hmong tribal people have accounted for a large number of refugees fleeing from Laos into Thailand, and many Hmong have been resettled in the United States.

Isan (*Īsān*): literally, "northeast, northeastern"; used to refer to the northeastern region of Thailand and to the dominant, Lao-speaking people living in the region.

kamma (**Pali; Thai,** *kam;* **Skt.,** *karma*): morally relevant actions; in Thai usage, refers primarily to the consequences of morally relevant actions of the past, including past lives, while the terms *bun* (Pali, *puñña*) and *bāp* (Pali, *pāpa*), "merit" and "demerit," are used to refer to the consequences of present morally relevant actions.

kamnan: headman of a commune (*tambon*), that is, an administrative collectivity of villages.

Karen: the largest tribal population of Thailand. Most Karen live in Burma.

kharatchakan (*khārātchakān*): literally, "servants of the crown"; officials, civil servants.

Khon Muang (*Khon Mŭang*): literally, "people of the domains"; self-designation used by northern Thai.

khru (*khrū*): teacher.

khwan: vital essence of a person. If the *khwan* becomes detached or if it wanders, the person will be left vulnerable to illness and eventually to death. Thus, on any occasion (such as moving house, marriage, or serious illness) when the *khwan* might become detached, it must be "called" back and "secured" to the person.

kin muang (*kin mŭang*): literally, "to eat the country." Traditionally, used to refer to the right, conferred by a king, of a local lord or governor to appropriate part of the taxes levied on the people for his own use. In contemporary usage, refers to the practice (but not the right) of an official to demand "extra" payments for government services or to expect "gifts" from the people in the official's administrative domain.

krom: department or bureau; traditionally used also as part of a title conferred on royalty by the king.

maechi (*māēchī*): ascetic woman; i.e., Buddhist nun.

Mahanikai (**Thai,** *Mahānikāi;* **Pali,** *Mahā-nikāya*): literally, "the great order"; the largest order (*nikai*) of monks in Thailand. This order was created in the nineteenth century to include all monks who were not members of the new reformed order, the Thammayutnikai.

Mahayana (**Pali and Skt.,** *Mahāyāna;* **Thai,** *Mahāyān*): literally, "the great vehicle"; refers to the Buddhist tradition that uses texts written in Sanskrit rather than Pali and that gives greater prominence to beliefs in bodhisattvas, "Buddhas-to-be," who effectively are Buddhist gods, than does Theravada Buddhism. Mahayana Buddhism is dominant in Tibet, East Asia, and Vietnam in contrast to Theravada Buddhism, which is dominant in Thailand, Laos, Burma, Cambodia, and Sri Lanka. Some Chinese and Vietnamese in Thailand follow the Mahayana tradition.

Meo: *See* Hmong.

mǫ (mǭ): specialist in traditional arts; usually refers to a curing specialist.

myang (mūang): domain, country, town.

muban (mūbān): administrative village.

nai amphoe (nāi amphōē): district officer.

*nibbana (**Pali,** nibbāna; **Thai,** niphañ; **Skt.,** nirvāna):* ultimate salvation according to Buddhist thought; in achieving *nibbana* one is freed forever from the cycle of birth, death, and rebirth.

Pali *(Pāli):* the language in which the scriptures and related texts of Theravada Buddhism are written. Pali is not associated with a distinctive script; in Thailand, texts in Pali are written and printed in Thai script; in Burma, they would be written and printed in Burmese script and in Sri Lanka, in Sinhala script.

phansa (phansā; vassa **in Pali):** Buddhist lent; a period of three lunar months during the rainy season when monks are required to remain in one *wat* and when many laypersons adopt more ascetic practices. In Thailand, it has long been customary for men to be ordained temporarily as novices or monks for a lenten period.

phi (phǐ): spirit, ghost.

phikkhu: See bhikkhu.

phra: a title used to indicate that someone or something is sacred in a Buddhist sense; also used as part of the titles of kings. When used alone refers to or is a title for a Buddhist monk.

phuyaiban (phūyaibān): headman of an administrative village *(mūbān).*

rai: unit of land measure, equal to two-fifths of an acre.

sakdi na (sakdi nā): literally, "rank (as indicated by) paddy fields." During Ayutthayan times and the first half of the Bangkok era, every person in the realm was accorded a status associated with a specific acreage of rice land; the greater the acreage, the higher a person's position in a social hierarchy headed by the monarch. This hierarchy constituted the *sakdi na* system. Despite the association of a status with an area of cultivated land, a particular status did not indicate control over a specified amount of land. Some recent scholars, following the work of Jit Poumisak, use the term *sadki na* to refer to a Thai system of "feualism" as well as to elements of that system that still persist in Thai society today.

samanen (samanēn; **Pali,** *samanera):* novice in the Buddhist sangha.

sangha (Pali; Thai, *song* **or** *phra songi;* **also transliterated as** *samgha* **from the Sanskrit):** the collectivity of people who have been ordained as Buddhist monks and novices; nuns *(mae chi)* are not part of the sangha.

sangharat (Thai, *sangharāt;* **Pali and Skt.,** *sangharāja*): the supreme patriarch of the Thai sangha; appointed by the king.

stupa (*stūpa*): *See cedi.*

tambon: commune; an administrative collectivity of villages (*muban*).

Thammayutnikai (**Thai,** *Thammayut-nikāi;* **Pali,** *Dhammayuti-nikāya*): order of Buddhist monks and novices whose practices are based on reforms instituted by King Mongkut; differentiated from Mahanikai.

Theravada (**Pali,** *Theravāda;* **Thai,** *Thērawāt*): literally, "the way of the elders." The Buddhist tradition that traces its origin to the practice of the early sangha (the theras) and is based on scriptures written in Pali. The Theravada tradition is differentiated from the Mahayana tradition, the former being practiced in Thailand, Laos, Cambodia, Burma, and Sri Lanka while the latter is practiced in Tibet, East Asia, and Vietnam.

thǫt kathin (*thǫt kathin*): Buddhist ritual held following the end of Buddhist lent at which laypeople offer robes and other gifts to members of the sangha who have spent lent in a particular *wat.*

Tripitaka (**Pali,** *Tipitaka;* **Thai,** *traipitok*): literally, "the three baskets." The Buddhist scriptures, consisting of the *sutta-pitaka,* "the basket of discourses" (of the Buddha); the *vinaya-pitaka,* "the basket of the discipline" (incumbent on members of the sangha); and the *adhidhamma-pitaka,* "the basket of metaphysics."

wat: the center of Buddhist religious practice; includes both shrines to the Buddha (image halls and *cedi*) and the monastic residence of members of the sangha; thus, "temple-monastery."

Selected Annotated
Bibliography

GENERAL AND INTRODUCTORY

Ayal, Eliezer B., ed. 1978. *The Study of Thailand*. International Studies, Southeast Series, Paper no. 54. Athens, Ohio: Ohio University Center for International Studies, Southeast Asia Program. A collection of "state of the field" papers in anthropology, history of art, economics, history, and political science. See, especially, "Ethnography and Anthropological Interpretation in the Study of Thailand" by Charles F. Keyes and "Studies of the Thai State: The State of Thai Studies" by Benedict R. O'G. Anderson.

Brown, J. Marvin. 1965. *From Ancient Thai to Modern Dialects*. Bangkok. Social Science Association of Thailand Press. A good guide to the Tai languages and dialects spoken in Thailand.

Bunge, Frederica M., ed. 1981. *Thailand: A Country Study*. Washington, D.C.: Government Printing Office for the American University, Foreign Area Studies (DA Pam 550-53). The latest of the handbooks prepared for the U.S. Department of the Army. Contains useful information, with a slant toward political and security issues.

Donner, Wolf. 1978. *The Five Faces of Thailand: An Economic Geography*. London: C. Hurst and Company. A detailed work that is not only the most up-to-date geography of Thailand but also a good source on the Thai economy through the mid-1970s.

Ishii, Yoneo., ed. 1978. *Thailand: A Rice-Growing Society*. Trans. Peter and Stephanie Hawkes. Monographs of the Center for Southeast Asian Studies, Kyoto University, English-language Series, 12. Honolulu: University Press of Hawaii. Contains articles on the ecology and economics of rice production, the history of Thailand as an agrarian society, contemporary rural society, and the political structure of Thailand prior to the 1973 revolution.

Keyes, Charles F. 1979. *Southeast Asian Research Tools: Thailand*. Southeast Asia Paper no. 16, part 6. Honolulu: Southeast Asian Studies, Asian Studies

Program, University of Hawaii. Includes annotated bibliography of major sources for the study of Thailand organized by form and by subject.

Pendleton, Robert L. 1962. *Thailand: Aspects of Landscape and Life.* New York: Duell, Sloan and Pearce. Although now dated, this work still remains a useful source on the physical environment of and land use in Thailand.

HISTORY

Akin Rabibhadana. 1969. *The Organization of Thai Society in the Early Bangkok Period, 1782–1873.* Data Paper 74. Ithaca, N.Y.: Cornell University Southeast Asia Program. This work by a Thai scholar who has been trained both as a lawyer and as a social anthropologist, has become the major source for understanding "traditional" nineteenth-century Thai society. The study is based primarily on Thai legal documents, which has led the author to idealize the character of traditional society somewhat, although he depicts the ideological basis of that society well.

Batson, Benjamin A. 1984. *The End of the Absolute Monarchy in Siam.* Publication of the Asian Studies Association of Australia, 10. Singapore: Oxford University Press. An excellent study of the reign of King Prajadhipok (1925–1935), the last absolute monarch of Thailand.

Charnvit Kasetsiri. 1976. *The Rise of Ayudhya: A History of Siam in the Fourteenth and Fifteenth Centuries.* Kuala Lumpur: Oxford University Press. An interpretive history of the early Siamese kingdom of Ayutthaya. Places historical events in the context of Siamese notions of history and cosmology.

Chatthip Nartsupha and Suthy Prasartset, eds. 1981. *The Political Economy of Siam 1851–1910.* Bangkok: Social Science Association of Thailand Press. This and the following study contain translations of major documents relating to the political economy of Siam during the reigns of King Mongkut (1851–1868) and King Chulalongkorn (1868–1910). The introduction to this volume offers an interpretation of the history of Siam during this period from the perspective of leaders of the political economy group of Thai intellectuals.

————. 1977. *Socio-Economic Institutions and Cultural Change in Siam, 1851–1910: A Documentary Survey.* Southeast Asian Perspectives Series, 4. Singapore: Institute of Southeast Asian Studies.

Chatthip Nartsupha, Suthy Prasartset, and Montri Chenvidyakarn, eds. 1978. *The Political Economy of Siam, 1910–1932.* Bangkok: Social Science Association of Thailand. A similar volume to the two previous ones relating to the reigns of King Vajiravudh (1910–1925) and King Prajadhipok (1925–1935). The introduction traces the political and economic changes of the period.

Direk Jayanama. 1978. *Siam and World War II.* English edition prepared and edited by Jane Godfrey Keyes. Bangkok: Social Science Association of Thailand Press. Memoirs of the man who served as foreign minister and as ambassador to Japan during World War II. Includes many important documents relating to the period.

Reynolds, Craig J. 1976. "Buddhist Cosmography in Thai History, with Special Reference to Nineteenth-Century Culture Change." *Journal of Asian Studies* 35:2, pp. 203–220. A seminal study in Thai intellectual history.

Steinberg, David J., et al. 1971. *In Search of Southeast Asia: A Modern History.* New York: Praeger. Reissue; Honolulu: University of Hawaii Press, 1985. Includes discussions of the traditional Buddhist monarchical order, of the history of Thailand from the mid-eighteenth century to World War II, and of postwar developments situated within a general history of Southeast Asia.

Stratton, Carol, and Miriam McNair Scott. 1981. *The Art of Sukhothai.* Kuala Lumpur: Oxford University Press. A general introduction to the history as well as the art of the first major Tai kingdom in what is now Thailand. Also provides references to the scholarly literature on which current understanding of Sukhothai is based.

Tej Bunnag. 1977. *The Provincial Administration of Siam, 1892–1915.* Kuala Lumpur: Oxford University Press. Traces in considerable detail the impact of the administrative reforms instituted under King Chulalongkorn at the end of the nineteenth century.

Thak Chaloemtiarana, ed. 1978. *Thai Politics: Extracts and Documents, 1932–1957.* Bangkok: Social Science Association of Thailand. A good source book on the political history of Thailand during the period.

Thamsook Numnonda. 1977. *Thailand the Japanese Presence, 1941–1945.* Research Notes and Discussion Papers, 6. Singapore: Institute of Southeast Asian Studies. This and the following work are the best studies of Thailand during World War II.

―――. 1978. "Pibulsongkram's Thai Nation-Building Programme During the Japanese Military Presence, 1941–1945." *Journal of Southeast Asian Studies* 9:2, pp. 234–247.

Thompson, Virginia. 1941. *Thailand: The New Siam.* New York: Macmillan for the Secretariat, Institute of Pacific Relations, International Research Service. Reissue; New York: Paragon Book Reprint Corporation, 1967. A detailed account of Thailand in the 1930s.

Vella, Walter F. 1957. *Siam Under Rama III, 1824–1851.* Association for Asian Studies Monographs, 4. Locust Valley, N.Y.: J. J. Augustin. A good description of Siam just prior to the socioeconomic transformation that occurred after the Bowring Treaty of 1855.

Vella, Walter F., assisted by Dorothy Vella. 1978. *Chaiyo! King Vajiravudh and the Development of Thai Nationalism.* Honolulu: University of Hawaii Press. Detailed and admiring study of the reign of King Vajiravudh, who is credited both with shaping modern Thai nationalist ideology and with undermining the prestige of the Thai monarchy.

Wales, H.G. Quaritch. 1934. *Ancient Siamese Government and Administration.* London: Bernard Quaritch. Reprint; New York: Paragon, 1965. A pioneering study of the traditional political order in Siam as it developed in Ayutthayan times. Based primarily on study of Ayutthayan law codes. Although outdated and subject recently to considerable criticism, the book remains important for students of traditional Thai society.

Wenk, Klaus. 1968. *The Restoration of Thailand under Rama I, 1782–1809.* Trans. from the German by Greely Stahl. Association for Asian Studies Monographs, 24. Tucson: University of Arizona Press. The only extended study of the important reign of Rama I, the founder of the Chakri dynasty who not only "restored" the Siamese order following the destruction of Ayutthaya but also laid the foundation for the fundamental transformation of that order in the latter half of the nineteenth century.

Wilson, Constance M. 1970. "State and Society in the Reign of Mongkut, 1851–1868: Thailand on the Eve of Modernization." Ph.D. dissertation, Cornell University. The basic source for the history of Thailand during the reign of King Mongkhut. Gives particular emphasis to economic and social history of the period.

Wyatt, David K. 1969. *The Politics of Reform in Thailand: Education in the Reign of King Chulalongkorn.* New Haven: Yale University Press. This study not only traces the roots of the modern system of national education in Thailand but also provides an excellent account of court politics during the reign of King Chulalongkorn.

————. 1982. "The 'Subtle Revolution' of King Rama I of Siam." In *Moral Order and the Question of Change: Essays on Southeast Asian Thought,* ed. David K. Wyatt and Alexander Woodside, pp. 9–52. Southeast Asia Studies, Monograph Series, 24. New Haven: Yale University. A stimulating interpretation of the founding of the Chakri dynasty and of the type of social order that Rama I instituted.

————. 1984. *Thailand: A Short History.* New Haven: Yale University Press. An overview of Thai history, with emphasis on reign history.

POLITICS AND EXTERNAL AFFAIRS

Anderson, Ben. 1977. "Withdrawal Symptoms: Social and Cultural Aspects of the October 6 Coup." *Bulletin of Concerned Asian Scholars* 9:3, pp. 13–30. An excellent analysis of Thai politics for the period from the mid-1960s through 1976. Also provides one of the few accounts of the significance of the emerging middle class in Thai society.

Chai-anan Samudavanija. 1982. *The Thai Young Turks.* Singapore: Institute of Southeast Asian Studies. The best study of the role of the Thai military in politics since 1973, with particular reference to the "Young Turks" who staged the abortive coup of 1981.

Darling, Frank C. 1965. *Thailand and the United States.* Washington: Public Affairs Press, 1965. An account of the development of the "special relationship" between the United States and Thailand.

Elliott, David. 1978. *Thailand: Origins of Military Rule.* London: ZED Press. A Marxist and rather polemical analysis of Thai politics up to the mid-1970s.

Girling, John L.S. 1981. *Thailand: Society and Politics.* Ithaca, N.Y.: Cornell University Press. The best recent study on the culture of politics in Thailand, with particular reference to the period from 1963 to 1977.

Jacobs, Norman. 1971. *Modernization Without Development: Thailand as an Asian Case Study.* Praeger Special Studies in International Economics and Development. New York: Praeger. Jacobs, a comparative sociologist, interprets the Thai polity with reference to the Weberian model of patrimonial bureaucracy. Although providing interesting insights, the study is limited by the author's lack of firsthand knowledge of Thai society and culture.

Lobe, Thomas. 1977. *United States National Security Policy and Aid to the Thailand Police*. Monograph Series in World Affairs, vol. 14, bk 2. Denver: University of Denver, Graduate School of International Studies. A detailed study of the way in which U.S. aid in the 1960s and 1970s was used to bolster coercive forces employed by the Thai government to ensure "national security."

Morell, David, and Chai-anan Samudavanija. 1981. *Political Conflict in Thailand: Reform, Reaction, Revolution*. Cambridge, Mass.: Oelgeschlager, Gunn and Hain. A detailed study of the elements involved in the Thai political process in the 1970s.

Neher, Clark D., ed. 1976. *Modern Thai Politics: From Village to Nation*. Cambridge, Mass.: Schenkman Publishing Company. Rev. ed.; Cambridge, Mass.: Schenkman, 1979. A good collection of mainly previously published articles that deal with the traditional Thai political structure and with the political process in the 1950s and 1960s. Covers the period up to the 1973 revolution.

Nuechterlein, Donald E. 1965. *Thailand and the Struggle for Southeast Asia*. Ithaca, N.Y.: Cornell University Press. Describes how Thailand's foreign policy was shaped in the 1950s and 1960s by the anti-Communist policy of the United States.

Randolph, R. Sean. 1978. "Diplomacy and National Interest: Thai-American Security Cooperation in the Vietnam Era." Ph.D. dissertation, Fletcher School of Law and Diplomacy. A comprehensive and insightful analysis of U.S. involvement in Thailand during the 1960s and 1970s.

Riggs, Fred W. 1966. *Thailand: The Modernization of a Bureaucratic Polity*. Honolulu: East-West Center Press. Rigg's model of the "bureaucratic polity" is based on researches carried out in the 1950s, but it continues to have utility for understanding the contemporary Thai polity.

Siffin, William J. 1966. *The Thai Bureaucracy: Institutional Change and Development*. Honolulu: East-West Center Press. A basic source for understanding how the Thai bureaucracy developed and came to dominate Thai political life.

Thak Chaloemtiarana. 1979. *Thailand: The Politics of Despotic Paternalism*. Bangkok: Social Science Association of Thailand and Thai Khadi Institute, Thammasat University. By far the best source on the rise of the military during the period from the 1947 coup to the 1957 coup as well as an excellent introduction to the political culture and character of military rule in Thailand.

Thompson, W. Scott. 1975. *Unequal Partners*. Lexington, Mass.: D. C. Heath. Concerns the impact of U.S. policy on Thailand.

Turton, Andrew; Jonathan Fast; and Malcolm Caldwell, eds. 1978. *Thailand: Roots of Conflict*. Nottingham, Eng.: Spokesman. A radical look at Thai politics and society with primary reference to the 1973–1977 period. See, especially, Turton's "The Current Situation in the Thai Countryside."

———. 1984. "Limits of Ideological Domination and the Formation of Social Consciousness." In *History and Peasant Consciousness in South East Asia,* ed. Andrew Turton and Shigeharu Tanabe, pp. 19–74. Senri Ethnological Studies, 13. Osaka: National Museum of Ethnology. Considers the hegemonic and coercive domination by the Thai state of its rural citizenry. Reviews studies of peasant movements, particularly those in the 1970s.

Wilson, David A. 1962. *Politics in Thailand.* Ithaca, N.Y.: Cornell University Press. Based on research carried out in the 1950s, Wilson's book was long the standard source for understanding Thai politics. It has been criticized in recent times for its overly functional and static interpretation.

SOCIETY AND ECONOMY

Anan Ganjanapan. 1984. "The Partial Commercialization of Rice Production in Northern Thailand (1900–1981)." Ph.D. dissertation, Cornell University. A detailed and insightful study of how the economy of a northern Thai village in the Chiang Mai Valley was restructured with reference to world market forces.

Boonsanong Punyodyana. 1971. *Chinese-Thai Differential Assimilation in Bangkok: An Exploratory Study.* Data Paper, 79. Ithaca, N.Y.: Cornell University, Southeast Asia Program. A report of research carried out a decade after that in which Skinner carried out his pioneering work on the Chinese community in Thailand.

Brummelhuis, Han ten, and Jeremy H. Kemp, eds. 1984. *Strategies and Structures in Thai Society.* Publikatieserie Vakgroep Zuid- en Zuidoost-Azië, 31. Amsterdam: Universiteit van Amsterdam, Antropologisch-Sociologisch Centrum. See, especially, "Abundance and Avoidance: An Interpretation of Thai Individualism" by Han ten Brummelhuis; "The Manipulation of Personal Relations: From Kinship to Patron-clientage," by Jeremy H. Kemp; "Change and Consciousness in a Southern Countryside," by Ruth T. McVey; and "Political Monks: Personalism and Ideology," by Somboon Suksamran.

Chayan Vaddhanaphuti. 1984. "Cultural and Ideological Reproduction in Rural Northern Thai Society." Ph.D. dissertation, Stanford University. An excellent study, based on research in a northern Thai village, that shows how the state has intruded itself into rural life and reshaped local culture.

Embree, John F. 1950. "Thailand—A Loosely Structured Social System." *American Anthropologist* 52, pp. 181–193. Ever since Embree's paper first appeared, scholars have debated the utility of his characterization of Thai society as a "loosely structured social system." Because much of the debate has turned on misrepresentations of Embree's argument, it is worth reading the original.

Evers, Hans-Dieter. 1966. "The Formation of a Social Class Structure: Urbanization, Bureaucratization, and Social Mobility in Thailand." *Journal of Southeast Asian History* 7:2, pp. 100–115. One of the very few studies to consider the bases for class stratification in Thai society. The study is, however, quite dated both in terms of the research on which it is based and in terms of the theory of stratification it employs.

Evers, Hans-Dieter, ed. 1969. *Loosely Structured Social Systems: Thailand in Comparative Perspective*. Southeast Asia Studies Cultural Report Series, 17. New Haven: Yale University. A symposium volume with contributions by anthropologists and sociologists who consider whether ethnographic and historical data about Thai society can be interpreted with reference to Embree's formulation. This volume exhausted the potentialities contained in Embree's insight; subsequent work has, with some exceptions, not taken that formulation as the starting point for constructing interpretations of Thai culture or society.

Feeney, David. 1982. *The Political Economy of Productivity: Thai Agricultural Development 1880–1975*. Vancouver: University of British Columbia Press. A detailed economic history of the political economy of agriculture in Thailand, with primary emphasis on developments prior to World War II.

Fraser, Thomas M., Jr. 1960. *Rusembilan: A Malay Fishing Village in Southern Thailand*. Ithaca, N.Y.: Cornell University Press. Although dated, this and the following book remain the best studies of Malay-speaking fishing villages in southern Thailand.

_____. 1966. *Fishermen of South Thailand: The Malay Villagers*. New York: Holt, Rinehart and Winston.

Haas, David F. 1979. *Interaction in the Thai Bureaucracy: Structure, Culture, and Social Exchange*. Boulder, Colo.: Westview Press. Considers how local officials define themselves as a class apart from the local populace.

Hanks, Lucien M. 1962. "Merit and Power in the Thai Social Order." *American Anthropologist* 64:6, pp. 1247–1261. Next to Embree's (1950) paper, this essay is probably the most cited of any interpretive study of Thai society and culture.

_____. 1972. *Rice and Man: Agricultural Ecology in Southeast Asia*. Chicago: Aldine-Atherton. A good general introduction to the practice of rice cultivation in Thailand. Based primarily on case material from central Thailand.

Hewison, Kevin. 1981. "The Financial Bourgeoisie in Thailand." *Journal of Contemporary Asia* 11:4, pp. 395–412. An excellent study of the control of domestic capital markets by a small number of Sino-Thai banking families. Points to a new type of class analysis of Thai society.

Ingram, James C. 1971. *Economic Change in Thailand, 1850–1970*. Stanford: Stanford University Press. Based primarily on research on the period before 1950, with some updating for the period 1950–1970. This work remains the basic source for understanding the economic history of Thailand.

Johnston, David. 1980. "Bandit, *Nakleng*, and Peasant in Rural Thai Society." *Contributions to Asian Studies* 15, pp. 90–101. Johnston has shown that roots of discontent in rural central Thailand date from the earliest capitalist development of the area and the restructuring of relationships between peasants and the state.

Kaufman, Howard J. 1960. *Bangkhuad: A Community Study in Thailand*. Monograph no. 10. Locust Valley, N.Y.: J. J. Augustin for the Association of Asian

Studies. Reprint; Rutland, Vt., and Tokyo: Charles E. Tuttle Company, 1976. Describes a central Thai village close to the "Cornell Village" of Bang Chan before the rapid changes of the 1960s and 1970s.

Keyes, Charles F. 1967. *Isan: Regionalism in Northeastern Thailand.* Data Paper, 65. Ithaca, N.Y.: Cornell University Southeast Asia Program. This study remains the major source for understanding ethnoregionalism in northeastern Thailand.

————. 1977. *The Golden Peninsula: Culture and Adaptation in Mainland Southeast Asia.* New York: Macmillan. Chap. 3, "Rural Life in Theravada Buddhist Societies," discusses patterns of social organization and culture in rural Thailand as well as in Laos, Burma, and Cambodia. Chap. 5, "Cities in Changing Societies in Mainland Southeast Asia," summarizes findings from the few available studies on urban life in Thailand.

Keyes, Charles F., ed. 1979. *Ethnic Adaptation and Identity: The Karen on the Thai Frontier with Burma.* Philadelphia: Institute for the Study of Human Issues. Concerns the largest tribal population in Thailand and situates the Karen within the context of Thai history and the contemporary political economy.

Kingshill, Konrad. 1965. *Kudaeng: The Red Tomb.* Rev. ed. Bangkok: Bangkok Christian College. The village of Ku Daeng, a community near Chiang Mai, was first studied by Konrad Kingshill in the 1950s, restudied by him in the mid-1960s, and again (although not identified as such) studied by Jack Potter (in *Thai Peasant Social Structure*) in the mid-1970s. Their works thus provide some understanding of the changes villages in this area underwent over a twenty-year period.

Kunstadter, Peter, ed. 1967. *Southeast Asian Tribes, Minorities, and Nations.* 2 vols. Princeton: Princeton University Press. Nearly half of this work consists of essays about the adaptation of minority groups (Thai-Lue, Haw Chinese, Yao, Lua or Lawa, and Karen) to Thai society and about government programs (the Thai Mobile Development Unit Program, the Hill Tribe Program of the Public Welfare Department, and the Tribal Research Center in Chiang Mai) directed at such peoples in the early 1960s.

Kunstadter, Peter; E. C. Chapman; and Sanga Sabhasri, eds. 1978. *Farmers in the Forest: Economic Development and Marginal Agriculture in Northern Thailand.* East-West Center book. Honolulu: University Press of Hawaii. A collection of articles concerned primarily with the practice and implications of slash-and-burn (swidden) cultivation and opium production among tribal peoples in northern Thailand.

Lewis, Paul, and Elaine Lewis. 1984. *The Peoples of the Golden Triangle.* London: Thames and Hudson. Provides descriptions of all the tribal peoples in Thailand as well as excellent photographs of them.

London, Bruce. 1980. *Metropolis and Nation in Thailand: The Political Economy of Uneven Development.* Boulder, Colo.: Westview Press. This work considers the causes and implications of the markedly uneven development of Bangkok compared to the rural hinterland.

Mabry, Bevars D. 1979. *The Development of Labor Institutions in Thailand.* Data Paper, 112. Ithaca, N.Y.: Cornell University Southeast Asia Program. The single most comprehensive study of the history of labor institutions in Thailand, with particular reference to the period from the mid-1960s to the early 1970s.

McKinnon, John, and Wanat Bhruksasri, eds. 1983. *Highlanders of Thailand.* Kuala Lumpur: Oxford University Press. Contributions by scholars who have carried out recent research among tribal (and other) groups in northern Thailand. James A. Matisoff's essay, "Linguistic Diversity and Language Contact," is a good introduction to all the languages found in Thailand. In addition to general essays, there are specific essays on the Yuan (Northern Thai), Shan, Yunnanese, Lua (Lawa), Karen, Hmong, Yao (Mien), Lisu, Lahu, and Akha.

Maxwell, William Edgar. 1975. "Modernization and Mobility into the Patrimonial Medical Elite in Thailand." *American Journal of Sociology* 81:3, pp. 465–490. Maxwell, a sociologist who carried out research in Thailand in the early 1970s, shows in this and the following study how certain professions, the medical profession in particular, have become dominated by assimilated Chinese or Sino-Thai.

————. [1976?] "The Ethnic Assimilation of Chinese Students into the Thai Medical Elite." In *Intergroup Relations: Asian Scene*, ed. Tai S. Kang, pp. 97–104. Buffalo: Council on International Studies, State University of New York at Buffalo.

Moerman, Michael. 1965. "Ethnic Identity in a Complex Civilization: Who Are the Lue?" *American Anthropologist* 67, pp. 1215–1230. Although this paper focuses primarily on the ethnic identities of people living in a village in Chiang Rai Province, northern Thailand, it provides a model for understanding the hierarchical structure of ethnic identities that is applicable to other peoples in Thailand.

————. 1968. *Agricultural Change and Peasant Choice in a Thai Village.* Berkeley and Los Angeles: University of California Press. Considers how villagers in a community in far northern Thailand confronted economic and technological changes in the late 1950s and early 1960s.

Nantawan Haemindra. 1976–1977. "The Problem of the Thai-Muslims in the Four Southern Provinces of Thailand." *Journal of Southeast Asian Studies*, Part 1, 7:2 (1976), pp. 197–225; Part 2, 8:1 (1977), pp. 85–105. A good introduction to the place of Thai-Muslims in Thai society.

Oey Astra Meesook. 1979. *Income, Consumption, and Poverty in Thailand, 1962/63 to 1975/76.* World Bank Staff Working Paper, 364. Washington, D.C.: World Bank. A detailed study by an economist of the changing character of poverty within Thai society in the 1960s and 1970s.

Pasuk Phongpaichit. 1980. "The Open Economy and Its Friends: The 'Development' of Thailand." *Pacific Affairs* 53:3, pp. 440–460. An economist's view of the implications of intense involvement in the world's capitalist economy for Thai society.

Phillips, Herbert P. 1965. *Thai Peasant Personality.* Berkeley and Los Angeles: University of California Press. This study, based on research in the "Cornell Village" of Bang Chan, concludes that Thai peasants "are people who for their own distinctive psychocultural reasons—their Buddhist ethos, their child-rearing practices, their loose and simple social system—have heightened [an] essential human need to be left alone." This thesis has not been sustained in studies carried out in villages in most other parts of Thailand and probably reflects the rather unusual anomic character of certain central Thai villages.

Poole, Peter A. 1970. *The Vietnamese in Thailand: A Historical Perspective.* Ithaca, N.Y.: Cornell University Press. Based on research carried out in the 1960s, considers the characteristics and political status of immigrants and refugees from Vietnam who have settled in Thailand, with primary focus on those refugees who went to Thailand after the division of Vietnam in 1954.

Potter, Jack M. 1976. *Thai Peasant Social Structure.* Chicago: University of Chicago Press. An ethnographic analysis of a northern Thai village previously studied by Kingshill (Ku Daeng).

Sharp, Lauriston, and Lucien M. Hanks. 1978. *Bang Chan: Social History of a Rural Community in Thailand.* Ithaca, N.Y.: Cornell University Press. Bang Chan was the "Cornell Village," a community in central Thailand near Bangkok that was originally studied by a team of researchers from Cornell University from the late 1940s through the end of the 1950s. By the 1970s, the village had ceased to exist and had been incorporated as a suburb of Bangkok. This study, by the two scholars who directed the project from the outset, traces the history of the village from its beginnings in the nineteenth century to its ultimate disappearance.

Silcock, Thomas H., ed. 1967. *Thailand: Social and Economic Studies in Development.* Canberra: Australian National University. A number of the essays in this book, notably those by Silcock and D. Usher, provide good summaries of aspects of economic change in Thailand from World War II to the early 1960s. Also useful is Wijeyewardene's essay on rural Thailand and Evers and Silcock's one on elites.

Skinner, G. William. 1957. *Chinese Society in Thailand: An Analytical History.* Ithaca, N.Y.: Cornell University Press. An excellent historical account of the Chinese community in Thailand and the best analysis of social stratification in Thailand in the 1950s.

————. 1958. *Leadership and Power in the Chinese Community of Thailand.* Ithaca, N.Y.: Cornell University Press. A seminal study not only of the Chinese economic elite and its relationship to the Thai political elite but also of urban society in Thailand more generally. Although based on research carried out in the 1950s, this work remains a basic work for understanding social stratification and urban society in Thailand.

Skinner, G. William, and A. Thomas Kirsch, eds. 1975. *Change and Persistence in Thai Society: Essays in Honor of Lauriston Sharp.* Ithaca, N.Y.: Cornell University Press. A collection of historical and ethnographic studies. Particularly noteworthy are Akin Rabibhadana's "Clientship and Class Structure in the Early Bangkok Period"; David K. Wyatt's "Education and the Modernization of Thai Society"; A Thomas Kirsch's "Economy, Polity, and Religion in Thailand"; Lucien M. Hanks's "The Thai Social Order as

Entourage and Circle"; and Steven Piker's "The Post-Peasant Village in Central Plain Thai Society."

Steinberg, David F. 1985. "The Role of External Assistance in the Economic and Development and Planning of Thailand: Dichotomies of Security and Growth in the American Aid Program." Paper presented at the United States–Thailand Bilateral Forum, sponsored by the Institute of East Asian Studies, University of California; American Studies Program, Chulalongkorn University; and the Asia Society, Berkeley, California, March 25–28. The single best analysis of the economic impact of U.S. aid in Thailand.

Sternstein, Larry. 1984. "The Growth of the Population of the World's Preeminent 'Primate City': Bangkok at Its Bicentenary." *Journal of Southeast Asian Studies* 15:1, pp. 43–68. A historical study of the development of Bangkok.

Surin Pitsuwan. 1985. *Islam and Malay Nationalism: A Case Study of the Malay Muslims of Southern Thailand.* Bangkok: Thai Khadi Research Institute, Thammasat University. The most detailed account of the Malays in southern Thailand by a scholar who himself is a Thai Muslim.

Szanton, Cristina Blanc. 1983. "People in Movement: Social Mobility and Leadership in a Central Thai Town." Ph.D. dissertation, Columbia University. Szanton argues, on the basis of research in a town in southeastern Thailand, that a distinctive Sino-Thai element in the town has acquired local power. Her findings raise questions about the thesis of previous studies, especially those by Skinner, that the Chinese in Thailand ultimately assimilate to the point of losing their distinctive ethnic identity.

Thomlinson, Ralph. 1971. *Thailand's Population: Facts, Trends, Problems, and Policies.* Bangkok: Thai Watana Panich. A good introduction to and evaluation of Thai censuses through the 1960 census, with some reference to the 1970 census.

Turton, Andrew. 1976. "Northern Thai Peasant Society: Twentieth-Century Transformations in Political and Jural Structure." *Journal of Peasant Studies* 3:3, pp. 267–298. An analysis of the historical transformation of rural society in northern Thailand that has been brought about by the increasing impingement of the Thai state.

van Roy, Edward. 1971. *Economic Systems of Northern Thailand.* Ithaca, N.Y.: Cornell University Press. A good introduction to the types of economic systems that incorporate both tribal and lowland peoples in northern Thailand in the 1960s.

Watson, Keith. 1982. *Educational Development in Thailand.* Hong Kong: Heinemann Asia. Historical overview of education in Thailand with primary reference to the 1970s.

World Bank (International Bank for Reconstruction and Development). 1959. *A Public Development Program for Thailand.* Baltimore: Johns Hopkins Press. This and the following World Bank report, based on missions sent to Thailand in the mid-1950s and the mid-1970s, provide insights into the major changes in the Thai economy over the twenty-year period and especially into the characteristics of the economy deemed relevant to policy formulation.

————. 1978. *Thailand: Toward a Development Strategy of Full Participation—A Basic Economic Report.* Report no. 2059-TH. Washington, D.C.

RELIGION AND CULTURE

Amara Pongsapich, ed. 1985. *Traditional and Changing Thai World View.* Bangkok: Chulalongkorn University, Social Research Institute and Southeast Asian Studies Program. Collection of essays written as part of the Thai World View Project started in early 1977 as part of a five-ASEAN-country comparative studies activity sponsored by the Southeast Asian Studies Program. See, especially, essays by Chai Podhisita on "Buddhism and Thai World View"; Sombat Chantornvong on "The Political World of Sunthonphu"; Navavan Bandhumedha on "Thai Views of Man as a Social Being"; and Kobkul Phutharaporn on "Country Folk Songs and Thai Society" as well as the introduction by Amara Pongsapich.

Anderson, Benedict R. O'G., and Ruchira Mendiones, eds. and trans. 1985. *In the Mirror: Literature and Politics in Siam in the American Era.* Bangkok: Duang Kamol. Not only does this volume contain a collection of short stories by many of the leading writers in Thailand today, but the introduction by Anderson provides a stimulating interpretation of the relationship between literature and politics in Thailand.

Anuman Rajadhon, Phya. 1961. *Life and Ritual in Old Siam: Three Studies of Thai Life and Customs.* Trans. and ed. William J. Gedney. New Haven: Human Relations Area Files Press. This and the following work bring together most of Phya Anuman Rajadhon's writings in English or in English translation. Until his death in 1969, he was considered the doyen of Thai cultural studies. His essays treat aspects of language and literature, Thai folkloric and cultural studies, and religious customs.

————. 1968. *Essays on Thai Folklore.* Bangkok: Social Science Association of Thailand Press.

Golomb, Louis. 1985. *An Anthropology of Curing in Multiethnic Thailand.* Illinois Studies in Anthropology, 15. Urbana: University of Illinois Press. Compares the uses of alternative systems of curing found among Buddhists and Muslims in southern Thailand. The best single work for showing the cultural tensions between Buddhists and Muslims in the region.

Keyes, Charles F. 1971. "Buddhism and National Integration in Thailand." *Journal of Asian Studies* 30:3, pp. 551–568. A study of the creation of a national Buddhist "church" in Thailand and the subsequent use of Buddhism as an instrument of national policy.

————. 1977. "Millennialism, Theravāda Buddhism, and Thai Society." *Journal of Asian Studies* 36:2, pp. 283–302. Although primarily concerned with a peasant uprising in northeastern Thailand in 1901–1902, this article also considers the general relationship between Buddhist ideology and popular notions of power.

————. 1983. "Economic Action and Buddhist Morality in a Thai Village." *Journal of Asian Studies* 12:4, pp. 851–868. Considers the relevance of

Buddhist values for villagers who have experienced a radical change in the political-economic conditions of their lives as a consequence of the incorporation of Thailand into a world economy and the growing intrusion of the state into rural society.

———. 1984. "Mother or Mistress but Never a Monk: Buddhist Notions of Female Gender in Rural Thailand." *American Ethnologist* 11, pp. 223–241. This and the following work offer an interpretation of the traditional "culture of gender" in Thailand, with particular reference to northern and northeastern Thailand. They argue that males and females are conceived of in popular Buddhist thought as having different psychological natures, which, in turn, leads to different ways for males and females to follow the religious teachings of the Buddha. The thesis offered is controversial, as can be seen in Kirsch's riposte to the first of these works (see Kirsch 1985).

———. 1986. "Ambiguous Gender: Male Initiation in a Buddhist Society." In *Gender and Religion: On the Complexity of Symbols,* ed. Caroline Bynum, Stevan Harrell, and Paula Richman. (Forthcoming.) Boston: Beacon Press.

Khin Thitsa. 1980. *Providence and Prostitution: Image and Reality for Women in Buddhist Thailand.* London: Change International Reports: Women and Society. Offers a feminist view of how Buddhist culture has served to relegate women in Thai society to an inferior position vis-à-vis men.

Kirsch, A. Thomas. 1977. "Complexity in the Thai Religious System: An Interpretation." *Journal of Asian Studies* 36:2, pp. 241–266. Kirsch believes Thai religion consists not only of Buddhist elements but also of "folk Brahmanistic" and animistic elements. This essay provides an excellent introduction to the relationship between religion and society in Thailand.

———. 1982. "Buddhism, Sex-Roles, and the Thai Economy." In *Women of Southeast Asia,* ed. Penny Van Esterik, pp. 16–41. Monograph Series on Southeast Asia, Occasional Paper, 9. De Kalb: Northern Illinois University, Center for Southeast Asian Studies. In this and the following paper, Kirsch argues that Buddhist ideology leads women to adopt more "worldly" roles than men. The second work reasserts this thesis in response to Keyes's argument in "Mother or Mistress but Never a Monk" (Keyes 1984).

———. 1985. "Text and Context: Buddhist Sex Roles/Culture of Gender Revisited." *American Ethnologist* 12:2, pp. 302–320.

Manas Chitakasem. 1982. "The Development of Political and Social Consciousness in Thai Short Stories." In *The Short Story in South East Asia: Aspects of a Genre,* ed. Jeremy H.C.S. Davidson and Helen Cordell, pp. 63–100. Collected Papers in oriental and African Studies. London: School of Oriental and African Studies, University of London. A good introduction to modern Thai literature, with particular reference to short stories. Considers the relationship between literature and politics.

Reynolds, Frank E., and Mani B. Reynolds, trans. 1982. *Three Worlds According to King Ruang: A Thai Buddhist Cosmology.* Berkeley Buddhist Studies Series 4. Berkeley: University of California, Group in Buddhist Studies, Center for South and Southeast Asian Studies, and Institute of Buddhist Studies.

The Three Worlds According to King Ruang, written in the fourteenth century by a Thai prince, became the major source for popular Buddhist cosmological ideas not only among Thai but also among other Southeast Asian Buddhists. The worldview based on this Buddhist cosmology was dominant in Thailand until the end of the nineteenth century and remains significant for many sectors of the population in Thailand. Useful introduction and notes provided by the translators.

Schweisguth, P. 1951. *Etude sur la littérature siamoise.* Paris: Imprimerie Nationale. The only source in a Western language that surveys the history of literature of Siam/Thailand from the Sukhothai period to the 1930s.

Smith, Bardwell L., ed. 1978. *Religion and Legitimation of Power in Thailand, Laos, and Burma.* Chambersburg, Penn.: Anima Books. An excellent collection of essays that treats the relationship between Buddhism and political power in traditional Siam (and traditional northern Thailand) and in contemporary Thailand. See especially, "The Holy Emerald Jewel: Some Aspects of Buddhist Symbolism and Political Legitimation in Thailand and Laos," by Frank E. Reynolds (on the traditional relationship); "Modernizing Implications of Nineteenth-Century Reforms in the Thai Sangha," by A. Thomas Kirsch (on the origins of reform Buddhism); "Sacral Kingship and National Development: The Case of Thailand," by Frank E. Reynolds; "Sangha and Polity in Modern Thailand: An Overview," by S. J. Tambiah; and "Political Crisis and Militant Buddhism in Contemporary Thailand," by Charles F. Keyes (on the contemporary relationship).

Somboon Suksamran. 1976. *Political Buddhism in Southeast Asia: The Role of the Sangha in the Modernization of Thailand.* New York: St. Martin's Press. This and the following book by a Thai political scientist provide a detailed analysis of the relationship between some individuals in the Buddhist sangha and the ruling elite from the time of Sarit (1957) to the immediate period following the coup of October 1976. Primary attention is given to "political monks," that is, monks who have taken explicit political stands.

―――. 1982. *Buddhism and Politics in Thailand.* Singapore: Institute of Southeast Asian Studies.

Sulak Sivaraksa. 1980. *Siam in Crisis.* Bangkok: Komol Keemthong Foundation. This and the following collection of essays are by arguably the most prolific intellectual critic of Thai culture and society. Sulak is a leading advocate of social justice and human rights based on Buddhist ethical principles.

―――. 1981. *A Buddhist Vision for Renewing Society: Collected Articles by a Concerned Thai Intellectual.* Bangkok: Thai Watana Panich Company.

Swearer, Donald K. 1981. *Buddhism and Society in Southeast Asia.* Chambersburg, Penn.: Anima Books. A general introduction to Theravada Buddhism as practiced in Thailand and elsewhere in Southeast Asia.

Tambiah, Stanley J. 1968. "Literacy in a Buddhist Village in North-East Thailand." In *Literacy in Traditional Societies,* ed. Jack Goody, pp. 85–131. Cambridge: Cambridge University Press. The best and most detailed account of the types of knowledge contained in traditional texts in local temple-monastery libraries.

———— . 1970. *Buddhism and the Spirit Cults in North-East Thailand.* Cambridge: Cambridge University Press. A highly detailed study of the religious practices of villagers in northeastern Thailand. Links these practices to an underlying structure rooted in Buddhist cosmology. Best single work on popular religion in rural Thailand.

———— . 1976. *World Conqueror and World Renouncer: A Study of Buddhism and Polity in Thailand Against a Historical Background.* Cambridge: Cambridge University Press. About half of this book is devoted to an analysis of the relationship between Buddhism and the monarchy in the history of various Thai states and other Southeast (and South) Asian societies. Tambiah's basic thesis is that there is an underlying structure to this relationship, which—with oscillating permutations—has persisted from earliest Buddhism, through all of Thai history since the introduction of Buddhism, right up to the present. The book also contains a study of the urban sangha in Bangkok based on the author's research.

———— . 1984. *The Buddhist Saints of the Forest and the Cult of Amulets.* Cambridge: Cambridge University Press. Based on research carried out in the late 1970s, this work considers the model of the Buddhist saint and how this model has been employed in shaping the roles of monks in Thailand today. It also examines the way in which the charismatic power of monks is believed to be made concrete in the form of Buddhist amulets.

Tobias, Stephen F. 1977. "Buddhism, Belonging, and Detachment—Some Paradoxes of Chinese Ethnicity in Thailand." *Journal of Asian Studies* 36, pp. 303–326. A stimulating interpretation, based on research in a central Thai town, of the Buddhist worldview adopted by Sino-Thai.

Wales, H.G. Quaritch. 1931. *Siamese State Ceremonies: Their History and Function.* London: Bernard Quaritch. A study based primarily on firsthand observations made by Wales, who was trained as an anthropologist, of royal rites performed during the reign of King Vajiravudh. Wales also drew heavily on "The Royal Ceremonies of the Twelve Months," a work written by King Chulalongkorn. Wales's study is useful for understanding the Hindu influences in court rituals as well as for the sources of some royal rites still performed today.

Wells, Kenneth E. 1975. *Thai Buddhism, Its Rites and Activities.* 3d rev. ed. Bangkok: Suriyabun Publishers. Wells describes and translates the relevant texts associated with the major *wat*-centered rituals performed in Thailand. He also describes the formal role of the sangha in establishment Buddhism.

Wibha Senanan. 1975. *The Genesis of the Novel in Thailand.* Bangkok: Thai Watana Panich. A good introduction to the development of modern fiction in Thailand.

Index